Code Breaking

Code Breaking
A History and Exploration

RUDOLF KIPPENHAHN

Translated from the German, in collaboration
with the author, by Ewald Osers

THE OVERLOOK PRESS
WOODSTOCK & NEW YORK

First published in the United States in 1999 by
The Overlook Press, Peter Mayer Publishers, Inc.
Lewis Hollow Road
Woodstock, New York 12498

Library of Congress Cataloging-in-Publication Data

Kippenhahn, Rudolf.
[Verschlüsselte Botschaften. English]
Code breaking : a history and exploration / Rudolf Kippenhahn.
p. cm.
Includes bibliographical references and index.
1. Cryptography. 2. Cryptography—History. I. Title.
Z103.K56   1999   652.8'09—dc21   98-48791

Book design and type formatting by Bernard Schleifer
Manufactured in the United States of America
First Edition
1 3 5 7 9 8 6 4 2
ISBN 0-87951-919-3

In memoriam Arno Gutberlet (1906–1996),
the teacher of my school days, whom we called the Sheikh
and whose teaching in the subjects of mathematics and
physics determined the direction of my life

CONTENTS

PREFACE

IN MY YOUTH I was no more interested in secret writing than other boys, who are all attracted by mystery. Of course I had read the Sherlock Holmes story "The Dancing Men," but I do not recall that secret scripts held a particular fascination for me. Even as a student of mathematics I was unaware of the close relation between my subject and the art of encoding and decoding. Not until the seventies, when a friend told me about an entirely new development in cryptology, did I begin to concern myself with it: unexpectedly I was captivated by the fascination that comes from it. I came to know the destinies of people whose lives had been molded by cryptology, either because they had dedicated themselves to encryption and decryption or because secret writings had protected them or, when decoded, had been their doom.

At some point I felt a need to share that fascination with others. That is how this book came to be written. The more I concerned myself with the subject, the more deeply I was drawn into the events of World War II. For that reason part of my book deals with the German cipher machine Enigma and with the people who succeeded in breaking its codes.

My intention, however, was not to write history, let alone war history. I am interested in cryptology as such. I write about historical events only because the history of cryptology reveals the close links between science and human destinies.

I could not have completed this book had I not received help from many quarters. I had discussions with a great many friends, and also with people whom I met only in connection with my investigations, and I learned a lot as a result. I wish to thank them all. But I would like to single out Franz Leo Beeretz, Joachim Heinke, Reimar Lüst, Hartmut Petzold, Wolfgang Scondo, and Helmut

Steinwedel. I am grateful, moreover, to the president of the Hamburg Regional Court. I am grateful to Rolf Spindler, who did photographical work for me. But my very particular thanks go to my friend, the mathematician Hans-Ludwig de Vries, not only because he encouraged me to take up this subject but also because, as with my earlier books, he went through the entire text with me, critically, page by page. Finally I am grateful to the staff of Rowohlt Verlag for their loyal cooperation.

All the graphics in this book were created by the *Corel-Draw!* program. For some of them, pictures from the program's clip-art library were used.

—RUDOLF KIPPENHAHN
Göttingen, March 17, 1997

PREFACE TO THE AMERICAN EDITION

WHEN I HEARD THAT my book would also be published in the English-speaking world, I was overcome with joy. America has played a big part in my life ever since I first stepped on American soil in 1961.

I soon realized the major task that an English edition of a book on cryptology would mean. I had written a book that was to show German readers how to encode German texts and how to make encoded German texts legible again. Now I was confronted with the need to rework the book so that an English-speaking reader could learn to encode and decode English texts. This meant more than just the translation of the German examples, since the methods of decoding vary with different languages. Tricks that can be applied in one instance fail in another.

I could never have mastered this task without a translator with empathy not only for the language but also for the cryptological problems. Collaboration with Ewald Osers was a real pleasure. We enjoyed working on the book together, finding new texts and entirely rewriting parts of the book. Despite the geographical distance between England and Germany, our work progressed smoothly. I owe him special thanks. In Osers I have made a friend electronically—except that I still don't know what he looks like.

My thanks are also due to the staff of The Overlook Press, without whose helpful cooperation this book would not have seen the light of day.

—RK

Göttingen, October 5, 1998

1. SECRET WRITING IN WAR AND PEACE

> I am fairly familiar with all forms of secret writings, and
> am myself the author of a trifling monograph upon the
> subject, in which I analyze one hundred and sixty sepa-
> rate ciphers.
>
> —SIR ARTHUR CONAN DOYLE, "The Dancing Men"

"IF I AM SENTENCED TO DEATH, Ohashi-san, I will come back to haunt
you," said the prisoner to the secret police inspector. During the
many interrogations a familiar tone had developed between the two
men. Inspector Ohashi had been present on that Saturday in October
1941, when in the early morning his men burst into the Tokyo home of
the journalist Richard Sorge and took him to the police station in his paja-
mas and slippers.

Since then the prisoner had had plenty of time to reflect on his life.
During the first few weeks in his cell, this defeat, a new experience, drove
him to despair. Then an initially feeble but gradually strengthening realization awoke in him that, after all, he had successfully accomplished his
mission. This consoling thought made the uncertainty about his fate more
bearable. After Hitler's attack on the Soviet Union, Sorge had signaled
the Fourth Department in Moscow to the effect that Japan would not
attack the Soviet Union from the east. It had been these reports that
enabled Marshal Zhukov to withdraw divisions, tanks, and aircraft from
Siberia and employ them against the Germans outside Moscow. Had
he, Richard Sorge, not made world history? From the questions put by
his interrogators he was able to conclude that the Japanese had not succeeded in deciphering the coded messages that his radio operator sent by
the thousands to the Soviet stations in Shanghai and Vladivostok.

RADIO OPERATOR KLAUSEN TRANSMITS TO MOSCOW

On this summer day the air over Tokyo is oppressive. Max Klausen glances at the sheet before him. It will take a while to encode it. He reads it—another report from "Otto." His boss never told him, but Klausen knows that Otto is a Japanese collaborator of the group. His messages are always important.

Since June 22, 1941, German troops have been pushing ever deeper into Soviet territory. Long before then, Klausen sent the warning, complete with the correct date of the German attack, to Moscow, but no one there reacted to it. Will the Soviet Union shortly have to defend itself not only against Germany but also, despite the nonaggression treaty, against Japan? Japan has been mobilizing over the past few days. Will these newly assembled troops be ordered toward the south or toward the north, against the Soviet Union?

The report from Otto holds the answer. On no account will Japan attack Russia; it has its hands full enough with the Chinese incidents. Until it is clear how the negotiations with the Americans develop, no one in Japan wants war with Russia.[1] If Japan attacks the Soviet Union at all, it will be next year at the earliest. But now the German forces have advanced far into Russian territory. It looks as if Hitler intends to be in Moscow before the onset of winter. The news that no attack should be expected from the Japanese must come as a great relief to the Soviets. Max Klausen, the radio operator, starts encoding.

He knows the first step by heart, but this time he uses a sheet of paper that he will afterward destroy. The first step requires the assigning of numbers to the letters of the alphabet. To do that he has to use his code word. It is *SUBWAY*. He writes down the six letters of the word, next to one another, then in four additional lines below he inserts the remaining letters of the alphabet, in their normal order, as well as a period and a slash (to indicate word division). He thus obtains the table in figure 1.1, top.

As he invariably sends his messages in English, the most frequent letters in that language—*a, s, i, n, t, o, e*, and *r*—play a special role. The phrase "A sin to err" consists of just these letters—a mnemonic aid that Klausen does not need. These eight letters will be assigned the numbers

s	u	b	w	a	y
c	d	e	f	g	h
i	j	k	l	m	n
o	p	q	r	t	v
x	z	.	/		

s	u	b	w	a	y
0				5	
c	d	e	f	g	h
	3				
i	j	k	l	m	n
1					7
o	p	q	r	t	v
2			4	6	
x	z	.	/		

s	u	b	w	a	y
0	82	87	91	5	97
c	d	e	f	g	h
80	83	3	92	95	98
i	j	k	l	m	n
1	84	88	93	96	7
o	p	q	r	t	v
2	85	89	4	6	99
x	z	.	/		
81	86	90	94		

Fig. 1.1. How Max Klausen, using the keyword *SUBWAY* and the mnemonic *asintoer*, in three steps sets up the key table for converting the letters of the alphabet into numbers.

0 to 7. He enters them into this table, column by column, starting from the left. As soon as he encounters a letter from *asintoer*, he writes the numbers from 0 to 7 in sequence underneath. His table now looks like figure 1.1, center. He now writes under the remaining letters, column by column, left to right, the numbers from 80 to 99 and obtains the table in figure 1.1, bottom.

Now every letter of the alphabet has its own number. Klausen can therefore convert the letters of the message into a sequence of numbers. Let us take a simple radio message as an example. The words "no attack" become **729456658088**. This twelve-digit group can easily be reduced to numbers that correspond to pairs of numerals. Numbers not preceded by 8 or 9 correspond individually to letters in the table. If an 8 or 9 is encountered, it stands in conjunction with the number that follows it for a single letter in the table. In **729456658088** the figures 7, 2, 94 and 5 correspond to the letters (and punctuation symbol) *n*, *o*, /, and *a*. The two 6s are the double *t*. The 80 represents *c*, and the 88 the letter *k*. We now have "no attack" in encoded form. But this is only the first step. What Klausen has before him is the *provisionally* encoded text.

So far, nothing much has been gained. Any beginner can discover that in lengthy messages encoded in this manner the number 3 appears most frequently. This represents the letter *e*, the most frequent letter in English as well as in German. This would allow any unauthorized person to take the first step toward decoding the text. That is why Klausen now proceeds to the encipherment proper. From his bookshelf he takes the *Statistical Yearbook of the German Reich* for 1935 and opens it to a page filled with numbers. He notes down the page number, as well as the row and column of the table that contains the number with which he intends to start. These are data on tobacco production in different countries. They start with the number 4230, below it 5166, 7821, 9421, and so on. It has long been agreed between Moscow and himself that he must start with the third and fourth digits of the first number and then append the other figures, hence 30516678219421. . . . This numerical sequence is his real key. Klausen therefore writes down his provisionally encoded text and places his key below it:

729456658088

305166782194

He now adds, but if a sum exceeds 9, he does not carry the ten to the preceding place—hence not 7 + 8 = 15 but 7 + 8 = 5. Figure 1.2, top, demonstrates his calculation. Now he has to communicate the page number, row, and column of the annual to enable the recipient to take the same key from the book. For the page number two figures are sufficient; if 34 is transmitted, this can mean 34, or 134, or 234, but it will be easy for the recipient to decide which of them is the right page. For the row and column three figures are sufficient; 236 stands for row 23, column 6. Hence a total of five figures, 34236, is sufficient to indicate the beginning of the key. Klausen places these five figures at the beginning of his signal,

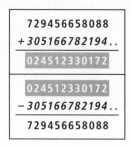

Fig. 1.2. **Top: from a numerical plaintext—that is, a plaintext converted into figures—via a key into a numerical ciphertext. Bottom: from the numerical cipher-text to the numerical plaintext.**

but he encodes them by adding the first five-figure group of his encoded text, again without carrying; hence 34236 + 02451 = 36687. His message therefore, divided into five-figure groups, reads: 36687 02451 23301 72. He then transmits these groups of figures. He knows that the receiver will start by subtracting the second five-figure group from the first: 36687 - 02451 = 34236. This gives the receiver the page number (34, 134, or 234) and the row and column (23 and 6), that is, all the information he needs to determine the key. He now has to subtract the key from the signal as received (without the first five-figure group he used for discovering the key), as shown in figure 1.2, bottom. This gives him the text encoded with the table in figure 1.1, bottom, and this he can easily convert back into the plaintext, since he, too, has the table.

Max Klausen would transmit each signal from a different location. One time he would transmit from his room, another time from the house of a Yugoslav member of the spy ring, and sometimes he would set up his transmitter and antenna in the homes of other friends. Thus the Japanese secret service did not succeed in locating the transmitter in the middle of the densely populated metropolis, even though it had long been aware of the numerous signals emanating from Tokyo.

To avoid being discovered by direction-finding vehicles, Klausen would change his position even during a single transmission. Continually lugging his transmitter from place to place, he could easily have run into a police checkpoint. Yet it was not the radio signals that eventually betrayed the spy ring. The unmasking took place by chance, when the Japanese secret service began to take a closer look at former sympa-thizers with the Communist Party of Japan.

In the evening of October 14, 1941, Richard Sorge intended to meet his Japanese collaborator Hotsumi Ozaki—his source, Otto—but Ozaki failed to turn up at the agreed time. Over the next few days Sorge could not reach him by telephone either. Klausen was arrested the night of October 17, and in the early hours of the next day the secret agents knocked at Sorge's door. The trial of Sorge and his comrades dragged on over three years. Ozaki and Sorge were hanged on November 7, 1944, while Klausen was sentenced to life imprisonment and his wife to three years. Following Japan's surrender, both were freed by the Allies and flown to the Soviet Union. For a long time afterward there was no news of them.

Not until October 29, 1964, nearly twenty years later, did the East Berlin newspaper *Neues Deutschland*, under the headline "Max Klausen Alive," report that the Berlin correspondent of the Moscow *Izvestiya* had, with the help of German comrades, tracked down "the Klausen couple living modestly and quietly in the capital of the German Democratic Republic." Now one story followed another. In 1945, after a rest-and-recuperation vacation, the couple had come into the then Soviet zone of occupation and lived there under the name of Christiansen. Later they moved to Berlin. The East Berlin papers described the two as upright Communists and citizens of the German Democratic Republic. Only then did the media discover that Max Klausen had on an earlier occasion attracted attention by his "exemplary constructive determination." From its archives *Neues Deutschland* dug up a nine-year-old story about the activist Maxe Christiansen, cadre instructor at the Köpenick yacht-building yard, shown in a photograph with a pickax, attacking some rubble. At the time the paper was unaware of the identity of the man in the picture.

It was said that simple modesty had kept him silent about his merits. But in 1964 the silence was broken. Klausen gave interviews and told of his work with Sorge in Japan. All of a sudden the Klausens emerged into the limelight. Evidently the news about the activist Maxe Christiansen was released only in 1964 because any historical examination of the work of the spy ring around Sorge would have revealed Stalin's blunders. After all, Stalin had dismissed Sorge's message about Hitler's impending attack on the Soviet Union. By 1964, however, this subject was no longer taboo. Now the longtime Communist Gerhart Eisler, member of the Central Committee of the Socialist Unity Party and chairman of the State

Broadcasting Committee of the German Democratic Republic, was allowed to recollect that he had once met Richard Sorge, and the Party veteran Hermann Siebler suddenly remembered his meetings with the until-then-unmentionable Sorge. And Hero of Labor Ehrenfried Navarra of the machine-tool factory in Gera pledged his brigade to a production competition in honor of Sorge's birthday. By the time Max Klausen died on September 15, 1979, at age eighty-one, he had been decorated with the Karl Marx Order, the Order of the Red Banner of the Soviet Union, and other high honors.

The Japanese never managed to decode the signals sent by Sorge and his faithful radio operator. Their encoding system was quite sophisticated and, above all, based on the use of a harmless book. A statistical yearbook would not have attracted any attention during a house search.

THE SECRET OF THE WAX TABLETS

The method by which the radio operator Max Klausen sent a message to Moscow in a form incomprehensible to the uninitiated must seem a bit primitive to today's encoder, who has a computer encode his letter to a business partner in Australia and then sends it over the Internet. But compared to the beginnings of encoding Klausen's system was not bad at all.

The first secret messages were exchanged as long as thousands of years ago. Legends of them surround many a major event in world history, such as the famous Battle of Thermopylae in 480 B.C.

Anyone driving down European Route 75 from Thessaloniki to Athens will, after leaving Mount Olympus behind him, come to the Gulf of Lamia, where the highway runs close to the coast. A memorial stone on a hill commemorates the battle in which King Leonidas of Sparta vainly tried to defend himself against the superior forces of the Persians. Leonidas had expected the arrival of the Persian army because he was notified of it in a secret message.

As the Greek historian Herodotus reports, a Greek in Persian exile sent wax tablets to his home city; more accurately, he sent wooden tablets with a layer of wax, such as were then used for writing. The man removed the wax, wrote on the wood the message of the imminent Persian invasion, covered the tablet with a fresh layer of wax, and sent it to Leonidas.

The message, no longer legible, reached Greece without mishap. It would have remained hidden if Gogo, Leonidas's wife, had not accidentally discovered the writing underneath the wax. Thus Leonidas was warned.

But, as so often happens in history, the secret message had no effect on the outcome of the battle. A Greek traitor guided the Persians along a secret path over the mountains to Leonidas's position on the pass of Thermopylae, and his forces were attacked from two sides. They fought to the last man.

In the case reported by Herodotus, the secret message was transmitted in such a way that no one could see the wax tablets contained a vital message. Presumably there was an innocent text scratched into the wax covering the real message, designed to distract attention from it.

THE SECRET MESSAGE TO COUNT SANDORF

Trieste in 1867 was an Austrian town, and to its north the biggest port in the Hapsburg monarchy was about to be created. But the prospects for the realization of that plan were not too favorable in the spring of that year. A few months earlier, Austria had lost the Battle of Königgrätz against Prussia, and the Hungarian freedom movement had never completely quieted down after the death of Lajos Kossuth, the leader of the rebellion crushed by the Austrians.

This tense atmosphere provides the background for Jules Verne's novel *Mathias Sandorf*. The hero, a Hungarian nobleman, is temporarily staying in Trieste. Carrier pigeons bring him encrypted messages about the liberation struggle back home in Hungary. But the message that everything is ready for a rising against Austria, and that his followers are only waiting for a signal from him, falls into the wrong hands. Here is the text:

```
SETVIETGGNRIAHYSELRTYFHEOIAUDIRYSNTA
RSVELNERMIDTSRURYEISFOFEONSRTREEWOIE
RHCUENEENSGDRKAEHAPRGPYEDNNPDSOEHINN
```

None of the Austrian agents is able to decode it. Only when a villain steals the key to it from Count Sandorf's writing desk is it possible to decipher it.

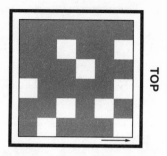

Fig. 1.3. The cipher template, or "turning grille" or "mask," described by Jules Verne in his novel *Mathias Sandorf*. It is placed on a clean sheet of paper, and the first nine letters of the message to be encrypted are entered into the cut-out fields or "cells" (white in the illustration) of the square. The grille is then rotated clockwise by ninety degrees, and the next nine letters are written into the apertures. This procedure is repeated until the grille has been used in all four positions. On the paper the letters thus entered now fill a square of six by six fields, which, read line by line, produce the encrypted text. If the message is longer, a new square is started with the same grille. Whenever a square is not completely filled, the text to be encrypted is extended by arbitrarily chosen letters to ensure all fields have letters in them.

The key is a square of six rows and six columns. Of the thirty-six square fields, nine are cut out. The result is a grille as shown in figure 1.3. For deciphering, the recipient writes down the ciphertext in three squares of thirty-six fields each, as shown at the top of figure 1.4. He now places the grille on the square with the ciphertext and reads through the nine apertures: EVERYTHIN (fig. 1.4, bottom left). He then rotates the grille clockwise through ninety degrees (fig. 1.4, bottom right) and reads: GISREADYA. Another ninety degrees: TTHEFIRST. One more turn: SIGNALYOU. This completes the first square. With the other squares, the following plaintext emerges:

everythingisreadyatthefirstsignalyousendusfromtriesteevery
onewillriseforhungarysindependencekhpnohnreesragdp

The end of the message is extended by sixteen random letters in order to make the secret text fit into the three squares.

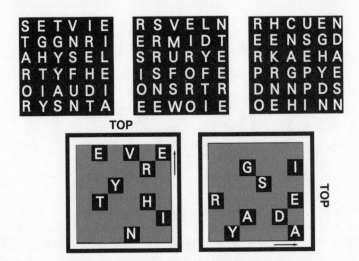

Fig. 1.4. This shows how the encrypted text on page 22 is decoded. The secret text has been written into three squares. Bottom left: the grille of figure 1.3 is placed over the first square in its basic position; bottom right: the grille has been rotated clockwise by ninety degrees. In these two positions the first eighteen letters of the original message are revealed.

HOW MARY, QUEEN OF SCOTS, WAS BETRAYED

In 1586, Philip II was king of Spain. He had inherited the empire of his father, Charles V, an empire comprising Spain, Sicily, Lower Italy, all the Hapsburg possessions, and the Spanish colonies scattered throughout the globe. Full of pride, Charles V had been able to exclaim: "In my empire the sun never sets!" When his son Philip was born in 1527, ten years after Luther had nailed his thesis to the door of the castle church of Wittenberg, Protestantism began to establish itself in the countries of Europe. The Zurich parish priest Ulrich Zwingli likewise opposed the papal teaching, and John Calvin followed him in the French part of Switzerland. Calvin's Reformed Church spread to France, the Netherlands, England, and Scotland. Philip II had his half brother Don John of Austria administer the Netherlands, still a Spanish possession. Previously, in the Battle of Lepanto in 1571, John had with the Italians successfully defended Catholicism against the Turks. Now, transferred to the Netherlands, he again saw it as his principal task to protect the Catholic dogma against Protestant heresy.

In England in the thirties, Henry VIII had quarreled with the pope when the pope refused to approve the annulment of his marriage to Catherine, an aunt of Charles V, and his subsequent marriage to a lady of the court. Henry thereupon declared himself head of the Church of England and compelled the clerics to recognize him instead of the pope as the supreme authority. That was the origin of the Anglican Church, which closely associated itself with the teachings of Calvin. The reform was enforced mainly under the reign of Henry's daughter, Elizabeth I. Thus England developed into the principal Protestant power.

In Scotland, too, Calvin's teachings had found followers. In a rebellion the Catholic Stuart queen, Mary, Queen of Scots, had been driven out. She found asylum in the country of her kinswoman Elizabeth, but relations between the two were tense. The English Catholics maintained that Mary was the lawful queen of England, which induced Elizabeth to put her under house arrest for twenty years.

Mary Stuart is said to have been an attractive woman, but that certainly was not the only reason why Don John considered landing his troops in England, marrying Mary, and ruling the country with her instead of Elizabeth. He confided this to others in his letters, naturally in encoded form, but apparently he did not allow for the English secret service.

There were so many intrigues and conspiracies in England during the reign of Elizabeth I that a secret police became necessary to preserve the state. Its creation was organized by Elizabeth's minister, Sir Francis Walsingham. Some years earlier, while traveling in Italy, Walsingham had come to realize the importance of ciphers, which had a long tradition there. He set up an organization that on the European continent alone maintained fifty-three secret agents. The usefulness of this was soon to become evident. A coded letter was channeled into the hands of a nobleman in the Netherlands, who had concerned himself extensively with secret writing, and within a month he succeeded in deciphering it. The letter was from Don John of Austria, and in it was revealed his dream of conquering England. One of Walsingham's men in Holland got wind of the contents of the letter and reported to the minister. Walsingham concluded that it was high time for a closer surveillance of Mary Stuart. It so happened that about the same time a petition from a prisoner, Gilbert Gifford, came into his hands, offering his services. When Gifford had completed his sentence, Walsingham took him up and employed him to observe everything that was going on around Mary Stuart.

He succeeded in infiltrating Gifford into Mary's staff as a messenger.

In 1586, when Mary had been an English prisoner for twenty years, one of her followers conceived the plan to murder Elizabeth and thereby trigger a rebellion of English Catholics, with the aim of crowning Mary queen of England. As instructed, the messenger Gifford smuggled out of the castle all letters from Mary to her followers. But before doing so he always made copies of the encoded messages and passed these on to Walsingham, who now had an experienced cryptologist able to decipher these letters quickly. In one letter to the originator of the murder conspiracy, Mary allegedly wished success to the enterprise. The decoding of this sentence sealed her fate. First Walsingham's agents seized the men who had planned the murder. Then the queen of Scots was accused of high treason. It has never been determined whether the agents who found numerous encoded letters in her rooms when they arrested her did not perhaps also plant some forged documents there. On February 8, 1586, she was taken to the scaffold. The executioner had to strike three times before severing her head from her body.

THE RIDDLE OF THE MAN IN THE IRON MASK

The mask probably was made not of iron but of velvet, and the truth of the story has never been proven. The story is as follows. In the 1670s the inhabitants of the town of Pignerol in the duchy of Savoy noticed a prisoner who was often to be seen on the ramparts of the fortress that served as a prison. His face was covered by a black mask. The soldiers of the guard reported that the prisoner was courteously treated and even dined at the table of the fortress commandant. Supposedly the man once threw a silver tablet from the wall, with various symbols scratched into it. A citizen of the town who had happened to walk past and pick up the tablet was immediately arrested by the guards. He is said to have sat in a cold cell for weeks before he succeeded in convincing his interrogators that he could neither read nor write and that he was not involved in any conspiracy to free the prisoner. Eventually the man in the mask was taken to the Bastille in Paris, where he died in 1703, after thirty years of imprisonment.

The mysterious prisoner excited the imagination of his contemporaries and subsequent generations. Alexandre Dumas, the author of *The Three Musketeers* and *The Count of Monte Cristo,* wrote a novel about the man in the iron mask. Rumors flew about the country. Had the man in the mask been the twin brother of Louis XIV? Had he been his illegitimate son?

In 1891, a French officer named Victor Gendron in the course of some historical studies discovered a coded letter. Not knowing what to do with it, he passed it on to Etienne Bazeries of the Cipher Bureau of the foreign ministry.

Bazeries was a French officer who had come into contact with secret writing when trying to decode various personal messages in the daily papers. At that time married persons would often exchange messages with their extramarital partners; the letters were sometimes so intimate that they afforded Bazeries's comrades in the officers' mess a lot of entertainment. Bazeries was becoming increasingly skillful at reading encoded texts. On one occasion, when he was forty-four, he boasted that he would have no difficulty in reading messages encoded by the cipher system of the French military. Put to the test, he proved his ability. The war ministry thereupon changed its system, but even before the new code went into operation, Bazeries had cracked it. His fame quickly grew, and he was assigned to the Cipher Bureau of the foreign ministry. At that time he began to develop an interest in century-old messages that had remained undecoded. He uncovered the secrets of texts written at the time of Louis XIV. He was also able to read secret correspondences of the Napoleonic age. It was to him, therefore, that Gendron sent the old coded text.

This consisted of numbers between 1 and 500 that followed one another in no regular sequence. Some of the numbers occurred with special frequency. Bazeries suspected that each number represented a syllable of the French language, but that individual letters might also be expressed by one or more numbers. The number **22** was the most frequently encountered—187 times—followed by **124**. Next came **42**, **311**, and **125**. Bazeries next tried to assign these numbers to the syllables that occurred most often in a French text. He assumed that **124** could mean the article *les,* **22** *en,* and both **146** and **125** could mean *ne;* he also came to the conclusion that the letter *s* was represented by a string of various numbers. He succeeded in almost completely decoding the message. It was from the war minister Louvois and addressed to the lieutenant general de Catinat, who was commanding the army in Piedmont.

In the message Louvois reported that General Boulonde was to be punished for refusing to obey orders. The king's command was that Boulonde be arrested immediately and taken to the fortress of Pignerol. The prisoner was to be locked in a cell every night but during the day allowed to walk the battlements with **330 309**. These two numbers did not occur anywhere else in the text, which is why Bazeries was unable to guess their meaning from the context. However, he knew the story of the man in the mask in the Bastille, knew that the man had originally been imprisoned at Pignerol, and knew that the prisoner had been treated as an important personage. Bazeries concluded that **330** must mean *masque*, the French for mask, whereas **309** was probably a closing sign. He announced that the man in the mask had been General Boulonde.

Whether the brilliant Bazeries solved the mystery is doubtful. It would be surprising if *mask*, a word not part of military language, had been encoded with just a single number. The five hundred possible numbers of the code were used only for frequent words; all others had to be spelled out by strings of numbers representing letters. Moreover, Boulonde was said to have still been alive five years after the death of the man in the mask.

THOMAS JEFFERSON'S WHEEL

Systems for the transmission of secret messages were usually invented by monks and military men, by mathematicians and secret agents, but on one occasion this brotherhood was joined by a famous politician and statesman. Thomas Jefferson, coauthor of the American Declaration of Independence, third president of the United States, invented a cipher machine, named the Jefferson wheel after him. A modern version of this is shown in plate 1.

It consists of thirty-six wooden disks of equal size, each disk divided into twenty-six equal sectors. These carry the letters of the alphabet in random sequence. The sequence is different for every disk, which presents no problem, since the number of possible arrangements of the twenty-six letters of the alphabet is enormous. The disks are marked at their apexes with the numbers 1 to 36, drilled at their center, and mounted on a metal axle—perhaps disk 27 at the extreme left, then 2, then 10, 13, and so on.

Sender and receiver must possess the same collection of disks and must have them arranged on the axle in the same order. Let us assume that the sender wishes to transmit the secret message "attacktomorrowatsunrise." He therefore holds the axle with the mounted disks horizontally before him and turns them individually so that the letters standing next to one another in a row form his text. Then he locks the disks so they can no longer turn. If he now rotates this fixed block of disks on their axle, it shows another line. Every one of the other twenty-five lines is an encoding of the message, in a form no unauthorized person can decode. Let us assume the sender chooses the line that reads **TOBQMVESBXUZKYGYMZAPXUW**. He sends this sequence of letters to the addressee, who then, on his little machine, adjusts the disks so that this same sequence of letters stands in a row. All he has to do now is look for a meaningful sequence of letters among the other twenty-five lines. Provided his disks are arranged in the same way as those of the sender, in one of the lines, he will come across "attackto-morrowatsunrise."

Whereas in Europe the art of encrypting has a long history, it seems that Jefferson thought up his invention independently. For an unauthorized person it is virtually impossible to decode a message encoded in this way, even when he has the identical thirty-six disks, if he does not know in what sequence these are threaded on the axle. Even Jefferson knew that the number of different ways of arranging the disks had forty-two digits. The Jefferson wheel proved so successful that the United States Navy was still using it in World War II.

SIGNS ON GRAVESTONES AND WALLS

Not far from the New York Stock Exchange on Wall Street stands Trinity Church, a church that is more than two hundred years old, tiny and lost between the skyscrapers around it. A relic of bygone centuries amidst the high tech and hubbub of New York's business district. In the churchyard beside it the visitor finds the gravestone of James Leason, who died on September 28, 1794. Leason had been a Freemason, a member of the "Jerusalem Lodge No. 4." Next to the inscription is a row of signs along the upper edge of the stone, as reproduced in figure 1.5, top. They are secret signs that can be read only by someone in possession of the key.

Each sign corresponds to a letter of the alphabet. The assignment of the letters is exceedingly simple; it can be understood from the bottom part of the figure. The inscription reads: "rememberdeath."

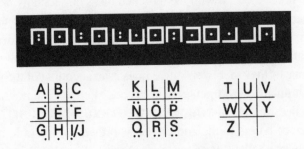

Fig. 1.5. Top: the coded inscription on James Leason's grave. Bottom: twenty-five letters of the alphabet are divided among three grilles. The number of dots in each sign indicates the grille in which the letter is found. The lines of the sign indicate the position of theletter in the grille. The signs are kept so simple to allow them to be incised into the stone with a hammer and chisel (after S. B. Morris, *Cryptology*, January 1983, p. 27).

As we will see later, this kind of code is easily deciphered. Presumably the Freemasons did not so much intend to keep the text secret by encoding it as to express the mystery of their fraternity.

Fig. 1.6. Top: a secret password of the Order of the American Union after the Civil War (1861-1865). Bottom: the cipher alphabet needed for deciphering the secret text.

They did not very effectively encode their real secrets either, and other fraternities were no better. The Order of the American Union (OAU), founded shortly after the Civil War, also had mysterious rituals. Anyone wishing to have access to its events had to give the password twice. Members were informed of these continually changing passwords in secret writing (fig. 1.6). They were not allowed to let the key out of their hands. This, too, was a code so simple, it could be read even without the key—as we will see. In this case, it seems that the motivation was the thrill of clandestine activity rather than the need to preserve a secret.

Secret signs were used not only by societies with noble aims. The Ku Klux Klan also had its secret writing, and thieves and murderers over the past three hundred years used secret signs on walls and the sides of houses to give advice or warnings to colleagues. Figure 1.7 shows some of these signs and their meaning.

Fig. 1.7. Crooks' secret marks, found in Graz about 1915. They say: "At dawn go to the crossroads by the tramcar stop at the *Volksgarten* (trees). Birdcall repeated four times. Support needed. Rich spoils. Attention (colon), meeting on 28th in the toilet at the *Volksgarten*" (from Hans Gross and Friedrich Geerds, *Handbuch der Kriminalistik*, vol. 1, Berlin 1977, p. 92).

THE ART OF ENCODING

The art of changing a text so that it becomes unreadable to an outsider is called *encoding, enciphering,* or *cryptography*. The science of encoding and decoding is *cryptology*. We will presently see that even with cryptographic methods that at first sight seem secure it is often possible to decode a coded message.

The example of Klausen's signals to Moscow already provided an opportunity for the explanation of a few basic concepts that will be encountered throughout this book. The message to be transmitted is the *plaintext*, which for Klausen was "no attack." He converted it into a sequence of numbers, in two separate steps. These numbers, **34236   02451   23301   72**, were the *secret text*, or *ciphertext*. In the case of James Leason's gravestone the plaintext was the warning "rememberdeath," the ciphertext the sequence of signs in figure 1.5, top. In this book all plaintexts will be printed (where possible) in lowercase letters and all ciphertexts in bold capital letters or as white letters against a black background.

The recipient of Klausen's signal in Moscow could make something of the ciphertext only because he knew the *key*. In other words, he knew how to restore the plaintext from the ciphertext. In the case of the OAU secret text, the key is reproduced in figure 1.6, bottom. For the key for James Leason's tombstone inscription, see figure 1.5, bottom. For Count Sandorf's ciphertext, the key is the template in figure 1.3. A key should be kept strictly secret, because anyone possessing it can convert a ciphertext into plaintext. In this book the keys (whenever possible) are written in capitals, and these capitals, as well as numbers if the key is a numerical sequence, are italicized. Hence:

plaintext, KEY, CIPHERTEXT

In this first chapter we already have come across two basically different kinds of encoding. The radio operator Klausen replaced the letters of his plaintext by numbers arrived at by a complicated method. Jefferson's wheel replaces the plaintext letters by other letters: a, b, c can become **F**, **X**, and **Y**, even if there is no f, x, or y in the plaintext. This type of encoding, when signs are replaced by other signs, is called *substitution*. Nearly all the chapters of this book deal with substitution procedures. In the ciphertext of Count Sandorf, however, the letters of the plaintext are preserved: they merely appear in different positions in the ciphertext. If there is no x or y in the plaintext, then neither one appears in the ciphertext. If the plaintext contains the letter f five times, then f must also occur five times in the ciphertext. This type of encoding is called *transposition*. It is discussed in chapter 8.

Whether substitution or transposition is used, the key has to be agreed upon between sender and receiver before transmission. In World War I, all naval vessels carried fat *codebooks*, comprehensive dictionary-like volumes in which every plaintext word was faced by its cipher sequence. As with a word-by-word translation into a foreign language by means of a dictionary, plaintext was converted into ciphertext. At the very beginning of World War I, the Russians got hold of one of the codebooks of the German navy (see chapter 3). It was therefore easy for Germany's opponents to decode the German naval signals.

In an effort to send as much encoded information as possible and to send it as fast as possible, and also to gain an equally fast insight into the opponent's signal traffic, encoding and decoding was not only done manually. In order to be able to read the signals encoded with the German cipher machine Enigma, which was developed in World War II (see chapters 9 and 10), and to read them with the least possible delay, British scientists and technicians developed the first electronic computers as decoding machines. After World War II, computers became an essential cryptological tool.

But better machines for ever faster code breaking were not the only development. A milestone in the history of cryptology was the development of procedures for which no secret key had to be exchanged. Until this point, anyone wishing to send a coded message also had to pass on the key, in one way or another. This involved the risk that unauthorized persons might get hold of it. Today it is possible quite publicly to send someone a ciphertext that only the authorized receiver can read, without the need also to give him the secret key.

Over the centuries increasingly sophisticated methods of encoding have been invented, but at the same time more and more sophisticated methods have been developed for reading a ciphertext without authorization. The reader will follow the development of cryptology in detail up to the present day. First, however, we will concern ourselves with the simplest forms of the transmission of secret messages. Klausen's signals consisted of numerical sequences that did not make immediate sense. Count Sandorf's ciphertexts were strings of letters. The secret texts of the Freemasons were sequences of symbols. Anyone encountering such texts would immediately assume that they were ciphertexts. Not so with the wax tablets sent to Leonidas. They got past the Persian frontier guards, because no one seeing them would suspect that a secret message might be hidden in them. This type of encoding, when an unauthorized person does not even suspect the presence of a secret message, is the subject of the next chapter.

NOTE

1. F. W. Deakin, and G. R. Storry, *The Case of Richard Sorge* (London: Chatto & Windus, 1966) 246ff.

2. HIDDEN MESSAGES AND CODEBOOKS

So-called steganography . . . reaches a veritable climax
on the computer. The programmer Romana Machado has
developed a subversive little program, named *Stego*, that
conceals data in any kind of electronic image.... It does
this so subtly that the viewer is totally unaware that the
portrait of the pope may perhaps in reality be an instruction on how to make bombs.

—*Der Spiegel* 36 (1996) 211

THE PRISONER WHO WISHES to change his lifestyle can hardly ask his
wife in a letter that she hide a stick of dynamite in his birthday cake.
Such a birthday request would seem inappropriate to the prison officer who reads his letter, even in a liberal penal institution. At the same
time, the prisoner cannot convey his request in code, because a letter containing a seemingly meaningless sequence of signs would not pass the
censor—indeed, the censor might feel obliged to decode the text himself.
The poor prisoner therefore has no other option but to send home a seemingly harmless letter, one that will not arouse anyone's suspicion but will
nevertheless contain his secret wish, which only his wife can detect
because she alone knows how to look for the message. How, then, does
one hide a secret text in an openly accessible document?

THE EXPLOSIVE MESSAGE IN A HARMLESS TEXT

History does not record how the mailman on Main Street in Los Angeles
tackled his problem on that day in the fall of 1943, the third year of the

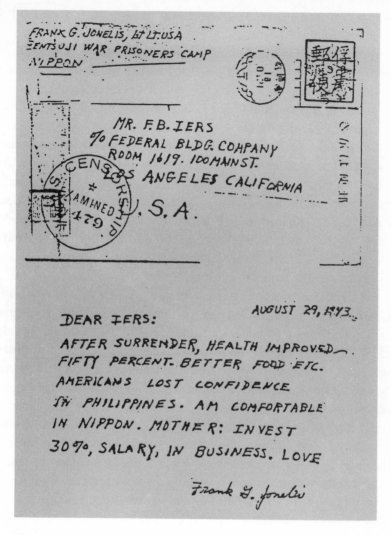

Fig. 2.1. A card sent from a Japanese POW camp to the FBI in Los Angeles passed the Japanese censor without difficulty. The first two words of every line, read after one another, contain information about American losses.

war. There he was, in front of Number 100, where a Mr. F. B. Iers was supposed to be working in room 1619 for a firm called Federal Building Company. However, in the building there was neither a firm of that name nor even a room 1619. Eventually the card ended up in room 619, where the FBI maintained an office. The initial letters of the addressee and the name of the firm suggested that the card (fig. 2.1) was intended for that destination. It came from a Japanese POW camp and had passed both the Japanese and the U.S. censors. The sender was a Lieutenant Frank G. Jonelis. The FBI people had a hunch there was something more to the text than met the eye. And indeed, if one reads the first two words of each line, one obtains the message: "After surrender fifty percent Americans lost in Philippines in Nippon 30%."[1] It was intelligence about American losses, concealed in a harmless card.

As early as the sixteenth century the Italian physician and mathematician Geronimo Cardano—of whom we will hear more—speculated on how one might hide a message in a text that would seem harmless to a naive reader. His suggestion was a template, similar to that of Count Sandorf (fig. 1.3), that lets only certain letters emerge from a text; read by themselves, the letters constitute the secret message. An illustration is shown in figure 2.2. Needless to say, sender and receiver must possess the same template. The template is the key.1976

But there does not have to be a template. Herbert W. Franke, in his book *The Secret Message*, illustrates a different method with a telegram: "Noch einmal tiefempfundene Anteilnahme. Rasche Rückkehr erforderlich. Von Norbert alles Liebe. Paula" (Once again profound sympathy. Speedy return necessary. Much love from Norbert. Paula.)[2] If the first letters of all the words are read from the end to the beginning, they disclose the message: "Plan verraten" (Plan betrayed). The wax tablets in chapter 1 are another example. This kind of news transmission, when an unauthorized person does not even realize that he has a hidden message before him, is called *steganography*. Steganography includes the emphasizing of certain letters in a way that would not occur to the uninitiated.

In Hamburg in May 1996, the master furrier Lutz Reinstrom was sentenced to life imprisonment. He had kept two women prisoner in a basement, tortured them, and eventually killed them. To cover his tracks, he had forced his victims to send greeting cards—which he would mail later—to their families, implying that the women had gone abroad. One of the women added a cry for help and gave the name of her tormentor by writing certain letters more thickly. Her effort was in vain: the hidden message was missed. Reinstrom dissolved the corpses of the women in barrels of acid. The emphasis on individual letters was discovered only subsequently by an expert and was used in the trial of the culprit. Figure 2.3 shows parts of two cards with the victim's call for help.

> dear martin,
> maybe you have already been told that the boss believes
> that at the last operation the police had been informed in
> advance. he therefore will send bob to all the people he
> considers trustworthy in order to get their opinion on where
> the leak could be. bob will come next monday at noon.
>
> greetings jack

b
h o b
a
s a
g
u n

Fig. 2.2. An exciting message hidden in a harmless text. It emerges only when the template (gray) is placed over it to reveal the letters of the text (white).

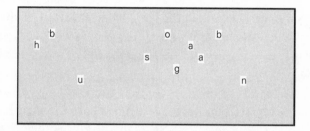

Fig. 2.3. The hidden cry for help of one of the victims of the "Hamburg acid murderer," who was sentenced in 1996. Emphasis on certain letters in the upper excerpt—"all the best in the New Year, mainly for your health"—spells out the word *hilf* (help), whereas in the lower excerpt the emphasized *l*, *u*, and *z* point to the murderer's first name, Lutz.

In a 1976 book that examined number combinations, the two German mathematicians Heinz Richard Halder and Werner Heise describe a classical mathematical problem, known as the Königsberg bridge problem. A close scrutiny of the text reveals that a few letters are printed a little bolder and are set slighly lower than the rest. Read by themselves they produce the sentence: "Nieder mit dem sowjetimperialismus" (Down with Soviet imperialism).[3]

Hidden messages also include those written with secret ink, a colorless liquid that becomes visible when warmed or when treated with some chemical. The messages are written in the margin of a letter or between its lines. Experienced agents who ran out of colorless ink have successfully used their urine.

During World War II, German intelligence conceived the idea of photographing messages and then reducing them to such a degree that the entire text fit on a thin strip of film, which was then placed under the period made by a typewriter ribbon at the end of a sentence in a typed letter.

It is in the nature of a message concealed in a seemingly harmless text that it may be missed not only by an unauthorized decoder but quite possibly also by the receiver. Had Sir John Trevelyan not been tipped off, he might never have discovered the suggestion that saved his life. Sir John, a convinced English Royalist, had fallen into the hands of Oliver Cromwell's agents and was being held prisoner at Colchester Castle. Two of his friends had already been executed there, so he too was waiting for his death sentence. Just then he received a letter signed R. T.—to this day historians have failed to discover the sender's identity. Here are the beginning and end of the letter in its archaic English:

> Worthie Sir John: —Hope, that is ye beste comfort of ye afflicted, cannot much, I fear me, help you now. That I would say to you, is this only: if ever I may . . .
>
> . . . have done. The general goes back on Wednesday. Restinge your servant to command. —R. T.

Although the story has been told and retold, I have never found an explanation for how Sir John discovered that every third letter after a punctuation mark was part of a hidden message. Its full text reads: "panelateastendofchapelslides." Sir John extracted this message from his letter and requested permission to meditate in the chapel for an hour—and disappeared.

It can, of course, also happen that a secret message is mistakenly believed to be hidden in a perfectly harmless report.

SHAKESPEARE AS A MATCHMAKER

The decoding during World War II of the Japanese cipher machine called Purple by the Americans is closely linked with the name of the world's most famous cryptologist, perhaps the greatest ever.

William F. Friedman was born in Russia in 1891. The following year, his parents emigrated to the United States. High school was no problem for the youngster; of more than three hundred students, he graduated among the top ten. He was initially employed by a firm manufacturing steam engines, then he went back to school, agricultural college, and finally studied horticulture at Cornell University in Ithaca, New York. To pay for his studies, he worked as a waiter in a restaurant. About that time, a wealthy textile merchant, George Fabyan, was looking for a horticulturist who would help increase the harvest of his farming enterprise. He inquired at Cornell about a suitable candidate and in the summer of 1915 hired Friedman.

Fabyan, who had no scientific training himself, maintained laboratories on his estate where researchers were working on projects in acoustics, chemistry, genetics, and also cryptology. Although Friedman's job was in the genetics laboratory, he was an expert photographer and therefore helped the cryptologists make enlargements of old texts. More than a dozen people were busy studying letters from the days of Queen Elizabeth I. Fabyan wanted to prove that Shakespeare's works had really been written by Sir Francis Bacon, Elizabeth's lord chancellor. This idea had been raising its head in scholarly literature for more than a hundred and fifty years. The American politician Ignatius T. Donnelly intended to get to the root of it. He wanted to discover if the word *Bacon* appeared anywhere in Shakespeare's works—if not in the plaintext then perhaps in some coded form. The champions of his theory therefore examined Shakespeare's works to discover if anywhere they contained cryptograms of *Bacon*.

It is a fact that Bacon himself was interested in secret writing. He had even invented his own system of ciphers. So what did all these investigations show? Do Shakespeare's works contain any hint of Bacon? In the play *Love's Labor's Lost*, in the third scene of the fourth act, we find the lines:

> But, with the motion of all elements,
> Courses as swift as thought in every power,
> And gives to every power a double power . . .

The first letter of line 1 and the first and second letters of lines 2 and 3 yield

> B
> CO
> AN

So here they are, the letters forming Sir Francis's surname. But this discovery and all the other "circumstantial evidence" like it were hardly accepted as convincing proof. A joker made fun of the supporters of the Bacon-alias-Shakespeare hypothesis by demonstrating that Shakespeare had written the forty-sixth psalm: in the English translation of the psalm, the forty-sixth word, if one counts from the beginning, is "shake"; the forty-sixth word, if one counts from the end, is "spear."

But Fabyan, a self-tutored man, was not discouraged. He made every effort to prove that Bacon had used the name *Shakespeare* as a pseudonym, and to this end in 1916 he also employed Elisebeth Smith, the youngest daughter of a banker and politician. Soon Friedman and she were working closely together. They developed a liking for cryptology—and for each other. They were married in May 1917. Thus the Bacon-alias-Shakespeare hypothesis brought two people together, though both realized at an early stage that Shakespeare's works contained no secret indication whatever of another author. Later the two wrote a book about it.

By the time the United States entered World War I, Friedman had advanced to the head of Fabyan's cryptology department. Now, in addition to combing through Shakespeare's writings, serious work began to be done. The department soon became known, and government agencies made use of its skills, for instance, asking them to solve cryptograms sent from India to Berlin. A group of Hindus hoped to achieve their country's independence with German help. Friedman was able to crack these and other codes. Later he lectured to U.S. Army officers on cryptology; these lectures opened entirely new pathways in that discipline. Friedman succeeded in determining the length of the keyword in Vigenère ciphers, a useful method when the Kasiski method fails (see chapter 6).

Less well known is the fact that in 1924 he was asked to crack the code of the Martians. That year, the planet Mars came especially close to Earth, closer than during the whole preceding millennium. Suddenly several radio stations of the U.S. Navy believed they had intercepted strange signals. But Friedman was unable to make any sense of them. They were probably just radio interference.

In August 1940, Friedman began his attack on the Japanese Purple and after twenty months of hard work he was able to present the first deciphered Purple signals.

PLAYING DICE IN THE AIR-RAID SHELTER

On December 7, 1941, the Japanese without warning attacked Pearl Harbor. A month later, the FBI agent Robert L. Shivers from Honolulu drew the attention of J. Edgar Hoover, the FBI director in Washington, to the fact that the November 22 issue of *The New Yorker* carried an advertisement on page 86 for a game of dice (fig. 2.4, left).

The upper part of the picture shows a night sky illuminated by searchlights above a barren landscape; its lower part shows an evidently cheerful party rolling dice. Underneath the players are the words "Achtung, Warning, Alerte!" This is followed by a text suggesting that in addition to tinned food, candles, bottled water, sweaters, blankets, books, and vitamin tablets, one should take the game *The Deadly Double* along to the air raid shelter. The game is available for $2.50 in all leading sports stores and supermarkets. Several lesser ads point to this big one; each of these also shows two dice (fig. 2.4, right). If one interprets XX as a death symbol, the first die as the month, and the second as the date, then the picture hints at either December 5 or December 7. Did the numbers on the dice represent a secret message? The attack on Pearl Harbor took place on December 7. Is it possible that Japan had placed this ad to warn Japanese in America of the opening of hostilities two weeks in advance?

Shivers's report was the first in a string of references to the advertisement of the Monarch Publishing Company, all of them were followed up by the FBI. In the course of the investigation into why the attack on Pearl Harbor had caught the Americans totally unprepared, the Monarch

Fig. 2.4. An advertisement published in *The New Yorker* in 1941, showing a game of dice. After the December 7 Japanese surprise attack on Pearl Harbor, the Monarch Publishing Company was suspected of having pointed to this date beforehand. Were agents to be told of the date of this attack by the dice in the picture on the right?

Publishing Company was naturally scrutinized. The firm belonged to one Mr. Craigh, who was most cooperative during the investigation. The authorities found no grounds for action against him. In a letter dating from that time, addressed probably to a journalist or radio reporter, he protested his innocence, and the editor of *The New Yorker* spoke of a witch hunt against a harmless citizen.

The investigation raised a number of questions, but Mr. Craigh could not answer them, since he died in 1946. He supposedly came from Boston, Massachusetts, but it was not possible to uncover any details of his past. He never presented a birth certificate.

It seems probable that the dice show the fatal date by accident, because it was discovered that an advertisement for the same game, showing the same position of the dice, had been published a year earlier. Nobody can seriously believe that the exact date of the attack on Pearl Harbor could have been predicted as early as 1940.

As recently as 1979—that is, forty years later—a Dartmouth graduate student came across the old advertisement while working on his doctoral thesis and likewise noticed that the date of the attack on Pearl Harbor was hidden in it.[4]

THE HIDDEN MESSAGE IN THE ACCOUNT NUMBER

It is not always that some information is added to a text in order to transmit a secret. Often the hidden message is intended merely as a protection against writing or transmission errors. Thus every one of our account numbers contains a hidden code. In most cases the code permits a check on whether the account is in fact held by the bank given.

Take, for example, an account with the Deutsche Bank. Let its number be 0291864. We will now examine whether this is in fact an account number of the Deutsche Bank. To do this, we first drop the last digit. What remains is the account number proper: 029186. We now count the digits, starting from the right: 6 is in the first position, 8 in the second, 1 in the third, 9 in the fourth, 2 in the fifth, and 0 in the sixth. Next we take all digits in the odd positions (counting from the right) and double them: 4, 2, 12. If the result has two figures, as 12 does here, we replace the number by the sum of its figures. For 12, the sum $1 + 2 = 3$:

$$029186$$
$$4\ \ 2\ \ 3$$

Next we enter the digits in the even positions, not changing them, in the lower line:

$$029186$$
$$049283$$

and add them together: $0 + 4 + 9 + 2 + 8 + 3 = 26$. If we now take the last digit of the complete account number, which we first dropped, and add it, $26 + 4 = 30$, the result is a multiple of 10, that is, a number ending with a 0, indicating a genuine account number of the Deutsche Bank. Had we instead taken the account number 0291865, the result of our test would not have been a multiple of ten, indicating that the account could not be held by the Deutsche Bank. The final figure of an account number is therefore a *test figure*, used for checking whether an error has crept in during the writing down of the number. The account number is said to be coded. If for instance we had transposed two neighboring figures, such as the 8 and the 1, the result would not have been divisible by ten. The same applies if we had made an error in writing, if for instance we had put a 3 instead of 2. Admittedly, even if the test works, the account number may not be correct. We might make a mistake by transposing not two adjacent figures but two that have another between them, for instance, we might transpose the 9 with the 8. Then the test would find no fault with the number. The secret message in the account number, while helpful in many cases, is not a complete guarantee that no mistake has been made.

For our illustration we have used an account number of the Deutsche Bank. Other financial institutions have other codes, that is, other calculation rules for discovering writing mistakes by means of a test figure. Your credit card is coded in the same way.

THE TEST FIGURE IN A CREDIT CARD

Take a Visa card with the number

0699 0043 1313 9642

Count the separate figures, starting from the right. The 2 thus becomes the first figure and the 0 on the left the sixteenth. Now write down under the number all the figures in the odd positions:

0699 0043 1313 9642
6 9   0 3   3 3   6 2

Double the figures in the even positions and again enter the result below the original number. If the result of doubling a figure is greater than 9, subtract 9.
This gives us

0699 0043 1313 9642
0699 0083 2323 9682

Now add the figures in the bottom line:

$$0 + 6 + 9 + 9 + 0 + 0 + 8 + 3 + 2 + 3 + 2 + 3 + 9 + 6 + 8 + 2$$

With a Visa credit card number, the result must be divisible by 10. In our case the sum is 70, as it should be. The opposite does not apply: if a number divisible by ten is obtained, it does not necessarily follow that the original number was a Visa credit card number.

Other credit cards also have a test figure that, by some rule or other, must fit the credit card number.

EVERY BOOK IS UNIQUE

Every book, even if its author has done nothing but copy from other sources, from the first page to the last, is unique. Its uniqueness is ensured by the ISBN code, the International Standard Book Number, a ten-digit sequence that enables any book published today to be unambiguously identified. Simply give your bookseller the ISBN number of the book you wish to have ordered. If it is available, the bookseller can get it for you. The ISBN number of the book you are now reading is

0-87951-919-3

It consists of four groups. The first indicates the primary language of the country in which the book was published. English-speaking countries, like the United States, Britain, and Canada, have a 0; France has 2; the German-speaking region has 3; the People's Republic of China has 7. The next group of digits is the publisher's number. The Overlook Press has the number 87951, Princeton University Press has 691, Rowohlt Verlag has 498 and 499.

The third group is the number of the book in the internal numbering of the publishing house. Now the book is unambiguously characterized. We know its country group (by language), its publisher, and the number under which it is listed there. The fourth group consists of a number from 0 to 9, or 10 written as the roman numeral X. This is the test figure that spots any mistake that may have crept into the preceding figures, so that when you order *Lady Chatterley's Lover*, you don't get the *Annual Report of the Smithsonian Institution*. If the ISBN is correct, the following conditions must be satisfied. Multiply the first figure by 10, the second by 9, the third by 8, and so on, until you get to the penultimate figure, which you multiply by 2. Add the result to the final figure. The sum must be divisible by 11. If it is not, something has gone wrong.

Let us take, by way of illustration, the number 0-285-63066-0. As we already know, the 0 at the beginning of the ISBN number tells us that the book was published in the United Statees, Britain, or Canada. The 285 tells the informed reader that the book was published by Souvenir Press,

London. Is the number correct? Below the individual figures, write the numbers 1 to 10 in descending order:

$$0\ 2\ 8\ 5\ 6\ 3\ 0\ 6\ 6\ 0$$
$$10\ 9\ 8\ 7\ 6\ 5\ 4\ 3\ 2\ 1$$

Multiply each number with the one immediately below it and add them all up:

$$(0 \times 10) + (2 \times 9) + (8 \times 8) + (5 \times 7) + (6 \times 6)$$
$$+ (3 \times 5) + (0 \times 4) + (6 \times 3) + (6 \times 2) + (0 \times 1) =$$
$$18 + 64 + 35 + 36 + 15 + 18 + 12 = 198$$

This number is divisible by 11. You may be sure therefore that with this number you will receive David Kahn's U.K. edition of *Seizing the Enigma*.

If you had made a mistake and, instead of 2, written 3 in the second position, the result of the calculation would not have been divisible by 11 and your bookseller's clever computer would have noticed this at once. It would also have noticed if you had transposed two figures, like writing the group 63066 as 63606. Try it out yourself. The test figure is a message concealed in the ISBN number that makes it possible to trace errors in transmission.

FROM JARGON TO CODEBOOK

Let us return to crucial messages packaged in an innocent text to prevent unauthorized persons from reading them. The most primitive form is the replacement of certain words or sentences by others. Military people are fond of giving their operations harmless names. Hitler's attack on the Soviet Union was Operation Barbarossa. The conquest of Sicily by the Allies had the code name Huskeyland. Overlord was the Allied landing in Normandy. Walküre was the code for the unsuccessful attempt on Hitler's life on July 20, 1944.

During World War I, a British censor noticed that two businessmen were negotiating by telegram daily about great quantities of cigars from British ports. On closer inspection, the businessmen were found to be German spies. If one of them ordered five thousand coronas from Newcastle, this meant that there were five cruisers in that naval port. Haicke Janssen and Wilhelm Ross were arrested and in 1915 executed at the Tower of London.

In 1944, shortly before Operation Overlord, the invasion of Normandy, French Resistance fighters were on alert to make their contribution to the liberation of France. In order to notify them of the imminence of the invasion, the BBC in its French service broadcast the opening line of Paul Verlaine's famous poem: "*Les sanglots longs des violons de l'automne*" (The long sobs of the violins of autumn). That was the signal for impending invasion. The next line of the poem, "*Blessent mon cœur d'une longueur monotone*" (wound my heart with monotonous longing), was the signal that the attack would begin within the next forty-eight hours.

The more elaborate the system of word substitution, the more necessary it becomes to compose long lists as dictionaries. As in a glossary, the concept in plaintext stands on the left and its secret equivalent, a series of letters or numerical combinations, or a mixture of both, on the right. In the sixteenth century, the nomenclator—as such a word list was then called—that Philip II gave his officials contained about four hundred code words. In the New World, George Washington's agents used word lists containing roughly eight hundred entries.

The first massive use of codebooks was in the American War of Independence. On July 15, 1780, a year before General Charles Cornwallis was forced with his British army to surrender at Yorktown, Virginia, Benedict Arnold sent a coded message to John André, a young British secret service officer. Arnold was commander of the military base at West Point, the location of the future U.S. military academy. He looked for the words of his plaintext in a then-well-known legal commentary and determined the page, line, and place within the line where the word stood. If he could not find the word he wanted in that volume, he encoded the word letter by letter, again by giving the page, line, and position of a word that began with the letter he needed, and by underlining indicated that he meant only the initial letter of that word. This made for rather complicated encoding. Imagine that you must encode the sentence "There was blood at the door" and as a codebook are using the Peregrine Smith paperback edition of Jack London's *The Road*. "There" is the first word of line 4 on page 5, so you write 5.4.1. You write "was" as 1.12.3. After some search you find "blood" on page 54, at the beginning of line 12, and write 54.12.1. And so on. You can see what a tedious business this is. And yet this text has only simple words. The task becomes really difficult if the plaintext contains a word such as *plutonium*, of which Jack London could not know about. You would then have to write 5.4.6 for *p*, 1.12.3 for *l*, and so on. A tedious business indeed.

Arnold soon switched to a dictionary, whose alphabetical arrangement made finding the words speedier. Letter-by-letter encoding of rare words, however, could still not be avoided. In his coded letter to André, Arnold offered, for twenty thousand pounds sterling, to supply the British General Sir Henry Clinton with information that would enable him to capture West Point and other garrisons. Nothing came of the deal, since the British secret service agent was taken prisoner by American troops. He was found in possession of material on West Point and was hanged as a spy. Arnold succeeded in escaping to British territory.

In 1786, President Thomas Jefferson, together with James Madison, his successor in office, designed a code in which certain words were represented by combinations of figures. The word *peace* was **1370**, *paper* was **207**, *Paris* was **1042**. But Jefferson replaced only certain words by numerical codes, using plaintext between them.

Soon the lengthy lists became books, the codebooks. From 1630, we can differentiate between good ones and bad ones. Until then, plaintext words were replaced by ciphertext words in such a way that a lexicographical ordering of the one also produced a lexicographical ordering of the other. Let us assume the ciphertext consists of five-figure groups. The beginning of the list might look something like figure 2.5. The advantage of such an arrangement is that one and the same codebook can be used for encoding and decoding. As in a dictionary, the alphabetical arrangement makes it easy to find every plaintext word, and equally, with the numbers in ascending order, every cipher.

abandon	**10020**
aberration	**10021**
accident	**10030**
accusation	**10035**
action	**10120**
address	**11444**
...	
...	

Fig. 2.5. **Pattern of a one-part nomenclator.**

The disadvantage is obvious. An unauthorized decoder, who may have identified *address* with **11444**, is bound to realize that the plaintext word of **20451** cannot come before *address* and therefore cannot possibly stand for *action*. Antoine Rossignol, the cryptologist of Louis XIV, was the first to introduce the so-called *two-part code*, which required two codebooks. In one, the plaintext words were arranged alphabetically; in the other, the ciphers were arranged in ascending order. The two volumes resembled our modern two-volume dictionaries: French-English, English-French. The drawback, of course, was that you had to work with two books.

Codebooks came into use also in the business world. Anyone wishing to keep telegram costs as low as possible should avoid those long words that German, for instance, is so fond of. He would be well advised to compose a codebook. He would save even more if he included in it not just individual words but entire phrases, such as "Unless payment is received within thirty days" or "with best regards." Such codebooks do not aim to make messages incomprehensible to the uninitiated, they aim merely to save telegram costs. But from here there is but a short step to the secret codebook.

Strangely enough, the German navy used a one-part code as recently as World War I (fig. 3.1 shows part of a page). Anyone therefore who had discovered that **53435** stood for *böig* (gusty), was bound to conclude that the plaintext word for **62280** must come well beyond *b* in the alphabet. In point of fact, it stood for *märz* (March).

THE CODEBOOK OF THE POPE

At the time of the Renaissance, the pope had the best cryptologists in the world in his service, such as the Argenti family, who introduced the concept of an easily remembered keyword. Rome then was a world power, and where power is, there is also intrigue and jockeying for position. To be able to decode your opponent's secret messages was a must. With the decline of the pope's secular power, the standard of his cryptologists also declined. Yet as recently as the nineteenth century there was a cipher section in the Vatican. Three cryptologists (*cifristi*) worked under a cipher secretary. Messages between the Vatican and its nunciatures in the principal countries continued to be exchanged in encoded form. But there were not many secrets to transmit. Months would sometimes elapse without a single secret message being exchanged between Rome and, for instance, the papal nuncio in Spain, and these messages were basically so undramatic as to make encoding not worthwhile. In such a climate, the art of encoding was bound to wither.

946	ra-e	983	democratico
948	congresso	984	dispo
949	ottanta	985	en
950	sospen	986	es
951	subito	988	grazia-e
952	quindici	989	ebbero
953	quattro	990	ncrisi
954	ud	991	piu
955	f	992	o
956	n	993	at
958	ro	994	ar
959	nove	995	c
960	po	996	risolu
961	fra	998	va-e-u
962	proclam	999	ur
963	opportuno	7700	Damao
964	culto-i	7701	S. Tommaso
965	cinquanta	7702	Coccino
966	ogni	7703	imperatore
968	ad	7704	pacifico
969	alla-e	7705	Faro
980	an	7706	Austria
981	avano	7708	marchese
982	canonica-o	7709	concilio

Fig. 2.6. **Part of a page from the two-part codebook about 1910 for the exchange of messages between the Vatican and the nuncio's office in Lisbon.**

As a rule, it was recommended to count off the sentences in a message, and in each odd-numbered sentence to state the opposite of the plaintext. The various nuncios' offices developed their own coding systems. The nuncio in The Hague wrote **MUSEUM** for *Vatican* and

MR.CERNI for *Austria*. The nuncio in Vienna invented a nomenclator with numerical combinations of groups of three and four figures. Proper names were represented by four-figure groups starting with **7**; the group **7690** meant *Napoleon Bonaparte*. An interesting role was played by **5**, which had no meaning and could be inserted anywhere to make life more difficult for the unauthorized reader.[5]

Nor were the papal cryptologists much better in the twentieth century. An insight into the secret writing of the pope is provided by two code-books in the papal nunciature in Lisbon, used before World War I.[6] One of them served encoding, the other decoding. Again, plaintext and cipher in the form of numerical groups face each. The secret ciphers are 739 three-figure groups from 000 to 999, which do not contain 7, since 7 plays the role of 5 in the example above. Each three-figure group means a letter (**643** = t), a number (**005** = 13), or a sequence of letters frequent in Italian (**833** = zione). It can also stand for a whole word (**655** = Italia). Figure 2.6 shows part of a page of the decoding volume of the papal code-book in Lisbon. No distinction was made between singular and plural. The groups were placed next to one another without a space between them. The decoder ignored the figure 7, divided the ciphertext into three-figure groups, and in his decoding volume looked up the plaintext designated by each three-figure group. It was not a very sophisticated method.

The opposing parties in World War I used codebooks mainly for the secret transmission of military and diplomatic information. In this the Germans suffered two heavy defeats that were to go down in history.

NOTES

1. *Cryptologia* (April 1980) 120.

2. Herbert W. Franke, *Die geheime Nachricht* (Frankfurt/Main: Umschau Verlag, 1982) 28.

3. Heinz Richard Halder and Werner Heise, *Einführung in die Kombinatorik* (Munich/Vienna: Carl Hanser Verlag, 1976) 118.

4. L. Kruh, "The Deadly Double Advertisements," *Cryptologia* (July 1979) 170.

5. A. Alvarez, "The Papal Cipher Section in the Early Nineteenth Century," *Cryptologia* (April 1993) 219.

6. A. Alvarez, "A Papal Diplomatic Code," *Cryptologia* (April 1992) 174.

3. CODEBOOKS IN WORLD WAR I

The last man to have the signal book was Radio Chief Petty Officer Neuhaus. He is seen in the water, but apparently without the book. . . . The signal key of the radio transmitter is still frantically clutched by Radio Petty Officer Kiehnert while already overboard. He is thrust below the water by those following him. By the time he surfaces again, the key has been lost.
—MATTI E. MÄKELÄ, *Das Geheimnis der* Magdeburg
(*The Mystery of the* Magdeburg)

THE BALTIC IN JULY 1915, one year after the outbreak of World War I. There is a lot of signal traffic, but the radio operators of the German warships cannot read all the signals, because there are also Russians transmitting, sending encoded messages. The Germans are not quite sure who is sending and to whom the signals are addressed, and they have no idea at all of the contents of the commands being radioed into the ether. The Russians, however, can decode the German signals; they know where the various ships are and on what missions they sail. Thus the Russian commander, Rear Admiral Bakhirev, can employ his force with great accuracy and, for example, sink the German minelayer *Albatross*. The Russian naval units owe their advantage to an event that occurred, also in the Baltic, a year before.

THE MAGDEBURG RUNS AGROUND

It is August 25, 1914. On the first day of this month, Germany declared war on Russia. Rear Admiral Behring, with his two cruisers *Augsburg* and *Magdeburg* and two escort destroyers, waits at the entrance to the Gulf of

Bothnia. There he intends to attack Russian battleships with torpedoes and, on his return, hunt for enemy destroyers. At 1700, both ships fix their position. Their positions differ by a nautical mile, but no one takes any notice. The *Magdeburg* is supposed to follow the *Augsburg*: the flagship carries the rear admiral at a distance of about a thousand meters, so that in case the *Augsburg* strikes a mine, he can get out of the danger zone. In the fog the sailors can barely make out the other vessel. The Germans suspect a Russian mine barrage. For that reason the *Augsburg* at 2303 hours notifies the *Magdeburg* in a coded signal that henceforth a southwesterly course is to be followed. This happens at 2307. Both vessels now sail along their new course at fifteen knots. Officers and lookouts are standing on the bridge of the *Magdeburg*. Thick fog envelops the ship. The Russians must be somewhere quite close. The *Magdeburg* now steers for the island of Odensholm. As soon as it is clear that the mine barrage has been circumnavigated, the boat will turn east again, away from the island and into the gulf in the direction of St. Petersburg. The men on board do not realize that they are about a nautical mile nearer Odensholm than they believe on the strength of their last location fix. Moreover, the crew of the *Magdeburg* are unaware at that moment that the flagship turned eastward some time ago. For reasons that have never been clarified, the order to change course arrives only at 0027 hours. Four minutes later, the signal has been decoded and Lieutenant Commander Habenicht orders, "Port fifteen degrees!" It is too late, and the ship reacts too slowly. She is still turning when at 0038 hours the men feel a violent bump, followed by several more. Eventually the ship stops so rapidly that everyone not holding on to something is flung down. The *Magdeburg* has run aground. Water enters the vessel. The depth of the sea at starboard is now only two and a half meters; to port, the sounding line shows five meters.

All attempts to free the ship fail, even after the anchor with chains has been jettisoned and the washing and drinking water tanks emptied. Ammunition and all dispensable loose iron parts are thrown into the water. The vessel does not budge. Then follow the bulkhead doors. Even at full force astern, the engines are unable to move the ship.

When daylight comes, the crew can see stones at the bottom of the Baltic. They realize that the ship has run aground a mere three hundred meters from the island of Odensholm. Lieutenant Commander Habenicht orders 120 shells to be fired at the island's transmitter station to prevent Russian units from learning about the plight of the *Magdeburg*. Too late.

The sentry on Odensholm has already reported to Captain Nepenin, the chief of the Russian observer service, that German words can be heard through the fog and that it seems a German ship is stuck fast off the island.

After the third attempt to free the ship, her commander gives up. Now it is time to destroy all secret material. The signal book of the imperial German navy of January 7, 1914, contains the instruction: "If there is a danger of the signal book falling into enemy hands, it is to be thrown overboard or destroyed (by fire)." Given the slight depth of the water, the only option is to burn the secret documents. Lively Russian signal traffic suggests that enemy forces will shortly appear on the horizon. A feverish destruction operation begins. In the boiler rooms, sailors are throwing books and papers into the fire. There are three copies of the signal book aboard the *Magdeburg*, and two of these are overlooked in the hurry. Moreover, naval charts containing information about German mine barrages in the Baltic are left lying on the chart table.

Some of the crew are saved by a German escort destroyer. But when a Russian lieutenant boards the ship shortly afterward, the six sailors who have stayed on board surrender. The commander, too, is still in his cabin and is taken prisoner. Over the months that follow, the wreck of the *Magdeburg* is thoroughly searched. All papers are collected and studied. To prevent suspicion being aroused, the rumor is spread that the *Magdeburg* carried major amounts of gold and money, whose salvage is taking some time. On the sea bottom, Russian divers find two signal books weighted with lead.

Eleven days after Lieutenant Commander Habenicht surrenders the *Magdeburg*, the Russian naval attaché in London reports to Winston Churchill, First Lord of the Admiralty, that the Russians are in possession of the signal book of the German imperial navy and that they have already succeeded in decoding some radio signals. He offers to make all the documents available to the British. Churchill is delighted, and as early as October two Russian officers bring one of the two signal books, along with other material, to London.

THE SIGNAL BOOK OF THE MAGDEBURG IN ROOM 40

What the Russian officers brought to England was a codebook. One of its pages is reproduced in figure 3.1. Churchill passed it on to a group that had been concerning itself with ciphers ever since the outbreak of the war.

On the first day of World War I, the British cable ship *Telconia* had put to sea in order to cut the German overseas cable off Emden. Almost entirely surrounded by enemies, Germany was now reduced to using international cables

Zahlen-	Buchſtaben- Eignal		Bedeutung
534 27	C a E		Bodenanſtrich
28	C a F		Bodenbeplattung
29	C a G		Bodenbeſchaffenheit
534 30	C a H		Bodenbeſchlag
31	C a I		Bodenſtück
32	C a J		Bodenventil (Nr. n)
33	C a K		Bodenverſchluß +
34	C a L		Bodenzünder
35	C a M		Bö -ig
36	C a N		Bogen
37	C a O		bogenförmig
38	C a Ö		Bogenlampe
39	C a P		Bohle
534 40	C a Q		Bohne (n kg)
41	C a R		bohren -ung, Bohr- *[s. Grund]*
42	C a S		Bohrer
43	C a T		Boje, Bojen- *[s. Anker, Kohlen, Leine]*
44	C a U		Boje auf den Anker ſtecken
45	C a ü		Boje aufnehmen (fiſchen)
46	C a V		Boje auslegen
47	C a W		Boje beleuchten
48	C a X		Boje über Bord
49	C a Y		eine Boje über Bord werfen und wieder fiſchen
534 50	C a Z		an der Boje feſtmachen
51	C a γ		an die Boje gehen
52	C γ A		Boje falſch hinlegen
53	C γ Ä		Boje legen

Fig. 3.1. Section from the codebook of the *Magdeburg*. Curiously, a one-part codebook was used.

running through enemy territory or communicating with the rest of the world by radio. In consequence all messages had to be encoded. This circumstance induced the British to set up a cryptology section, and Rear Admiral Henry F. Oliver soon found a suitable person to build such an organization.

Any physics student nowadays learns in his first year about a property of magnetic materials discovered in 1880 simultaneously by a British and a German scientist. The British discoverer James Alfred Ewing coined for it the term *hysteresis*, which is used to this day. Ewing had worked for five years at the University of Tokyo, where he set up a seismological observatory. After his return to England, he taught at Cambridge University. He was knighted for his scientific achievements.

Shortly before the outbreak of World War I, Ewing became interested in cryptology. This is what induced Rear Admiral Oliver to invite the fifty-nine-year-old scientist to establish a cryptology section in Naval Intelligence. Ewing accepted and set about studying all the commercial codebooks he could lay his hands on, including German ones. His progress was slow. In the meantime, the coded German messages that had been intercepted by radio were accumulating. Ewing acquired several collaborators for his project, especially colleagues from the naval college whom he knew to have a command of German. And now, suddenly, the codebook of the *Magdeburg* lay before him. But even with its aid the German signals could not be deciphered. Then one of Ewing's staff discovered that the codewords were themselves encoded—by a simple method, as was found, but a method that nevertheless took Ewing's team nearly three weeks to solve. After that, however, he was able to read the signals of the German navy.

As more experts joined Ewing's group, it moved to room 40 in the Admiralty building in November 1914. Henceforth the group was known as Room 40. It grew rapidly. By 1917, when it deciphered the famous Zimmermann telegram, Room 40 employed eight hundred radio operators and almost eighty cryptologists and office staff. The physical room 40 had long become too small for them, but the name stuck even after they moved to more spacious premises.

The people of Room 40 were a motley but illustrious bunch. They included a professor of classical archaeology and several university teachers of foreign languages, especially German. One member of the team later became a priest and made a name for himself as a Bible translator. Another was the son-in-law of the famous actress Eleonora Duse.

Yet another member of the team, William F. Clarke, the son of the attorney who had defended Oscar Wilde at his trial, became one of the famous code breakers of Bletchley Park during World War II (see chapter 10). Only the daughters or sisters of naval officers were employed as secretaries; they had to have command of at least two foreign languages. The lady who supervised them is reputed to have smoked cigars.

The codebook of the *Magdeburg* was not the only material from Germany that reached Room 40. At the beginning of August 1914, a group of Englishmen had taken the *Deutsches Handelsverkehrsbuch,* the German Trade Communications Book, from a German merchant ship whose crew were as yet unaware of the outbreak of war; and on November 30, 1914, a British fishing steamer brought in a tin box full of books and documents that had been jettisoned, in accordance with regulations, by a German destroyer before it was sunk. The team of Room 40 soon discovered that the codebook variant recovered from the tin box, the *Verkehrsbuch,* was used not only for radio traffic between warships but also for the exchange of messages between Berlin and the naval attachés of the German embassies abroad.

HOW WAS THE UNITED STATES TO BE KEPT OUT OF THE WAR?

It was the third winter of World War I. The enthusiasm with which Germany and its allies had entered the war had long evaporated. Both sides had already paid a heavy toll of lives. In the summer of 1916, the Germans had lost over 280,000 men killed in action, wounded, or taken prisoner at Verdun, and 220,000 in the Battle of the Somme. French losses amounted to 317,000 and British to 270,000. Neither belligerent had conquered significant enemy territory. Britain, the most dangerous opponent of the Central Powers, was safe thanks to its island position. There was only one way of hitting Britain painfully—by cutting off foreign supplies. Only if the wheat transports from the United States and Canada and the shipments of Swedish steel no longer reached the island could Britain be defeated. Thus, for the second time in this war, the plan was conceived of employing U-boats to sink all ships that made for the British Isles, including that of neutral countries, especially the United States. A U-boat hunt for merchant ships was therefore bound to drag

America into the war. The Central Powers had enough adversaries as it was; only quite recently Romania had also declared war on them.

The Germans, however, believed they could prevent America from joining the war on the Allied side. Ever since Mexico had to cede Texas to the United States, there was tension between the two countries. Frontier incursions by both sides had further aggravated the atmosphere. War between the United States and Mexico—so the German strategists speculated—would tie the Americans down in their own continent and prevent them from intervening in the war in Europe. In that case the U-boat war could bring Germany victory. There was, moreover, a chance that, in the event of a conflict between the United States and Mexico, the Japanese would land troops on the California coast. Mexico and Japan were at that time maintaining friendly relations, which worried the Americans.

The American government adviser Robert Lansing recognized the danger and issued this warning in a memorandum: "Germany wants us to embark on a war with Mexico, and that is precisely why we must not do so." But there were also counterarguments. The *Chicago Tribune* stated: "Fate offers us a golden apple in Mexico, but only bitter fruit in Flanders. If we start a war with Mexico we know what we will get—a secure continent. To lose is practically impossible."[1]

In Germany the issue of U-boat warfare was by no means uncontroversial. The German chancellor, Theobald von Bethmann Hollweg, was against it. But there were the hawks in the general staff, Hindenburg and Ludendorff, who were strongly in favor of the plan, and since 1916 they had supreme command of the entire German army. The decision was made in southern Upper Silesia at the Castle of Pless, where the German high command was located (Pless, at the Polish frontier, is now Pszczyna). With blue-eyed innocence the generals concluded that the United States's entry into the war was of no strategic significance. A mere six months of U-boat war would bring victory, they thought, and by that time the American war machine would not yet be running at full speed. Hindenburg and Ludendorff persuaded the still undecided kaiser. Bethmann Hollweg cautioned, quoting the reports of the German ambassador in Washington (Johann Heinrich Count von Bernstorff) and other experts on America, who had warned of the dangers if America entered the war. But the chancellor was not heeded. After all, there was still the Mexican card to play. The men at the Castle of Pless decided on unrestricted submarine warfare. It was to begin on February 1, 1917. Any enemy or neutral ship in the war zone was to be torpedoed without prior warning. Bethmann Hollweg's comment was *"Finis Germaniae"*—the end of Germany. He considered resigning, but as this would have a demoralizing effect on the public, he rejected the idea and dutifully set out for Berlin, where, against his better judgment, he was to obtain the endorsement of the Reichstag. His vice-chancellor, Karl Helfferich, was quoted as saying "Now Germany is lost for centuries."

This was the political background of a coded telegram that was to make history.

THE ZIMMERMANN TELEGRAM

Six weeks after that fateful conference at the Castle of Pless, Arthur Zimmermann was appointed director of the German ministry of foreign affairs—the first commoner to hold this post. Very soon, however, it was said that he was more a Hohenzollern than the kaiser himself. Worse still, he had an adventurous idea. In the event of a U-boat war, he believed, a Mexican-Japanese alliance could occupy the Americans to such an extent that they would not risk interfering in a European war. Felix von Eckhardt, the German ambassador in Mexico, had reported on developing friendly relations between his host country and Japan. Mexico, the German military leaders believed, might reconquer the lost Texan territories if, along with Japan, it embroiled the United States in a war on two fronts.

Zimmermann sent Eckhardt a telegram, which in English translation read:

> We intend to start an unrestricted U-boat war on February 1. An attempt will be made to keep the United States neutral nevertheless. In case we do not succeed in this, we propose an alliance to Mexico on the following basis: joint conduct of the war, joint conclusion of peace, extensive support and agreement from our side for Mexico to reconquer its earlier-lost territories in Texas, New Mexico, and Arizona.

> Detailed arrangements are left to Your Excellency. You will be good enough to disclose the above in strict secrecy to the president as soon as the outbreak of war with the United States is certain, adding the suggestion that he might invite Japan to join immediately and, at the same time, mediate between us and Japan. Please point out to the president that ruthless employ-

ment of our U-boats now holds out the prospect that Britain will be compelled to make peace within a few months. Confirm receipt. Zimmermann.

Originally Zimmermann had wished to send the message to Mexico by the merchant submarine *Deutschland*, due to sail January 15, but the voyage was canceled. Now the message had to be transmitted to Eckhardt telegraphically. The opportunity to do so was handed to him by the Americans themselves.

In Mexico, there were no radio stations sensitive enough to receive the signals of the Nauen transmitter near Berlin; but the American station of Sayville on Long Island had the necessary technical facilities. President Wilson was then trying to reconcile the European opponents. He made some peace proposals, but those fell upon deaf ears. As part of his endeavors to achieve a negotiated agreement, he permitted Count Bernstorff to correspond with his government in Berlin in cipher over American cables—a measure that earned Wilson fierce criticism in administration circles, since it gave the Germans an opportunity to exchange espionage messages. But the president stuck to his decision.

Zimmermann had three ways of sending a telegram to Bernstorff in Washington for forwarding to Eckhardt in Mexico. First, it could be radioed from Nauen to Sayville. Second, it could be transmitted by the American embassy in Berlin, which was in cable communication with its government and would forward coded telegrams without knowledge of their contents. Finally, he could take it to the Swedish embassy in Berlin, which, regardless of its country's neutrality, likewise permitted the dispatch of coded messages over its cables to America.

To be on the safe side, Zimmermann decided to use all three routes. Both the Swedish and the American cables ran via England, and thus the text reached the men of Room 40 in triplicate.

THE TELEGRAM IS DECODED

In the morning of January 17, 1917, a pneumatic-tube cartridge plopped into the basket in Room 40. In it was a sheet with numbers, arranged in groups of three, four, and five (fig. 3.2). William Montgomery and young Nigel de Grey[2] regarded the page. The second group of figures, **13042**, was reminiscent of the cipher that was normally found at the beginning of telegrams of the diplomatic service and that indicated the codebook used. Code 13042 was unknown to the men of Room 40, but they had in their safe Code 13040, and there was a book that listed the used variants of that code—the result of laborious study of hundreds of coded texts. The third to last number in the telegram was **97556**. Large numbers were normally used for names or for rarely occurring concepts. At the end, **97556** was probably a signature. In point of fact the codebook supplied for it the name Zimmermann. The head of the German foreign ministry had personally signed the coded telegram. But who was it addressed to? Montgomery and de Grey found **17214**, the sign for "top secret," and

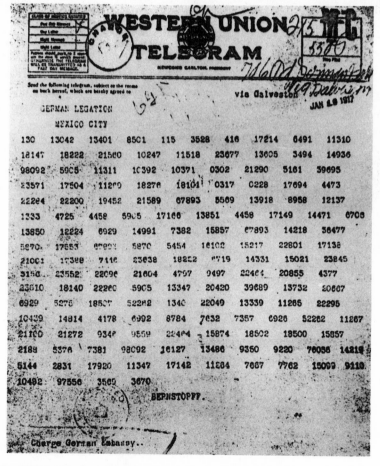

Fig. 3.2. **The Zimmermann telegram as Bernstorff forwarded it to Eckhardt in Mexico.**

23845, which meant "Your Excellency"—Code Book 13040 was equipped for correspondence requiring all kinds of courtesies. As the message had been intercepted en route to Washington, "Your Excellency" could only be the German ambassador, Count Bernstorff. Other words, too, were decoded with the aid of the codebook from the safe: **67893** meant "Mexico." What did a German telegram from Berlin to the German ambassador in Washington have to do with Mexico, which even occurred twice in the text? Next they found the word "alliance" (**12137**) and "Japan" (**52262**), which likewise occurred twice. The words were now beginning to come together, and the first fragmentary sentences emerged:

> We intend to start an unrestricted U-boat war on February 1. An attempt will be made to keep the United States neutral nevertheless . . . we do not . . . we propose an alliance to Mexico on the following basis . . . conduct of the war . . . conclusion of peace . . . Mexico . . . Your Excellency . . . disclose . . . in strict secrecy to the president . . . outbreak of war with the United States . . . Japan . . . at the same time mediate between us and Japan . . . Please point out to the president that . . . our U-boats . . . Britain will be compelled to make peace within a few months. Confirm receipt. Zimmermann.

Normally the Germans would encode their secret texts, produced with a codebook, a second time. With this telegram they had omitted to do so. The fragmentary sentences made sense, and their content was so startling that the code breakers could not believe their eyes. So far President Wilson had hesitated to come to the aid of the hard-pressed Allies. But now the devilish plan was revealed: the United States was to be squeezed simultaneously by Mexico and Japan. Surely that must change his mind.

Comparison with the complete text of the telegram shows that the passage between the words "conclusion of peace" (**17149**) and "Your Excellency" (**23845**), with the exception of the word "Mexico" had not at that point been decoded—that is, the passage in which Zimmermann promises to see to it that America, having lost the war, would return to Mexico its former territories in Texas, Arizona, and New Mexico. But even without this passage the telegram was explosive enough, and Montgomery immediately brought it to his chief.

Ewing had left the group in October 1916, to assume the vice-chancellorship of Edinburgh University. The new head of Room 40 was Admiral William R. Hall. As he glanced at the decoded passages, he realized what a crucial paper he held in his hands. Surely now the hesitant Americans would have to come to the aid of the Allies. As an experienced intelligence officer, however, he also realized that the telegram could only be used with the greatest caution. On no account must the Germans learn that their coded messages could be read in England.

Just then President Wilson was making his final attempt to get the belligerent parties in Europe to make peace. He had no idea of the existence of the telegram. In a speech to the senate on January 22, he appealed to the Europeans to conclude a "peace without victory." Many people in the United States hoped that the bloodshed in Europe would finally end. Only the German ambassador in Washington had no illusions. Bernstorff had received Zimmermann's telegram and already forwarded it to Eckhardt in Mexico City. Figure 3.2 shows the coded telegram.

Count von Bernstorff had tried for his eight years as German ambassador in the United States to keep America out of a European conflict. On January 31, eight hours before the start of the U-boat war, he presented his government's official statement on the subject to Secretary of State Robert Lansing. "I've had my fill of politics for the rest of my life," the disenchanted diplomat stated that evening. Three days later, the United States broke off diplomatic relations with Germany. But it remained neutral, with Wilson continuing to hope that he might get peace negotiations going in Europe, and the telegram, still not fully decoded, was still in the safe of Room 40. Not until February 5 did Admiral Hall hand it to Undersecretary of State Lord Hardinge.

Meanwhile German U-boats were sinking ships that approached the British Isles. There was talk of a naval graveyard in the Atlantic. Were the Germans to be proved right in their belief that Britain could take total U-boat war only for a brief time?

Lord Hardinge informed Arthur James Balfour, the British foreign secretary, of the contents of the telegram. Despite the still undecoded passages, Balfour wanted to bring it to President Wilson's notice. He hoped the fragment would be sufficient to induce the United States to join the war, though he agreed with Hall that the Germans must on no account learn where the leak in the transmission was located. Was there a way to deceive them?

Admiral Hall developed a plan. He would to get hold of a copy of the telegram that Bernstorff sent to Eckhardt in Mexico. If that telegram, which bore a different date and probably also Bernstorff's signature, was published, then the Germans were bound to believe that the leak was somewhere in the United States or Mexico. Through a liaison Hall succeeded in obtaining a copy. How this happened is an incredible story, almost as if out of a cheap thriller.

An English printer in Mexico one day discovered to his horror that one of his employees was producing counterfeit money on his presses. Counterfeiting then was punishable by death. While he was consulting with a Mexican friend what he had best do, the counterfeiter denounced him to the police to escape being prosecuted himself. The printer was arrested and, in a speedy trial, sentenced to death by hanging. Fortunately for him, this occurred on a weekend; the execution would not take place until Monday. The Mexican friend now asked a man he knew, a Mr. H. who worked for British Intelligence, to help. Alerted by Mr. H., the British ambassador intervened and succeeded in obtaining a grace period while the real culprit was proved guilty. The verdict was overturned and the printer released. Mr. H.'s effort bore fruit. The Mexican friend worked at the telegraph office; thereafter, out of gratitude, he supplied the Englishman with copies of whatever telegrams might be of interest to Intelligence. One of these was the copy of the coded Zimmermann telegram.

On February 20, 1917, it landed on Hall's desk, in the form in which Bernstorff had forwarded it to Eckhardt. In the meantime, the Room 40 staff had after much laborious work also decoded the missing passages. Figure 3.3 reproduces some of the figure groups of the telegram and the German plaintext words belonging to them. Hall was therefore able to assure the British foreign secretary that the telegram could now be used without revealing that the leak was located in England.

But what if President Wilson had to explain how he learned of the telegram? It was to be expected that many senators would regard it as a fake. Would the president not have to disclose that he received the text from the British? An American president cannot be seen to lie, and especially not President Wilson. Hall and the U.S. ambassador in London had an ingenious idea. When the copy of the coded telegram from Mexico arrived in London, de Grey went to the American embassy with his German codebooks and there once more "decoded" the long-familiar text.

Now President Wilson was able in all honesty to announce that the telegram had been decoded on U.S. soil. On February 24, Balfour informed the president of the contents of the telegram. Wilson began an investigation, wanting to be sure it was not a fake. On the morning of March 1, 1917, the readers of the *New York Times* were told that "Germany seeks allies against the USA and invites Mexico and Japan to join her. The text of the German proposal has become known in full." This news incensed the public more than the huge tonnage figures of merchant ships being

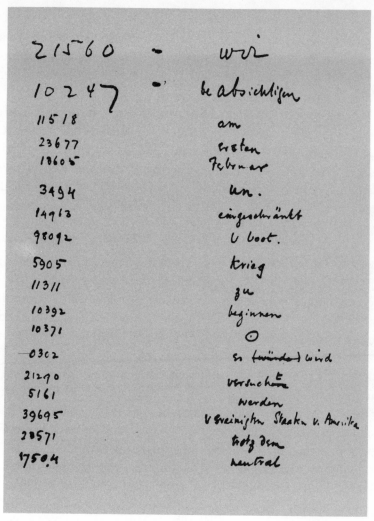

Fig. 3.3. One side of the worksheet used by Nigel de Grey in the decoding of the Zimmermann telegram "on American soil" in London.

sunk by the Germans. Eckhardt denied ever having received such a message. The Mexican foreign minister declared that no such proposal had ever been made to him. Was the telegram a fake after all? A surprise report from Germany removed all doubt: Zimmermann himself admitted to having drafted and dispatched the telegram. Now the mood in America changed. Even Americans of German extraction, on whose support the strategists of the Central Powers had always banked, turned their backs on the German Reich. The telegram put an end to the American illusion that the United States could live independently of the rest of the world and remain unmolested. The fact that Zimmermann had abused Wilson's friendly gesture of making the Long Island radio station available to the Germans, that instead he had used it for a conspiracy against America, was felt as a particular affront.

When Zimmermann learned that American citizens were able to read the text of the telegram over breakfast, he assumed that the plaintext had fallen into the wrong hands at the German embassy in Mexico. Furious, he sent several more telegrams to Eckhardt, still encoded in the old system, to discover where the leak had occurred. He evidently could not imagine that the enemy was in possession of the German code. The people of Room 40 had no more difficulties with these telegrams.

If Americans before had failed to agree on how to react to the German U-boat warfare, all doubts now disappeared. "How Zimmermann United the United States," observed a journal headline on March 17, 1917. The decoding of the Zimmermann telegram changed the course of world history. On April 6, the United States declared war on Germany. In another nineteen months, Germany and Austria-Hungary would surrender.

Codebooks were rather awkward keys. They often contained up to two thousand entries and could not easily be changed. Because of the danger that they might fall into enemy hands, they had to be continually replaced by new ones. We have seen that their use on board ship and in the diplomatic service had its weaknesses; their use was even more unsafe with ground troops, who had to take the codebooks with them whenever they moved to a different position. So it came about that other methods of coding were used. Preferable to codebooks were encrypting procedures that required only keywords. Such keywords could easily be changed from one day to the next. One of the oldest encrypting methods goes back to Julius Caesar.

NOTES

1. Barbara W. Tuchman, *The Zimmermann Telegram* (New York: Viking, 1958) 90 and 95.

2. De Grey also was one of the Enigma code breakers at Bletchley Park in World War II.

4. HE CAME, HE SAW, HE ENCODED

A monalphabetic substitution with a CAESAR encryption step was introduced in 1915 in the Russian army after it turned out to be impossible to expect the staffs to use anything more complicated.

—FRIEDRICH L. BAUER, *Decrypted Secrets*

WE KNOW THAT THE WORD *kaiser* is derived from the name of Gaius Julius Caesar, the Roman politician and general who, as we all learned at school, came, saw, and conquered. We also know that *Cesarean section* bears his name, because it was allegedly through such a procedure that he came into this world. Hardly anyone, however, knows that a simple encoding method to this day bears his name.

THE SECRET WRITING OF JULIUS CAESAR

The biographer Suetonius reports that Caesar sent letters of a confidential nature to Cicero in secret writing. Full of admiration, Suetonius explains that the words could be read only if instead of the letter *d* one read *a*, if instead of *e* one read *b*, and so on. The method is shown in figure 4.1. The letters in the upper row are those of the plaintext, the letters in the bottom

Fig. 4.1. If one alphabet is written below another, displaced by several (here, three) places to the left, and the missing letters are put in the empty spots on the right, we obtain a translation table in which the upper row contains the plaintext alphabet and the lower row the corresponding coded letters.

row those of the ciphertext. Had Caesar wanted to warn a friend:

never trust Brutus

he would have written:

QHYHUWUXVWEUXWXV

Caesar's secret writing simply consisted in the alphabet of the ciphertext being displaced by three letters from that of the plaintext, with the first three letters put in the empty spaces on the right. Obviously, instead of a displacement by three letters he could just as easily have chosen one by five or by twenty. There are only twenty-five displacements in all; the twenty-sixth would produce the plaintext alphabet. If Brutus had intercepted the text and realized that the secret writing resulted from a displacement of the alphabet, he would have had the plaintext before him after, at most, twenty-five attempts.

The displacement is more easily pictured if the plaintext and coded letters are written not in two rows but on two disks that can be rotated with regard to each other, as shown in figure 4.2. The outer disk carries the letters of the plaintext, the inner disk those of the encoded text. In the initial position the two alphabets face each other. If the inner disk is now

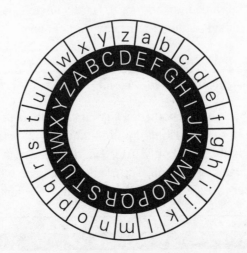

Fig. 4.2. Two disks that can be rotated against each other, with alphabets on them, operate in the same way as alphabets displaced against each other (as in fig. 4.1). The outer ring carries the plaintext letters, the inner the coded letters. Rotation of the bigger and smaller disks against each other permit all Caesar codes.

turned, as has been done in the illustration, we have a confrontation of alphabets that enables us to read off for every plaintext letter the coded letter corresponding to it. The disk in figure 4.2 can be used not only for coding by Caesar's system but also for more complicated coding methods. That is why the American agency concerned with ciphers, the National Security Agency (NSA), has the disk in its seal (fig. 4.3).

For anyone wishing to crack modern codes, a Caesar code produces just a weary smile. Yet even modern systems preserve remnants of it. The simple Caesar contains two elements important to coding. First, there is the *instruction*. It states: "Replace a letter at a particular place in the alphabet by one occurring a certain number of letters later." The more learned word for instruction is *algorithm*. The number by which the displacement is effected—in the historical Caesar, the number 3—is the key. In simple Caesar ciphers, the key is only a number.

We will encounter methods in which the key is a word, or a word and a number. There are also methods that use an entire book as a key. We have already seen codebooks and the statistical yearbook that were used by Richard Sorge's spy ring. Instruction and key are needed both for encoding a message and for reading it again. If someone wants to send an encrypted message to only one definite addressee, the key presents a

Fig. 4.3. The American authority on ciphers, the National Security Agency, chose a cipher disk for its emblem.

problem, because the sender and the receiver must agree on it beforehand and because, whichever way the key is conveyed, there is the risk of its falling into the wrong hands, like the template of Count Sandorf. Then the encoded secrets are secrets no longer.

That is why the best methods are those in which sender and receiver use a short key. Klausen's *SUBWAY* was a good example. We will see (in chapter 5) how a married man might send his mistress coded letters with a simple keyword like *POPSY*. *Popsy* he can easily remember; he does not have to write it down and risk his wife's discovering it and reading his letters. And when he gets too old to remember the keyword, he will not be much use to Popsy anyway. We will also see how his wife can decode the secret correspondence even though she does not know the keyword.

To this day, cryptologists accept the principle that it is more important to keep the key secret than the instruction. Thus, for instance, the cipher machine used by the Germans during World War II, the legendary Enigma, was internationally known even before the war and, in a basic version, commercially available. Its letter wheels and *plugboard* contained the coding instruction. But it was the key that was necessary for decoding, and this had to be kept secret. Often it was changed several times a day, confronting the opponents with a new key even before they had cracked the old one.

But let us stay with the Caesar code. The method becomes especially transparent if numbers are used instead of letters, in other words, if the letters of the alphabet are numbered as in figure 4.4. Caesar's message can therefore also be written in plaintext, as follows:

14 05 22 05 18 20 18 21 19 20 02 18 21 20 21 19

The ciphertext then runs:

17 08 25 08 21 23 21 24 22 23 05 21 24 23 24 22

Now we see how the Caesar works. Increasing the numeric value of the plaintext letters by the key number, we obtain the numeric value of the encoded letters. If the result is less than 26, there are no problems. But if it exceeds 26, we must subtract 26 and use the remainder. This can be clearly seen on the disk. If, starting from A, you count twenty-seven, twenty-eight, or twenty-nine places, you get to B, C, or D, exactly where you would have ended up by counting one, two, or three places. Hence for counting on the letter disk, 27 = 1, 28 = 2, and 29 = 3. Strange mathematics!

a	01	n	14
b	02	o	15
c	03	p	16
d	04	q	17
e	05	r	18
f	06	s	19
g	07	t	20
h	08	u	21
i	09	v	22
j	10	w	23
k	11	x	24
l	12	y	25
m	13	z	26

Fig. 4.4. The alphabetic assignment of letters to the numbers 1 to 26.

CALCULATING WITH REMAINDERS

Unlike the calculating rules of everyday life, what matters here is not the magnitude of a number but the remainder left by subtraction, often by repeated subtraction. We can also use the remainder left after division. We all know what it means when we say that two quantities are equal, that $3 + 4 = 7$. However, alongside equality there exists another, looser relation between two numbers: the equality of their remainders after division by a third number. If we divide the numbers 27, 28, and 29 by 26, the number of letters in the alphabet, we obtain the remainders 1, 2, and 3. If instead we divide by 17, the remainders are 10, 11, and 12. To avoid confusing the equality of numbers and the equality of their remainders, we add another stroke to the equals sign and write $27 \equiv 1$, but this example applies only to division by 26. Accordingly we now write $28 \equiv 2$ (mod 26), $29 \equiv 3$ (mod 26); or, if dividing by 17, $27 \equiv 10$ (mod 17), $28 \equiv 11$ (mod 17), and $29 \equiv 12$ (mod 17).

The remainders of numbers have a useful property. Let us consider the remainders of the number 31. There we have $40 \equiv 9$ (mod 31) and $55 \equiv 24$ (mod 31). Let us now take the sum of 40 and 55, that is, $40 + 55 = 95 \equiv 2$ (mod 31). Instead of adding those two figures together and forming the remainder mod 31, we could have added their remainders together: $9 + 24 = 33 \equiv 2$ (mod 31). It is the same with multiplication: $40 \times 55 = 2200 \equiv 30$ (mod 31). We get the same result by multiplying the remainders: $9 \times 24 = 216 \equiv 30$ (mod 31). So long as we are interested only in the remainders, we can replace the addition and multiplication of numbers by the addition and multiplication of their remainders. This has the advantage of preventing the numbers we work with from becoming too large.

REMAINDERS ON THE POCKET CALCULATOR

Do you know the remainder of 95728 in the domain of remainders of 73? You can easily calculate it. Take your calculator and divide 95728 by 73. The result is 1311.3425. This means that 73 is contained in 95728 as a whole 1311 times. But 1311 x 73 gives us 95703. The division leaves a remainder of 95728 - 97503 = 25. We can thus write: $95728 \equiv 25 \pmod{73}$.

What has all this to do with coding and the thrill of coded messages? The answer is that even in the most up-to-date coding methods, calculation with remainders plays a crucial part.

A CAESAR WITH A MNEMONIC

The twenty-five positions of the cipher wheel shown in figure 4.2 offer twenty-five different displacements. But we can make the decoder's life more difficult. To do this, we use a *mnemonic* in addition to the key number. Since we want a key that is easy to remember, we will choose a simple mnemonic.

The key number need not be greater than 26. Let 6 be our key number and the word *newspaper* our mnemonic. Now we proceed in three steps:

1. If a letter occurs in the mnemonic more than once, we include it only the first time, deleting it afterward. The word *newspaper* thus becomes the keyword *NEWSPAR*.
2. We write the plaintext alphabet in one line. Then, from the first letter we count by the key number to the right, in this case six digits, and write the keyword below. This has been done in figure 4.5, top. As a result, in the second line we have already obtained part of the ciphertext alphabet.
3. Now we fill the empty spaces of the second line, starting after the keyword, with the rest of the letters, needless to say in alphabetic order. When the spot under the plaintext letter *z* is reached, we continue from the beginning. The result is shown in figure 4.5, bottom. Now we have a ciphertext alphabet.

abcdefg h i j k l m n o p q r s t u v w x y z

N E W S P A R

---

a b c d e f g h i j k l m n o p q r s t u v w x y z

TU V X YZN EW S P A R B C D F G H I J K L M O Q

Fig. 4.5. A Caesar with a mnemonic. With the aid of the mnemonic *newspaper* and the key number 6, the matching of plaintext letters and coded letters is achieved.

Using this key,

never trust brutus

becomes

BYKYG IGJHI UGJIJH

The principle of this method was used as early as the sixteenth century in the papal secretariat.

Let us take a closer look at this type of coding. We have the key number 6 and the mnemonic *newspaper*—or, rather, the keyword *NEWSPAR*. So long as we do not change the key, the matching of plaintext letters and code letters always remains the same. It is always **Y** that corresponds to *e*, always **H** that corresponds to *s*. This unambiguous attribution is called *monalphabetic coding*. Every simple Caesar, just as every Caesar with a mnemonic, is monalphabetic.

The longer the keyword, the fewer letters have to be replenished in alphabetic order. The mnemonic *newspaper* supplies a keyword of seven letters; in the third step, therefore, nineteen letters are placed in the empty spots. The horrible German word

Donaudampfschiffahrtsgesellschaftskapitaenswitwe

as a mnemonic produces the keyword

DONAUMPFSCHIRTGELKW

which means that only seven letters have to be supplied in the empty spaces. With even longer keywords the coding of a Caesar with a mnemonic moves further and further away from a simple Caesar. In other words, the alphabetic order plays a progressively small part. If for instance you took the whole Bible as the mnemonic, then the "keyword" would contain all letters and none would have to be filled in later. In such a keyword, all twenty-six letters are arbitrarily shuffled. They form a secret alphabet, like that in figure 4.6. Admittedly we have then lost a key that we can easily remember. Nevertheless such shuffling of an alphabet plays a major role in cryptography to this day.

Fig. 4.6. **Matching of the plaintext alphabet to a randomly shuffled ciphertext alphabet.**

THE LAWS OF SHUFFLING

To recapitulate: in monalphabetic encoding we write the twenty-six letters in their normal sequence on one line and below it place the letters of a shuffled alphabet. If we want to encode a message, we look for the plaintext letter in the upper line and find our ciphertext letter below it. To understand this kind of coding better, we need to take a closer look at the nature of shuffling.

The number of shuffled alphabets is quite astonishing—or, in more general terms, the number of ways in which a series of things may be arranged is enormous. With four letters there are already twenty-four options. How rapidly the number of possible arrangements grows with the number of objects is reflected in a story told by the Austrian writer Egmont Colerus (1888-1939):

A respectable family of a long-past period consists of the two parents and twelve well-behaved, healthy children. The family is sitting happily at the dinner table. Suddenly a boy turns cheeky. He maintains that he always gets the leftover soup because his place at the table is unfavorable. The family is good-natured and used to settling differences of opinion by compromise. It is therefore decided to change the seating order every day, as the maid cannot be expected to change her way around the table when serving.

The event gives rise to a general discussion, and estimates are made of the time it will take before all possible seating orders are exhausted. "Well, a few days," suggests one boy. "Better say a few weeks," a girl corrects him. Eventually they agree on a year. "Surely there is a formula for this," the eldest son points out. . . . Paper and pencil are produced in the interval between soup and the meat dish, and the older children calculate with flushed faces. How large is . . . this magic number? The answer is: 87,178,291,200. What can one do with these billions of possibilities? How long will it take? A year has 365 days. Let us therefore divide by 365. More calculating . . . "I get . . . 238,844,633." "Do you know what this means?" the philosopher among the sons exclaims. "It means that it will take us nearly 239 million years to complete all the possibilities . . ." "And I shall die before I get a decent plate of soup," laments the youngest.[1]

With the formula mentioned in the story, the family of fourteen gets the desired number of possible seating orders by multiplying the numbers 1 to 14 with one another.

How many possibilities are there for shuffling the twenty-six letters of the alphabet and thereby creating cipher alphabets? How many possible shuffled alphabets must an unfortunate receiver of an important secret message examine if he has been careless enough to lose his key alphabet? Can every inhabitant of the earth, adult and child, create a secret alphabet that belongs to him or her alone? To answer that we must multiply the numbers 1 to 26 with one another. The number of possible secret alphabets is not in the range of billions but much greater:

$$403,291,461,126,605,635,584,000,000$$

Given a world population of nearly six billion, every person has more than sixty-five million billion secret alphabets available to himself or herself alone.

PERMUTATIONS

The transition from one sequence to another, for instance, in the shuffling of cards, is called *permutation*. If we number the individual cards of a pack, card 1 may be in position 25 after shuffling, card 2 in position 13, and so on. The sequence is changed, *permuted*. We have seen how great is the number of possible permutations of the twenty-six letters of the alphabet. For the thirty-two playing cards of euchre the number is much greater.

If we want to take a closer look at the possible arrangements of the alphabet, we are overwhelmed by the number of possibilities. Things would be a lot simpler if our alphabet had only a handful of letters.

Let us imagine that we live in a world whose inhabitants have developed an alphabet that stopped at four letters, A, B, C, and D. There exist twenty-four permutations of these four. They are listed in figure 4.7.

```
ABCD  ABDC  ACBD  ACDB  ADBC  ADCB
BACD  BADC  BCAD  BCDA  BDAC  BDCA
CBAD  CBDA  CABD  CADB  CDBA  CDAB
DBCA  DBAC  DCBA  DCAB  DABC  DACB
```

Fig. 4.7. **The different arrangements of the letters A, B, C, and D.**

ABCD can become DBCA by permutation. Figure 4.8, top left, indicates the transition from one arrangement to another. A becomes D, B becomes A, C and D become B and C. Let us call this permutation X; it transposes ABCD into DABC. To the right is another permutation, Y, which transposes ABCD into BDCA. Just as a deck of cards can be shuffled several times in succession, so any number of permutations can be performed one after another. In the second line of figure 4.8, ABCD is changed into DABC by permutation X; from this the sequence ABDC is produced by permutation Y. Permutations X and Y, performed consecutively, therefore give rise to a new permutation, given in the third line, left. But care must be taken of the order in which permutations are performed. If Y is performed first and X afterward, the result is a different sequence, ACBD.

Let us assume that we have turned a plaintext into a secret text by means of a permuted alphabet. Would the message become even more secret if we encoded it again, by another permuted alphabet? Would it be more difficult to decode? Would a text that we encoded fifty times, each time with a different permuted alphabet, present an insuperable obstacle

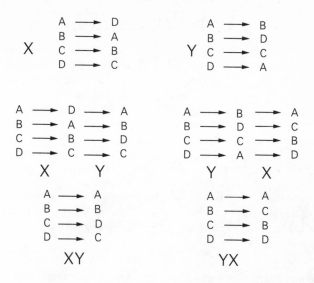

Fig. 4.8. Permutations X and Y (top). A becomes D, B becomes A, C becomes B, and D becomes C. For Y, A becomes B, an so on. X and Y yield a new permutation. But the permutation depends on the sequence in which X and Y follow each other. If Y follows X (center left), the arrangement of the alphabet is different from that when X follows Y (center right). The combined permutations XY and YX are shown at the bottom.

to an unauthorized decoder? After all, the decoder does not know our fifty different permuted alphabets, nor does he know the order in which we performed the permutations.

The answer is no. Fifty permutations performed one after another are no better than one. No matter how many we perform, the end effect is always that of a single permutation. This is not surprising. A well-shuffled pack of cards cannot be shuffled any better, whether we reshuffle it two or fifty more times.

In many respects permutations of things, be they playing cards or letters, are comparable to multiplications of numbers. Two or fifty performed in succession can be replaced by one. Instead of multiplying a number first by 3 and then by 7, we can equally well multiply it by 21. Two multiplications performed in succession can be replaced by a single multiplication. But whereas it makes no difference whether we multiply first by 3 and then by 7 or first by 7 and then by 3, in a permutation the order matters.

THE RECIPROCAL OF A PERMUTATION

Permutations share another similarity with multiplication. If we multiply 5 by 7, we get 35. If we multiply the result by 1/7, that is, by the reciprocal of 7, we return to 5. For every multiplication there is a reverse multiplication, the one by the reciprocal. If we perform the one after the other, it is as if we have multiplied by 1.

A permutation that transposes A to A and B to B may sound childish. Let us look at it anyway and call it permutation E. It is represented in figure 4.9, bottom right. It corresponds to multiplication by 1.

Just as with multiplication, each permutation has another permutation that annuls its effect. At figure 4.9, top, we find, alongside permutation X, another that we will call 1/X. It represents the *reciprocal permutation* of X. X and 1/X, performed after each other, no matter in what order, give the same result as E. If therefore we arrange the alphabet in a different sequence by means of a permutation, the reciprocal permutation will restore the original order.

But our alphabet has twenty-six letters, not four. Encoding with the table in figure 4.6 is based on a permutation of the plaintext alphabet, that is, the transposition of *a*, *b*, *c*, *d*, . . . into the cipher alphabet P, D, N, Z, . . . Every Caesar and every Caesar with a mnemonic is a permutation. Key tables like the one in figure 4.6 are therefore nothing other than permutations that transform the plaintext alphabet into a cipher alphabet. Every permutation of the alphabet produces a key table. If in our four-letter alphabet we encode the word ADAC by means of permutation X in figure 4.9, we get DCDB. For decoding we use the reciprocal permutation 1/X, which restores ADAC.

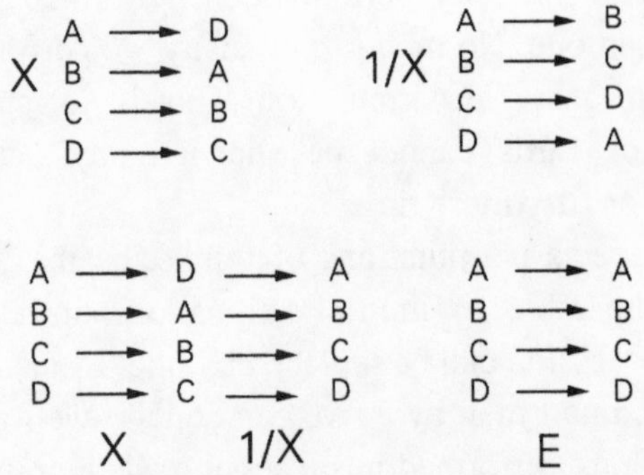

Fig. 4.9. Permutation X (top left) and its reciprocal (top right). The one revokes the other. If X and 1/X are performed consecutively (bottom left), the result is permutation E—no change.

THE UNIVERSAL LIBRARY

Obviously, monalphabetic encoding can use other signs than letters, such as numbers, playing cards, or domino blocks, but in any case the same symbol must always be assigned to the same letter. Any monalphabetic coding needs a key table of the type in figure 4.6. For decoding, the table is read backward.

The number of all possible key tables for the full alphabet is finite but very large. In principle a coded text might be decoded with the aid of a computer by testing that huge number of possible key tables one after another to discover if one of them produces a meaningful text. In practice, this is impossible. Even if a computer were capable of separating meaningful from meaningless plaintexts, and even if it required only one-thousandth of a second for each key table, the examination of all possibilities would take much longer than the age of the universe. To discover the right key table simply by trial and error is therefore hopeless.

Yet no cipher is truly secret. Suppose we have a secret text before us, ten letters long:

JCPRTETZTM

Whatever coding method was used, each coded letter corresponds to one plaintext letter. The plaintext, too, is a series of ten letters. In how many ways can the twenty-six letters of the alphabet be made into a group of ten? The answer is a 1 followed by twenty-six zeroes. Even though this number is large beyond our imagination, it is finite. Let us assume we have a computer that is able to set out all these sequences of ten letters in a line, line below line. One of the lines will certainly contain the correct plaintext. The difficulty is finding it among that colossal number of groups-of-ten. This is a thought that the philosopher, mathematician, and science fiction author Kurd Lasswitz developed in his short story "The Universal Library." He takes not groups-of-ten but entire books. The universal library contains all the books that can in principle be written.

The idea is simple. Let us take an English book. We have twenty-six letters, plus the punctuation marks, the space between words, ten numerals, and perhaps some Greek or mathematical symbols for scientific texts. Let us assume we have altogether fifty different symbols. The books in our library are to have six hundred pages with 3,300 symbols per page. If a book is shorter, then we complete it with empty spaces. Each book therefore contains 1,980,000 symbols or less. It consists of fifty different symbols that follow one another in ever new sequences. This means that only as many books are possible as the different ways our fifty symbols can be arranged in groups of 1,980,000. For this we have $50 \times 50 \times 50 \times \ldots$ possibilities, a multiplication in which the number 50 is written 1,980,000 times. The result is a number consisting of three million numerals. Walking along the shelves of this voluminous library, the librarian would have to cover distances by comparison to which even the distances to the most remote stars would seem minute. Most of the books, of course, contain only meaningless sequences of symbols. If, however, one were to search long enough, one would find among all that garbage the entire Bible and the text of the American Constitution, completed with empty spaces. Somewhere one would encounter Shakespeare's plays and Ian Fleming's James Bond novels. Moreover, the library contains not only all published texts but also all books yet to be written. You would be able to find there the doctoral thesis that one day would make your great-grandson famous.

The reason why the library does not exist is that it would vastly exceed the means available on earth—materials, space, labor. But even if it did exist, it would be useless. After all, who could find among the billions and billions of meaningless books one that made sense, at least linguistically, not to mention its contents?

Let us return to our coding. To this day, encoding methods are often preferred because it would take thousands of years to discover a plaintext by systematic trial and error. In World War II, the Germans believed they could rely on their cipher machine Enigma, because an unimaginably large number of attempts would be necessary to decipher a secret text. But this argument is false. We will see in the next chapter that, even if one does not know the key, one is not reduced to trial and error.

A SUPERFLUOUS MACHINE

Monalphabetic encoding and decoding a message is the simplest thing in the world. All we need is a strip as shown in figure 4.6; it leads us securely from the plaintext to the ciphertext and back. But let us imagine an electrical machine that performs this operation automatically. If, on a keyboard, the user presses a key with a plaintext letter, a little lightbulb illuminates the coded letter. We could also connect the keyboard directly to a printer; but as we are concerned here only with the principle, let us content ourselves with the little lightbulb.

The reader might ask why we have to build a machine for such a simple operation. The reason is that it will help us understand the principle of simple cipher machines. In the course of the next few chapters, we will develop this machine further. The small gadget we describe here is, in the most literal sense, only a tiny wheel in the elaborate machinery of Enigma. Again, for the sake of clarity, let us use a four-letter alphabet.

For our machine we require four little lightbulbs, four electrical switches, and a board, the heart of our gadget, which we can build ourselves. But we do not have to reach for our fretsaw or soldering iron. No handiwork is required. The board is a rectangular piece of flexible insulating material—cardboard will do—that has four electrical contacts on each of its two long sides. We now use a wire to connect each contact on the left side with one on the right side. There are twenty-four possible ways of connecting them. Let us decide on one. By using switches, the lightbulbs, and the contact board, we now create circuits as shown in figure 4.10, top. Each switch has a plaintext letter assigned to it (right) and each lightbulb a coded letter (left). Lightbulbs and switches are connected to a battery. When all switches are open, no current flows, all the bulbs remain off. Depressing switch c closes the circuit leading to lightbulb D. The plaintext letter c therefore corresponds to the coded letter D. You can see from the diagram that the following correspondences also exist: a to C, b to A, and d to B. The wiring of the board thus corresponds to the code table, top right. To decode, we use the machine shown in figure 4.10, bottom. We depress the switches in accordance with the coded letters, and the bulbs of the plaintext letters light up.

Let us now take twenty-six switches and twenty-six lightbulbs and on the board wire up twenty-six contacts on the left with twenty-six contacts on the right. We now have a gadget that works like the cipher strip in figure 4.6, and also like any other monalphabetic coding. Each cipher table has exactly one wiring, each wiring corresponding to one cipher table. For decoding, we need a board that is the mirror image of the original one, as illustrated by the four-letter alphabet at the bottom of

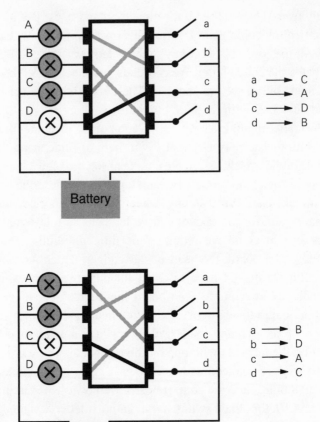

Fig. 4.10. **Coding by means of electrical switching. Top: four lightbulbs A, B, C, D can be turned on by four switches** *a, b, c, d.* **The plaintext letters are typed in by keys, and the letters of the corresponding lightbulbs then form the ciphertext. The permutation of the alphabet achieved by this wiring is shown on the right. Bottom: the wiring that decodes the ciphertext encoded by the arrangement above. If the coded letter is typed in, the lightbulb of the corresponding plaintext letter lights up. The permutation involved is again shown on the right. This is the reciprocal of the one above.**

the diagram. In the reciprocal machine, the keys represent the coded letters and the lightbulbs the plaintext letters.

The first encodings by an electrical machine were accomplished about 1915, when electric typewriters came into use. A depressed key closes a circuit, and an electromagnet presses the type head to the paper.

In a normal typewriter, pressing the *a* key operates the *a* lever. By changing the wiring the *c* key can be made to operate the *a* lever, the *d* key the *b* lever, and so on. Thus the machine automatically turns the typed plaintext into ciphertext. But it always supplies only a monalphabetic coding.

The present-day decoder is delighted when he comes across such a monalphabetic coding, because he can crack it at once. How to tackle such texts was known already to Edgar Allan Poe's hero William Legrand and to the famous Sherlock Holmes.

NOTE

1. Egmont Colerus, *Vom Einmaleins zum Integral* (Vienna/Hamburg, Umschau Verlag, 1937) 46ff.

5. HOW A MONALPHABETIC CODE IS CRACKED

> In the English language the frequency profile shows a
> marked *e*-peak and a somewhat smaller *a*-peak. There is
> also a marked elevation of the *r-s-t-u* ridge, and two
> smaller ones, the *l-m-n-o* ridge and the *h-i* ridge.
> —FRIEDRICH L. BAUER, *Decrypted Secrets*

NOW THAT THEY HAVE SPOTTED the bolt, the box is easily opened. Gold and jewels glitter and gleam in the light of the lantern. Legrand is excited, and Jupiter, the black man accompanying him, turns pale, sinks to his knees in the ditch, buries both his arms to his elbows in the gold, and leaves them there. The men have found the treasure of Captain Kidd, the Scottish pirate who in earlier days made the seas unsafe.

The story is an invention. The American author Edgar Allan Poe (1809-1849) published it in 1845 under the title "The Gold-Bug." The recluse William Legrand finds a parchment on the shore with a secret text that is monalphabetically encoded. He succeeds in decoding the message and thus learns where Captain Kidd, hanged some one hundred and fifty years ago, buried his treasure.

EDGAR ALLAN POE DECODES TO ORDER

Poe's tales are noteworthy for two reasons. Many are characterized by sharp deductive logic, which makes them precursors of the modern detective story. At the same time, Poe has written mysterious and eerie accounts of mental abnormalities and extrasensory phenomena. In "The Gold-Bug," he combines both aspects. There is the mysterious pirate treasure with its massive gold earrings, finger rings, and watches. And the directions on how to find it are weird: an object dropped through the left eye socket of a skull nailed to a tree will mark the spot on the ground. Legrand deciphers the text of the manuscript with the same analytic logic as that still used in the decoding of monalphabetic ciphers.

Cryptology was a hobby of the poet. In a periodical in 1839, he discussed the value of solving riddles, in particular the deciphering of secret texts. He invited his readers to invent monalphabetic codes and send him texts encoded by them. The texts were quick to come in. One of them was from a seventeen-year-old by the name of Schuyler Colfax, a future vice president of the United States.

Poe solved most of the cryptograms he received. Two of them, he discovered, were not a real text but signs arbitrarily strung together. Another contained fifty-one signs instead of the twenty-six of the alphabet, so it was not a monalphabetic code at all, as Poe had demanded. There was no end to the flood of secret texts, and Poe deciphered nearly all of them, which gained him a great reputation. Eyewitnesses claimed that he often took less time deciphering a text than its encoders had needed to encode it. It is thought that Poe's success in deciphering was based mainly on intuition. It was only later, from an article in an encyclopedia, that he learned about one of the most important methods of cryptology.

In every language, each letter of the alphabet occurs with a characteristic frequency. Thus in English, French, German, Italian, and Spanish, *e* is the most frequent letter; in Portuguese, it is *a*. In English and German, *q* is very rare, as is *w* in some other languages. Poe had made a name for himself as a decoding genius, and he kept his methods to himself in order to maintain that halo. But then he used his knowledge in his short story, where Poe the cryptologist dictated his words to Poe the poet. The secret text of Captain Kidd's parchment is reproduced in figure 5.1. Let us follow Poe's hero Legrand and see how he got from the ciphertext to the plaintext.

In one corner of the parchment, the drawing of a young billy goat can be made out: a kid. From this, and from the circumstances in which he found the parchment, Legrand concludes that it must be a message from Captain Kidd. It seems reasonable to assume therefore that the plaintext is in English. Legrand next examines the frequency with which the individual signs occur. The **8** occurs thirty-three times, far more often than

```
53≠≠†305))6*;4826)4≠.)4≠);806*;48†8 ]/ 60 ))85;1≠(;:
≠*8†83(88)5*†;46(;88*96*?;8)*≠(;485);5*†2:*≠(;4956*
2(5*- 4)8 ]/8*;40 69 285);)6†8)4≠≠;1(≠9;48 0 81;8:8 / 1;
48†85;4)485†52 8806*81( / 9;4 8;(88;4(≠?34;48)4≠;161;:
188;≠?;
```

Fig. 5.1. **Captain Kidd's coded message in Edgar Allan Poe's tale "The Gold-Bug."**

any of the other symbols. Legrand concludes that **8** stands for *e*. Added to this is the fact that five times it is doubled, corresponding to *ee* in English. In a monalphabetic code the frequent article *the* should be a repeated combination of three symbols ending in **8**. The combination **;48** does in fact occur seven times. Legrand therefore tries to interpret **;** as *t* and **4** as *h*. Let us now count back from the end to the thirty-third symbol. There begins the triple group interpreted as *the*. Next comes a *t*, followed by the still unknown symbol **(**, then come two *e*s, a *t*, and an *h*, that is, *t-eeth*. You can go through the whole alphabet to find a suitable letter for the empty space in *t-eeth*, but there is no such word in the English language. Legrand therefore concludes that the *th* at the end of the word belongs to the next word. This leaves us with *t-ee*. Running through the letters of the alphabet, we find that only *r* makes sense, giving us *tree*. So the passage decoded so far is "the tree." But we know the next three letters: they are *thr*. There follow the unknown symbols **≠?3**, followed in turn by an *h* and the word *the*. So we have "the tree thr---hthe". Legrand thinks of the word *through*.

If this assumption is correct, then three more symbols are identified: **≠**, **?**, and **3**, representing the letters *o*, *u*, and *g*. Near the start of the second line, we find the combination **†83(88**, that is, *-egree*, which Legrand concludes must be *degree*. This means that the symbol † stands for *d*. Five signs after "degree," we have the combination **;46(;88**. The symbols already known give *th-rtee*, so the word can only be *thirteen*. In consequence **6** and ***** stand for the letters *i* and *n*. At this point, Legrand replaces all ciphers whose meaning he already knows by their plaintext equivalents. The message is not yet legible, but Legrand continues his guesswork. The message begins with the symbols **53‡‡†**. The correspondences already known produce *-good*. There are only a few words in English consisting of just one letter. It seems reasonable therefore to replace **5** with *a*. Then the message starts: "A good." In this manner Legrand feels his way from one letter to another. Eventually he can read the text: "A good glass in the bishop's hotel in the devil's seat, forty-one degrees and thirteen minutes northeast and by north main branch seventh limb east side shoot from the left eye of the death's head a bee line from the tree through the shot fifty feet out."

The message is still mysterious, but its mystery is no longer a question of cryptology. Only a little detective work is now needed to interpret it.

The wretched Captain Kidd had placed an additional obstacle in the way of the decipherers by running all the symbols together without spaces. Had he indicated the beginning of each word by a space or a special sign, Legrand would have found his task easier.

SHERLOCK HOLMES AND THE DANCING MEN

Things were easier for Sherlock Holmes. In Sir Arthur Conan Doyle's story "The Dancing Men," Abe Slaney, "Chicago's most dangerous gangster," sends threatening messages to Elsie, his love of younger years, who is now married to the owner of an estate. For these Slaney uses a secret script that the two used in the past—he chalks a sequence of dancing stick figures in various positions on windowsills and on the door of the toolshed of the estate, near which he has rented a room. Elsie wants her husband to know as little as possible about her past, but he is worried about his frightened wife and the drawings that keep appearing. He copies the dancing-men drawings that he has discovered on his estate and leaves them with Sherlock Holmes. The top six lines of figure 5.2 show all the cryptograms available to the detective for deciphering.

The master detective immediately has a flash of inspiration. Some of the little men hold a flag. Holmes concludes that the flags indicate the end of a word. Then he proceeds exactly as Legrand. The most frequent figure in the cryptogram is the man standing with legs apart and both arms

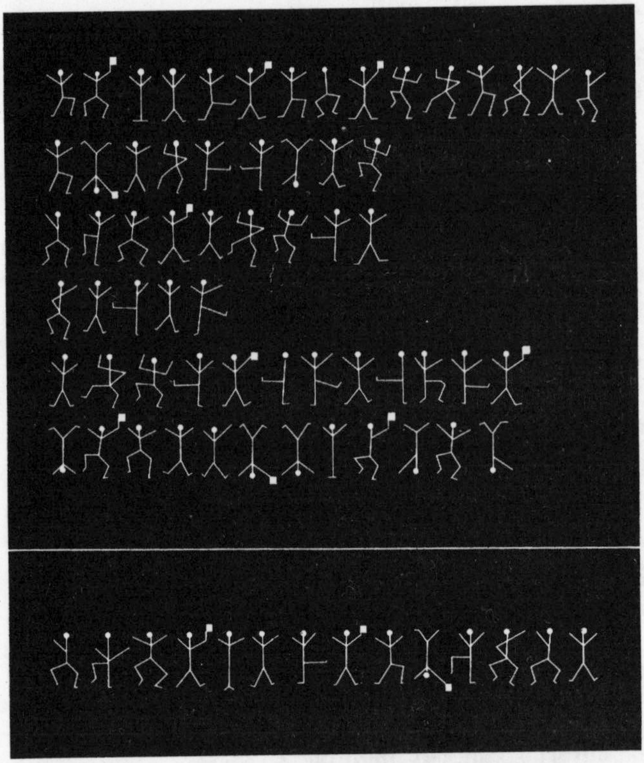

Fig. 5.2. Top: the different messages available to Sherlock Holmes in the story "The Dancing Men." Bottom: the coded message that the detective, having successfully broken the code, sends to the criminal.

stretched upward. Holmes decides that this corresponds to the letter *e*. Soon he has assigned a large part of the alphabet to the stick men—to so many, in fact, that he can himself encode simple messages by that system. From Slaney's messages he has learned where Slaney lodges, and now sends him the coded message "Come here at once." This is shown in the bottom line of figure 5.2. Slaney naturally assumes that it comes from his beloved—and so falls into the trap. Another success for the great detective.

These two examples from literature show the principle that has to be followed for the breaking of monalphabetic codes. Both examples contain English plaintexts, but matters are no different in most other languages.

But before embarking on the deciphering of monalphabetic cipher-texts, we need to equip ourselves with a few useful tools.

THE FREQUENT E AND THE INFREQUENT Q

In English, as in German, some letters are much more frequent than others. It is astonishing how consistently the individual letters of the alphabet occur in their respective frequencies in a text, no matter whether the text is a philosophical treatise or a romantic novel. As we are dealing here with a statistical regularity, the more extensive the available text material, the smaller the deviation. Words like *Labrador* or *Niagara Falls* are no counterargument; in a lengthy text containing them, the *e* will still be much more frequent that the *a* or the *u*.

The table in figure 5.3 shows the percentage frequency of the letters of the alphabet in an English text.[1] Figure 5.4 shows the same distribution, this time in graphic representation. We see that *e* and *t* are the most frequent letters, followed by *a*, *o*, *i*, and *n*.

a	8.04%	n	7.09%
b	1.54	o	7.60
c	3.06	p	2.00
d	3.99	q	0.11
e	12.51	r	6.12
f	2.30	s	6.54
g	1.96	t	9.25
h	5.49	u	2.71
i	7.26	v	0.99
j	0.16	w	1.92
k	0.67	x	0.19
l	4.14	y	1.73
m	2.53	z	0.09

Fig. 5.3. Frequency distribution of the letters in the English alphabet, in percentages.

Once one realizes which sign stands for *e*, one can work one's way further into the cipher alphabet. By far the most frequently paired letters in English are *th*, followed by *he*, *an*, *in*, *er*. The letters that follow *e* are, in order of frequency, *r*, *s*, *n*, and *d*.

Even the words in the English language occur with a characteristic frequency for nearly all texts. The most frequent short words, in descending order, are: *the, of, and, to, a, in, that, is, I*. These frequencies are especially helpful in decoding if the ciphertext does not show word separation.

Fig. 5.4. Frequency distribution of the letters in English, represented graphically. Bauer's words quoted at the beginning of this chapter refer to this chart.

A SECRET TEXT IS DECODED

Let us now tackle a ciphertext ourselves. It is an easy one, because its words are separated by spaces. One sees at once which are the short words—a great advantage, as we will see in a moment. Figure 5.5 shows a monalphabetically encoded text. Altogether it contains nineteen

```
ETNAN XFWN LYK Y RYETNA QF EBWKXF
LTX KYQP ETQK YPHQWN QK RXA DXB KXF
DXB PXFE LYKT DXBAKNMR LNMM
KX DXBA RNNE KCNMM MQUN TNMM
QR QF VNP LQET Y ZQAM
UNNI DXBA KTXNK XF
```

Fig. 5.5. A ciphertext.

different symbols. Arranging them according to their frequency, we get:

N	(16, 12.1 %)	**M**	(9, 6.8 %)
X	(14, 10.6 %)	**T**	(8, 6.1 %)
K	(12, 9.1 %)	**Y**	(7, 5.3 %)
Q	(10, 7.6 %)	**F**	(6, 4.6 %)

The first number in parentheses indicates the number of times the symbol appears in the text, the second number its percentage frequency.

The most frequent symbol is **N**, hence we must conclude that this stands for *e*. We can now search for the plaintext word *the*. Three times **N**, our presumed *e*, is preceded by the symbol **T**; could this be the frequent letter combination *he*? Two times we find **ETN**, that is, *-he*. Could that be *the*? If so, then the first word would be *the-e*. This suggests that **A** stands for *r*. Before examining what we have gained by these assumptions, let us look at the two words that consist only of the letter **Y**. Surely this is either *I* or *a*. But *a* is more frequent in English than *I*, so we replace **Y** by *a*. If we now write in all our assumed substitutions, we get the result shown in figure 5.6.

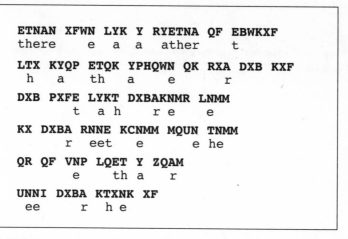

Fig. 5.6. With the letters *e*, *h*, *t*, and *a* identified, the ciphertext of figure 5.5 allows us to guess the letters *f*, *o*, *i*, *n*, *w*, and *s*.

The fifth word in the first line is bound to be *father*, which means that **R** equals *f*. The sixth word in the second line is probably *for*, hence **X** equals *o*. If this is correct, then the first word of the fifth line must be *if*; it cannot be *of*, since we already know *o*. This is followed by a two-letter word starting with *i*. It cannot be *it*, because we know *t* already. It could be *in*, in which case we can replace all **F**s by *n*. The first word in the second ciphertext line is *-ho*, which suggests that **L** is *w*. This is confirmed by the fourth word in the fifth line, which thus becomes *with*. The third word of the first line, *wa-* can only be *was*, which gives us the meaning of **K**. Figure 5.7 gives us an intermediate result.

```
ETNAN  XFWN  LYK  Y  RYETNA  QF  EBWKXF
there  on e  was  a  father  in t  son

LTX  KYQP  ETQK  YPHQWN  QK  RXA  DXB  KXF
who  sai   this a  i e   is  for  o   son

DXB  PXFE  LYKT  DXBAKNMR  LNMM
o    ont   wash  o rse f   we

KX  DXBA  RNNE  KCNMM  MQUN  TNMM
so  o r   feet  s e    i e   he

QR  QF  VNP  LQET  Y  ZQAM
if  in  e    with  a  ir

UNNI  DXBA  KTXNK  XF
ee    o r   shoes  on
```

Fig. 5.7. The plaintext fragment gained with figure 5.6 reveals to us the letters *c*, *u*, *y*, *d*, and *l*.

It is getting easier all the time. What else could the second word of the first line be besides *once*? This tells us that **W** is *c*. The opening line of the plaintext therefore reads: "There once was a father in T-cson". You do not have to live in Arizona to know that this must be Tucson. As a result we now have the *u*, and the second line, ". . . is for -ou son," tells us that **D** stands for *y*. Do I have to say that **P** is *d* (second ciphertext line, second word) and **M** is *l* (third ciphertext line, fourth word)? Figure 5.8 shows what we have discovered so far. I leave it to the reader to complete the decoding.

You may have the impression, if you have followed me, that I was guiding you in the decoding procedure to keep you from going down blind alleys. This is true. Why not try, at some point or other, not to follow my lead? For instance, you might assume that **P** is *d*. Sooner or

```
ETNAN XFWN LYK Y RYETNA QF EBWKXF
there once was a father in tucson

LTX KYQP ETQK YPHQWN QK RXA DXB KXF
who said this ad ice is for you son

DXB PXFE LYKT DXBAKNMR LNMM
you dont wash yourself well

KX DXBA RNNE KCNMM MQUN TNMM
so your feet s ell li e hell

QR QF VNP LQET Y ZQAM
if in  ed with a  irl

UNNI DXBA KTXNK XF
ee  your shoes on
```

Fig. 5.8. The plaintext almost completely decoded.

later you will encounter meaningless letter groups. I wanted to save you time. But if you wish to become a competent cryptanalyst, you will have to go your own way.

There are no clear, unequivocal prescriptions for tackling a monalphabetic ciphertext. There are only useful rules of thumb. The decoder must bring some adroitness and experience to the task.

THE FOUNDLINGS OF FRANKFURTER ALLGEMEINE ZEITUNG

In the puzzle corner of its weekly magazine supplement, *Frankfurter Allgemeine Zeitung* (*FAZ*) regularly, under the heading "Foundlings," publishes ciphertexts monalphabetically encoded by the mathematician and science journalist Thomas von Randow. The letters of the alphabet are replaced by symbols, sometimes Chinese ideograms, sometimes musical notations, sometimes hieroglyphs. Figures 5.9 and 5.10 present foundlings similar to those of the German paper. Try your skill on them, if you feel so inclined. The examples are relatively easy, as the words are separated. Moreover, the texts are of sufficient length and couched in ordinary language.

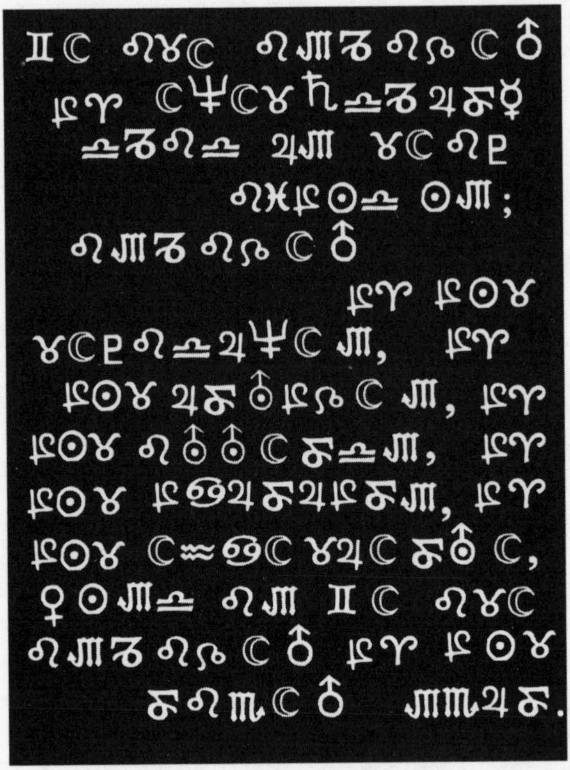

Fig. 5.9. A foundling in the style of *Frankfurter Allgemeine Zeitung*.

PENW LSYBKNI OYSBSNF UYM KYI UEND EN MYBI
PEN NYJPE FJZBPNI PEN MQD, ZQP EN UYM JBOEP;
PENW MYBI PEN UJBOEP ZJFPENJM UNJN LJYXW
UEND PENW PJBNI PF CSW, ZQP PENW IBI; PENW
MYBI KW QDLSN UBSZQJ UYM KYI YM Y EYPPNJ —
YDI EN UYM. OJYQLEF KYJV

Fig. 5.10. Another foundling.

Much greater difficulties are encountered with texts that have different letter frequencies. The mathematician Albrecht Beutelspacher, a cipher expert, in his book *Cryptology,* gives "traktat ueber die amoureusen aventueren des balthasar matzbach am rande des panamakanal" and "einfluss von ozon auf die zebras im zentrum von zaire" as examples of perverted frequency distributions. The following short ciphertext without word separation is a little more difficult to decipher than the foundlings of the *FAZ:*

YZIMZXOVYROORHZHGLMVLMNZIH

I leave it to you to decipher it. Anyone succeeding deserves as a reward a foundling containing two sentences of a well-known English author:

```
G XBLLXY EBNZYABLS BE G HGNCYAIJE LQBNC GNH
G CAYGL HYGX IP BL BE GUEIXJLYXS PGLGX.
A WGN ZGNNIL UY LII ZGAYPJX BN LQY ZQ IBZY IP
QBE YNYWBYE.
```

THE DECEITFULNESS OF TAPEWORMS

Frankfurter Allgemeine Zeitung prefaces each of its foundlings with the instruction "Frequently used letters and short words are the key to success." The recourse to identifying short words is lost when the encoder conceals spaces and punctuation marks, putting down a tapeworm of symbols. In the example in figure 5.11, we have no indication of short words and depend solely on statistics, but statistics tells us everything.

```
ZPMMZKHQUHMUXHKOLDHHCACZK
HXRCGKQMMFMCGHEHMQEHKOLEM
CHMRZZMZKHIAZGKHCOCLFOLHO
KOFOCLHEETOCLPAGKZKOZOFOC
POCZHLZMZOIHPAZKKAF
```

Fig. 5.11. A ciphertext without word separation.

The ciphertext letter **H** occurs most frequently, sixteen times, accounting for 13.4% of the letters. This is followed by **Z** and **O**, each with 10.9%. This suggests that **H** is *e*. The most frequent two-letter combination with *e* in English is *he*. We would therefore expect the ciphertext letter standing for *h* to occur with greatest frequency before **H**. Counting, we find that **K** occurs four times before **H**. This suggests that **K** is *h*. If this is correct, we should be able to discover the word *the*. Which letter occurs most often before **KH**? Twice we find **Z**. As **Z** is the second most frequent ciphertext letter, we have probably found the *t*. Figure 5.12 shows the result so far.

```
ZPMMZKHQUHMUXHKOLDHHCACZK
t  the  e   eh    ee    th

HXRCGKQMMFMCGHEHMQEHKOLEM
e    h      e e     eh

CHMRZZMZKHIAZGKHCOCLFOLHO
  e  tt the  t he       e

KOFOCLHEETOCLPAGKZKOZOFOC
h    e          hth t

POCZHLZMZOIHPAZKKAF
te t t  e   thh
```

Fig. 5.12. Having found *e, h,* and *t,* the reader is given hints as to the plaintext letter *a.*

After *e* and *t*, the most frequent letters in English are *a* and *o*. In the ciphertext the second most frequent letter is **O**. So does **O** stand for *a* or *o*? The penultimate ciphertext line contains **ZKOZ**, that is, *th-t*. This looks like *that*. So is **O** *a*? Let us risk it. Figure 5.13 shows what we have achieved so far.

How do we go on? The letter *o* is very frequent in English. In the ciphertext the next most frequent signs are **C** and **M**. In experimenting whether one of these might stand for *o*, we immediately find, in the third ciphertext line, *tothe*, which is *to the*, and in the last line another *to*. That seems to make sense. The first eight letters of the ciphertext, *t-oothe-* suggest *two other*. Let us try **P** as *w* and **Q** as *r*. A fairly frequent letter in the ciphertext is **C**; one of the more frequent English letters is *n*. Figure 5.14 shows what we know so far.

The last line cries out for *wanted*, which means **L** is *d*, and at the end of the penultimate line we find *thata-an*. Maybe **F** is *m*. See figure 5.15.

```
ZPMMZKHQUHMUXHKOLDHHCACZK
t  the  e  eha  ee   th

HXRCGKQMMFMCGHEHMQEHKOLEM
e  h    e e   eha

CHMRZZMZKHIAZGKHCOCLFOLHO
e  tt the  t he a   a ea

KOFOCLHEETOCLPAGKZKOZOFOC
h   e         hthata a

POCZHLZMZOIHPAZKKAF
a te t ta e  thh
```

Fig. 5.13. In the partially decoded text one can proceed to identify the plaintext letters *o, w, r,* and *n.*

```
ZPMMZKHQUHMUXHKOLDHHCACZK
twoother eo  eha  een nth

HXRCGKQMMFMCGHEHMQEHKOLEM
e  n hroo on e eor eha  o

CHMRZZMZKHIAZGKHCOCLFOLHO
neo ttothe  t henan  a ea

KOFOCLHEETOCLPAGKZKOZOFOC
ha an e   an w  hthata an

POCZHLZMZOIHPAZKKAF
wante tota ew thh
```

Fig. 5.14. Next we go on to find *d* and *m.*

```
ZPMMZKHQUHMUXHKOLDHHCACZK
twoother eo  ehad een nth

HXRCGKQMMFMCGHEHMQEHKOLEM
e  n hroomon e eor ehad o

CHMRZZMZKHIAZGKHCOCLFOLHO
neo ttothe  t henandmadea

KOFOCLHEETOCLPAGKZKOZOFOC
hamande   andw  hthataman

POCZHLZMZOIHPAZKKAF
wantedtota ew thh m
```

Fig. 5.15. The plaintext letters *b* and *i* emerge.

ZPMMZKHQUHMUXHKOLDHHCACZK
twoother eo ehadbeeninth

HXRCGKQMMFMCGHEHMQEHKOLEM
e n hroomon e eor ehad o

CHMRZZMZKHIAZGKHCOCLFOLHO
neo ttothe it henandmadea

KOFOCLHEETOCLPAGKZKOZOFOC
hamande   andwi hthataman

POCZHLZMZOIHPAZKKAF
wantedtota ewithhim

Fig. 5.16. Now *k* and *g* become apparent.

ZPMMZKHQUHMUXHKOLDHHCACZK
twoother eo ehadbeeninth

HXRCGKQMMFMCGHEHMQEHKOLEM
e n hroomon egeorgehadgo

CHMRZZMZKHIAZGKHCOCLFOLHO
neo ttothekit henandmadea

KOFOCLHEETOCLPAGKZKOZOFOC
hamandegg andwi hthataman

POCZHLZMZOIHPAZKKAF
wantedtotakewithhim

Fig. 5.17. Now we need add only the plaintext letters *u* and *c*.

ZPMMZKHQUHMUXHKOLDHHCACZK
twoother eo ehadbeeninth

HXRCGKQMMFMCGHEHMQEHKOLEM
e unchroomoncegeorgehadgo

CHMRZZMZKHIAZGKHCOCLFOLHO
neouttothekitchenandmadea

KOFOCLHEETOCLPAGKZKOZOFOC
hamandegg andwichthataman

POCZHLZMZOIHPAZKKAF
wantedtotakewithhim

Fig. 5.18. The nearly completed plaintext, without word spacing.

At the transition from the first to the second line, -*een-nthe* suggests *been in the*. Does this mean that **D** and **A** are *b* and *i* respectively? Figure 5.16 shows that this makes sense.

The last line suggests "wanted to take with him," which means **I** is *k*. Moreover, in the penultimate line, *hamande*-- calls for the filling of the two empty spaces with the same letter, as indicated by the two **E**s of the ciphertext. This must be "ham and egg." See figure 5.17.

In lines 2 and 3, we have "george had gone o-t to the kit-hen," hence **R** is *u* and **G** is *c*. The next result is shown in figure 5.18. I can now leave it to the reader to complete this text from Ernest Hemingway's short story "The Killers."

DISGUISED FREQUENCIES

Frequency analysis makes it possible to decipher virtually any monalphabetically encoded text, provided it is long enough. That is why efforts began long ago to change the principle of monalphabetic coding. The simplest possibility was discovered as long as six hundred years ago. In the correspondence of the officials of Mantua, a key was found dating to 1401. Figure 5.19 shows a key operating according to the same principle. In the top line we have the plaintext alphabet and below it the cipher alphabet consisting of letters and numbers. The encoder of the plaintext letters *e, i, n, r,* and *s* now has a choice of several cipher symbols. In this manner the natural frequency of the plaintext letters can be concealed. *Deepfreeze* can now become **SHCADBHULE**, and the greater frequency of *e* has disappeared.

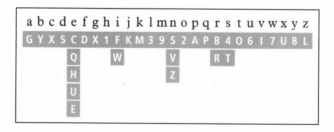

Fig. 5.19. To conceal the typical frequency of certain letters, the plaintext letters *e, i, n, r,* and *s* can be each represented by more than one cipher sign.

The key from 1401 tells us that the scribes of the Duke of Mantua had progressed a long way beyond Caesar. They knew about the weaknesses of monalphabetic coding. Nowadays we know the frequency distributions of every language. We can therefore assign to each plaintext letter just as many cipher letters as will ensure that in a lengthy ciphertext all signs appear with much the same frequency. The twenty-six letters of the English alphabet can be assigned the one hundred symbols **00, 01, 02,** . . . **98, 99**. If these symbols are distributed among the letters of the alphabet, c, m, p, y can be given two symbols each; f, l, u can be given three each; i, h, d can be given five each; a, s, n, r can be given seven each. The letters o and t are each given nine, and finally we assign thirteen symbols to e. The rest of the letters get one symbol each. Anyone can thus produce an individual cipher alphabet that conceals the frequency of the different letters. Although e is the most frequent letter, it appears in the ciphertext in thirteen different guises and therefore attracts no special attention.

One disadvantage of this so-called *homophone* coding is that sender and receiver cannot keep the key in their heads; they must carry it about with them. And, of course, it must be agreed on in advance. Moreover, the system is not as secure as one would expect. Although e can no longer be spotted, every language has some letter combinations that are more frequent than others. With a sufficiently long ciphertext, one can examine which symbol pairs occur with greater frequency. The decoder of a homophone cipher is not totally lost.

Another way of concealing the characteristic frequency of letters is provided by a square, as shown in figure 5.20. With letters occurring repeatedly, the encoder makes whatever choice he pleases, one time this one, the next time another. The letter e, for instance, can be **16, 96,** or **41** (using the square's number column for the first digit, the number row for the second). In this way the frequencies are blurred. The word *deepfreeze*, for instance, can become **70 03 28 42 21 85 82 89 62 41**. A frequency analysis would be of no use here to the unauthorized decoder.

A cryptologist will nevertheless notice that all the messages consist of an even number of symbols, since each letter is represented by a number pair. He may therefore suspect that the letters are set in a square of ten rows and ten columns, corresponding to the ten numbers 0, 1, . . . 9. He is still far from his objective, since he does not know in what arrangement the letters are placed in the fields of the square. Yet with sufficiently

	0	1	2	3	4	5	6	7	8	9
0	t	a	s	e	r	t	a	n	o	a
1	n	e	r	h	t	i	e	s	t	n
2	o	f	t	c	a	h	o	r	e	r
3	s	u	c	e	m	a	f	o	o	i
4	n	e	p	y	h	f	s	e	d	t
5	h	g	t	e	k	q	s	l	o	d
6	e	y	z	o	a	t	p	j	l	t
7	d	i	w	x	o	b	v	e	s	u
8	i	u	e	n	m	r	d	a	i	e
9	o	h	s	l	n	r	e	d	n	r

***Fig. 5.20.* A key table that can conceal the frequency distribution of letters. Each plaintext letter is represented by a number pair, such as *q* by 55, *f* by 45. For letters occurring more frequently, the encoder has at his disposal several number pairs: *e*, for example, can be 11, 41, 47, and so on.**

lengthy texts, certain frequent letter combinations—like *th*—will stand out as number-pair combinations.

Figure 5.20 shows but one example of a possible key table. It is easy to produce another, in which the letters of the alphabet are entered with the same frequency but in a different arrangement.

A method of this type was used for encoding one of the most important secrets in world history. General Leslie Richard Groves, the organizational head of the American atom bomb project in World War II, in his telephone conversations used number sequences for important words. He read these numbers off a table similar to the one in figure 5.20.

In the next section, we will learn about a different method of making frequency analysis difficult for an unauthorized decoder.

UNFAIR PLAY WITH PLAYFAIR

You are not playing fair with your spouse if you exchange coded messages with your lover and for this purpose use the cipher method bearing the name Playfair. Strictly speaking, the name is not correct. The first Baron Playfair of St. Andrews was a well-known figure in Victorian England, deputy speaker of the House of Commons and prominent in scientific and public life. He introduced reforms in British medical practice and was a friend of the physicist Wheatstone, whose name is familiar to us through the Wheatstone bridge in electricity.

Both men had chosen cryptology as their hobby. About that time, the London *Times* often carried private advertisements in coded form. The two men amused themselves by decoding these secret messages. Thus they were able to follow the correspondence between a student at Oxford and a married lady in London. When the young man suggested to the lady that they should elope, Wheatstone had a message published in the *Times* in the cipher of the two lovers, in which he admonished the lady. After that there was only one brief coded message in the newspaper: "Charles, don't write anymore; our cipher has been broken!"

Wheatstone could have proposed a superior cipher system, one invented by himself. His friend Playfair subsequently published it, without concealing the name of its inventor. Nevertheless it is known to this day as Playfair. It is based on the fact that not letters are encoded but letter pairs.

Here is how it works. First, a key table is produced—ideally a table that can be reconstructed out of one's head. One proceeds as with a Caesar that uses a mnemonic: taking a mnemonic and leaving out the letters that occur twice. Then one adds the remaining letters of the alphabet. No distinction is made between *i* and *j*, so the alphabet consists of twenty-five letters only. These can therefore be arranged in a square of five rows and five columns. The French mnemonic *orchidée* (orchid) yields the keyword *ORCHIDE*. This provides the square in figure 5.21.

```
O  R  C  H  I
D  E  A  B  F
G  K  L  M  N
P  Q  S  T  U
V  W  X  Y  Z
```

Fig. 5.21. An arrangement of the twenty-five-letter alphabet in a table of five rows and five columns, using the mnemonic *orchidée*.

Let us now, for an example, take the plaintext:

icomeonwednesday

and divide it into pairs:

ic om eo nw ed ne sd ay

When we look up the letters of one pair in the table, three situations are possible:

1. both letters are in the same row
2. both letters are in the same column
3. the letters are neither in the same row nor in the same column

We will treat each of these situations differently.

Situation 1. We encode the two letters by replacing them by the two following in the line: *oc* becomes **RH**. With *fe* we would have to proceed differently, because *f* has no follower. In this case we take the first letter of the row. Thus *fe* becomes **DA**. Similarly, *su* becomes **TP** and *nm* becomes **GN**.

Situation 2. If the two letters of a pair are in the same column, they are replaced by the two letters below them. Thus *sa* becomes **XL**. In the case of a letter that has no other letter below it, the first letter of the column is taken. Thus *zu* becomes **IZ**.

Situation 3. We proceed from the first plaintext letter of the pair toward the left or the right until we reach the column of the second plaintext letter. The letter standing there becomes the first letter of the cipher pair. We find the other by moving horizontally from the second letter of the plaintext pair to the column of the first. Thus *om* becomes **HG** and *mo* becomes **GH**.

A special procedure is necessary if a letter pair consists of two identical letters, such as when we divide up a plaintext word like *deepfreeze* into the pairs *de ep fr ee ze*. How are we to deal with *ee*? The rule is: Change the plaintext so that this does not happen. We could, for example, replace *de ep fr ee ze* by *de ep fr ex ez ex*, and an experienced decoder would soon recognize *deepfreeze*.

With a little practice, this is not as difficult as it may seem at first. Figure 5.22 shows several instances of pairs being assigned.

```
ic om eo nw ed ne sd ay
OH HG DR KZ AE KF PA BX
```

For decoding, we proceed in the reverse direction. In situations 1 and 2, the preceding letters or those above are taken; when the letters are first in a row or column, the final letters are taken. In situation 3, on the other hand, we act in the same manner as in encoding.

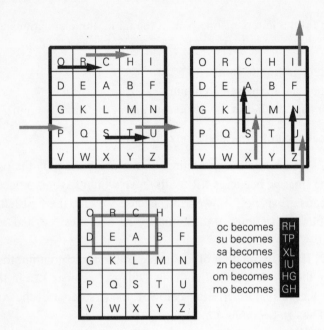

Fig. 5.22. **Encoding with a Playfair square for which the mnemonic** *orchidée* **was chosen.**

In the Playfair cipher, frequently occurring letters are no longer conspicuous—at most, frequently occurring letter pairs still are. Their frequency distribution, however, is more balanced than that of single letters. Nevertheless even this cipher method can be cracked, provided that a sufficient number of texts encoded by it are available.

PLAYFAIR IN WORLD WAR II

We can make the unauthorized decoder's life more difficult by modifying the Playfair method or by applying it a second time. For that purpose we arrange the alphabet twice in two five-by-five squares, in random sequence, again regarding *i* and *j* as the same letter. Figure 5.23 shows a key table of two squares of twenty-five letters each.

In World War II this was called *Doppelkasten* (double box) by the Germans. For encoding, we arrange the plaintext in rows in order to get

Fig. 5.23. The double box as used in World War II. Individual letters are not encoded; instead, letter pairs of the plaintext are converted into letter pairs of the ciphertext.

an even number of equal lines. If necessary, we complete the final line with random letters. With this procedure, instead of individual letters, vertical letter pairs are encoded. Let our plaintext be:

```
w  e  s  t  a  r  t  t  o

m  o  r  r  o  w  x  x  x
```

We start with the pair *w/m* and draw an arrow from the *w* in the left square to the *m* in the right (fig. 5.24). We then draw the horizontal mirror image of the arrow (gray in the illustration); this leads from the *x* in the right square to the *o* in the left.

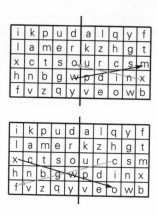

Fig. 5.24. Two-phase encoding with the double box. The letter pair *w/m* in the top figure is represented by an arrow running from the *w* on the left to the *m* on the right. A mirror image is now made of this arrow, producing the gray arrow running from *x* to *o*. In the first step, the plaintext letter pair *w/m* is turned into the cipher pair X/O. In the second step (bottom), the cipher pair X/O is turned into the cipher pair C/F.

This is the first step of the encoding process: *w/m* becomes *x/o*. We now take **X/O** as our new plaintext and perform the same operation once more. The result is the gray arrow running from *c* to *f*. Thus in two steps *w/m* has become the cipher pair **C/F**. We repeat this double operation with the second pair, *e/o*: the arrow goes from *e* on the left to *o* on the right, and the mirror image produces *h/q*. Next, from *h* on the left to *q* on the right, and the mirror image produces *i/i*. Our two lines of ciphertext therefore begin

```
        CI.....

        FI.....
```

We could go on like this. But things are not always so simple. It might happen that the letter pair to be encoded is in the same row in both squares, so that the connecting arrow is horizontal. For *n/x* the mirror arrow would then give us **X/N**, and after the second encoding we would be back at our original pair. To avoid this, we have to apply a rule for an exception (see below).

> The first arrow, which runs horizontally to the right, is mirrored and displaced to the left by one letter. Thus if we wish to encode *n/x*, the mirrored and displaced arrow connects *n* on the right with *h* on the left. The first step therefore yields *n/h*. Left *n* and right *h* give us a sloping arrow that, after mirror-imaging, leads to *i/a*. But there can be one more difficulty. Let us assume we want to encode the pair *x/r*. The arrow from left *x* to right *r* is horizontal. If we displace the mirrored arrow by one place to the left, it runs across the left edge of the left square. In that case, we take the corresponding letter of the last column of the right square, *m*. Thus *x/r* becomes *u/m* after the first encoding step. Then *u/m* becomes **F/S**.

Decoding proceeds analogously. With the cipher pair **C/F**, we go to *c* on the right and draw an arrow to *f* on the left, produce a horizontal mirror image and obtain *x/o*. The arrow from *x* on the right to *o* on the left after mirroring produces *w/m*, the original plaintext pair.

As for the arrangement within the two blocks, we can define this by two mnemonics. As before, we strip the mnemonic of recurring letters and write it down, letter by letter, as our keyword, into the first positions of the empty square. We then fill the square with the rest of the alphabet. Figure 5.25 shows a double box formed with the mnemonics *newspaper* and *orchidée*, or, rather, with the keywords derived from them, *NEWSPAR* and *ORCHIDE*.

n	e	w	s	p	o	r	c	h	i
a	r	b	c	d	d	e	a	b	f
f	g	h	i	k	g	k	l	m	n
l	m	o	q	t	p	q	s	t	u
u	v	x	y	z	v	w	x	y	z

Fig. 5.25. **A double box constructed with the mnemonics *newspaper* and *orchidée*.**

Double boxes were used in World War II by the German Security Service, the SS, and the armed forces. The key tables were changed every three hours. To express the missing *j* the combination *ii* was used. However, British Intelligence managed to read even these difficult Playfair ciphers.[2]

The double box method can be extended by the inclusion of numerals in the cipher tables. Thus, if we now regard the letters *i* and *j* as two separate symbols and if we add the numerals 0 to 9, we can create a cipher table of six by six symbols.

NOTES

1. The table in figure 5.3 is taken from Friedrich L. Bauer, *Decrypted Secrets* (Heidelberg–New York: Springer Verlag, 1997) 223.

2. Bauer, *Decrypted Secrets*, 63. J. S. Schlick, "With the 849th SIS 1942-1945," *Cryptologia* (January 1987) 29.

6. CAESARS IN RANK AND FILE

> Blaise de Vigenère was born April 5, 1523, in Saint-Pourçain. . . . He went to the Diet of Worms as a very young secretary, and subsequent travels through Europe in diplomatic missions widened his experience. . . . In 1570, at the age of forty-seven, he concentrated fully on writing. . . . He wrote his *Traicté des Chiffres* in 1585. . . . The book had more than six hundred pages and contained a lot more than cryptography—Japanese ideograms, alchemy, magic cabala, recipes for making gold, but also a reliable, precise reflection of the status of cryptology at that time.
>
> —FRIEDRICH L. BAUER, *Decrypted Secrets*

MONALPHABETIC CIPHERS ARE relatively easy to break. That is why, as early as the Renaissance, efforts began to use several alphabets simultaneously for encoding.

THE ABBOT WHO WAS NOT ENTIRELY TRUSTWORTHY

In fifteenth-century Germany there lived a scholar who became known chiefly as the author of several biographies. Johannes Trithemius (1462-1516) was born in Trittenheim on the Moselle, the son of a vintner, ten years after Leonardo da Vinci and thirty years before the discovery of America. He entered the monastery of Sponheim at the age of twenty, and a mere two years later he became its abbot. His interests, in line with the spirit of his century, included alchemy, astrology, and other occult sciences. He is reputed to have known the real Doctor Faustus, the model of

Goethe's Faust, whom he regarded as a charlatan. And yet he was a char-latan himself. In his research he discovered that there were four kinds of witches, that history revealed a cycle of 345 years, and that the world was created in 5206 BC. He claimed to know how one could make use of angels to send a message to another person, a kind of Renaissance e-mail. His boastfulness got him into trouble with the Church and even with the monks of his monastery. He had to leave Sponheim, but was received into a monastery in Würzburg, where he soon advanced to the post of prior. There he wrote six books on cryptology. He pretended to have needed only ten days for each of his books. He died in Würzburg at the age of fifty-four. Shortly afterward his books were published. The most impor-tant contribution was in his fifth book, where for the first time a square cipher table appears. In a slightly modified form this is reproduced in figure 6.1.

It is easy to see how the table came about. The headline is the plain-text alphabet. In the top line of the rectangular arrangement it is repeated, in the second line its first letter has moved to the final spot, then the first letter of the second row is moved to the end, and so forth. The first letter of one line always appears at the end of the next. Whereas in a monal-phabetic cipher one coded letter corresponds to one plaintext letter, here we have twenty-six cipher alphabets at our disposal.

Let us assume the plaintext "send help please" is to be encoded. According to Trithemius, encoding proceeds as follows. The first letter of the plaintext is encoded with the first line of the cipher table. This means that s becomes **S**. That is easy enough; but it gets more difficult. The second letter is encoded according to the second line, hence e becomes **F**. For the third letter, n, the third line supplies **P**. We can see now how it continues: d becomes **G**, h becomes **L**, e this time becomes **J**, and l becomes **R**. The whole ciphertext therefore reads **SFPG LJRW XUOLER**. If the plaintext contains more than twenty-six letters we start again from the beginning, so that the twenty-seventh letter is encoded with the alphabet of the first line again.

Basically this is nothing new. The different lines of the table are simply Caesar shifts. The difference is that the whole text is no longer encoded with the same Caesar; each letter is encoded with a different Caesar. This kind of cipher is called *polyalphabetic*. Each of the four es of the plaintext has been transformed into a different cipher. The letter's treacherous frequency has thus disappeared. Anyone realizing what

a b c d e f g h i j k l m n o p q r s t u v w x y z
A B C D E F G H I J K L M N O P Q R S T U V W X Y Z
B C D E F G H I J K L M N O P Q R S T U V W X Y Z A
C D E F G H I J K L M N O P Q R S T U V W X Y Z A B
D E F G H I J K L M N O P Q R S T U V W X Y Z A B C
E F G H I J K L M N O P Q R S T U V W X Y Z A B C D
F G H I J K L M N O P Q R S T U V W X Y Z A B C D E
G H I J K L M N O P Q R S T U V W X Y Z A B C D E F
H I J K L M N O P Q R S T U V W X Y Z A B C D E F G
I J K L M N O P Q R S T U V W X Y Z A B C D E F G H
J K L M N O P Q R S T U V W X Y Z A B C D E F G H I
K L M N O P Q R S T U V W X Y Z A B C D E F G H I J
L M N O P Q R S T U V W X Y Z A B C D E F G H I J K
M N O P Q R S T U V W X Y Z A B C D E F G H I J K L
N O P Q R S T U V W X Y Z A B C D E F G H I J K L M
O P Q R S T U V W X Y Z A B C D E F G H I J K L M N
P Q R S T U V W X Y Z A B C D E F G H I J K L M N O
Q R S T U V W X Y Z A B C D E F G H I J K L M N O P
R S T U V W X Y Z A B C D E F G H I J K L M N O P Q
S T U V W X Y Z A B C D E F G H I J K L M N O P Q R
T U V W X Y Z A B C D E F G H I J K L M N O P Q R S
U V W X Y Z A B C D E F G H I J K L M N O P Q R S T
V W X Y Z A B C D E F G H I J K L M N O P Q R S T U
W X Y Z A B C D E F G H I J K L M N O P Q R S T U V
X Y Z A B C D E F G H I J K L M N O P Q R S T U V W
Y Z A B C D E F G H I J K L M N O P Q R S T U V W X
Z A B C D E F G H I J K L M N O P Q R S T U V W X Y

Fig. 6.1. The Trithemius table. The lines in the square are, row by row, displaced to the left by one letter, and the letters displaced at the left margin are then placed in the free spots on the right. Above the table stands the plaintext alphabet. Coding is performed by replacing the first letter of the plaintext with the alphabet of the first row, which leaves it unchanged. The second letter is encoded with the second row, the third with the third row, and so on. This table can be used also for Vigenère encoding, which involves a keyword whose letters indicate which plaintext letter is to be encoded with which row. If, for instance, the keyword is *NEXT*, the plaintext letters will be encoded, one by one, using the rows beginning with N, E, X, T. After T, one starts again with N.

cipher method has been used can decipher the text by slavishly taking the separate lines one by one as encoding alphabets: for instance, decoding the seventeenth letter of the ciphertext with row seventeen. The advantage of the Trithemius system is that all twenty-five Caesar shifts are used before the first alphabet is drawn upon again.

From there it was only a short step toward breaking the rigid system of "first letter, first alphabet; second letter, second alphabet . . ." Several men of the Renaissance soon took that step. One was Giovanni Battista Della Porta (1535-1615), an all-around genius, an expert on natural science, but also with a marked inclination toward magic and conjuring. This contemporary of Galileo and author of a twenty-volume *Magia naturalis* believed, among other things, that a magnetic stone could be used for testing a woman's chastity. He also revealed what conjuring tricks could be used to induce women to take off their clothes. But Della Porta also made some important contributions to cryptology. The Italian mathematician, physician, and philosopher Gironimo Cardano (1501-1576) likewise wrote about everything under the sun, not confining himself to mathematics, astronomy, and astrology. He was the author of treatises on chess and games of chance, on poisons, dreams, urine, teeth, and wisdom. Two of his books were devoted to cryptology. The people interested in this science then seem to have been a rather motley crowd. Blaise de Vigenère (1523-1596) was no exception. As a young man, he worked as a diplomat for the Duc de Nevers and remained in his service nearly all his life. In Rome he met the cryptologists of the pope. He studied the works of Trithemius, Cardano, and Della Porta, and himself described numerous cipher systems, by no means confining himself to Caesar alphabets. After his death, his work was forgotten, until renewed interest in it was shown in the nineteenth century.

BLAISE DE VIGENÈRE'S TABLEAU

Nowadays a very simple cipher system is linked to the name of Vigenère. He goes one step beyond Trithemius but similarly bases his system on the table in figure 6.1. Encoding, however, becomes much more difficult if we depart from the "next letter, next line" pattern. Nor do we have to use all the rows. For instance, we can encode the first six letters, one by one, by means of lines 7, 1, 3, 6, 10, and 25. If the message is longer than six letters, we start again from the beginning. In our example, *send* thus becomes **YEPI**. The message can be deciphered by the receiver only if he knows the sequence 7, 1, 3, 6, 10, 25, which must be communicated to him by a route other than the ciphertext.

We again have a clear division between method (algorithm) and key. The sequence of lines 7, 1, 3, 6, 10, 25 is the key; the method lies in the easily reconstructable cipher table. A convenient way of fixing the sequence of the lines would be a date, such as one's anniversary, or a telephone number, naturally without the zeros. Instead of a sequence of lines we can also choose an easily remembered keyword that prescribes the lines. Let us take the keyword *NEXT*. In our plaintext "send help please," the first letter would then be encoded with the line starting with N. The letter *s* thus becomes **F**. For the second letter, the E line is the one to use: thus *e* becomes **I**. The third letter requires the X line: *n* becomes **K**. And so on. At the sixth letter we start again from the beginning with *NEXT*. Our plaintext becomes **FIKW UIII CPBTFI**.

To make encoding easier for us, we write down the keyword in a line in continual repetition and write the plaintext underneath, as shown in figure 6.2, top. Then step by step we can look up the ciphers in the table and write them underneath. The bottom part of the figure shows how we proceed when decoding. Instead of the cipher table we can also use the cipher wheel in figure 4.2. For encoding with the keyword *NEXT,* we set the disk for the first letter so that the plaintext *a* coincides with the cipher **N** on the inner disk. In this position we encode the first letter of the text: *s* becomes **F**. And so on.

The algorithm, the Vigenère tableau, is no secret. The keyword, on the other hand, agreed between sender and receiver, must be kept secret.

Fig. 6.2. Top: encoding with a Vigenère tableau and the keyword *NEXT*. Bottom: the corresponding decoding.

BLURRED FREQUENCIES

Polyalphabetic coding blurs the frequencies of the letters in a language, especially if the keyword has the least possible number of repeated letters. Anyone choosing *BBBBB* as a keyword will end up, even with the Vigenère tableau, with a monalphabetic cipher, indeed a simple Caesar.

Next we examine a plaintext of 331 letters encoded by the Vigenère method. I will not reveal the plaintext; we will work our way toward it by deciphering. Naturally I will not reveal the keyword either. But I will tell you that it consists of four letters. The frequencies of the letters in my plaintext match roughly those in figure 5.3. The letters e, t, n, a, and o in my plaintext occur with frequencies of 12.7%, 11.5%, 10.3%, 7.9%, and 7.5%, while k has a frequency of only 0.6% and p only 0.3%. The letters j, x, and z do not occur at all in the plaintext.

The ciphertext is reproduced in figure 6.3. For greater clarity I have divided it into five-letter groups. The most frequent letter, with 7.3%, is **A**. This shows that we are not dealing with a monalphabetic code, because then the cipher corresponding to e would have to occur with an approximate frequency of 12%. The rarest cipher is **J** (0.9%). The coding has smoothed out the frequency distribution. While plaintext frequencies are between 12.7 and 0%, those of the ciphertext range from 7.3 to 0.9%. The maximum frequency has become less, the minimum frequency greater.

```
WAFOO  YVHRE  HECOT  RDHPA  QOMGR
IZTBE  HGOAA  VXGJB  XTLFD  TONDC
VZOSV  SPIUA  OWFBB  KVAON  PTRTP
ADHLR  KRSLC  UTZOR  VSXIU  RDELA
DHPED  YZRFE  UBPCV  HBSLR  KTPAQ
CVADE  ZGCAY  RLYUB  WEHAC  AULDH
PAQNL  JKNKV  XFHPD  TORIA  YRAUP
GOAUB  ODMNC  HPBXE  KTKML  VXSVZ
OSLPD  IVACO  MGREJ  NENAE  ISBPR
AZGRE  ZBETO  NXDLN  CTIHD  TOVCI
ZGREM  VBSAO  SGWHL  LPPMO  UGOSA
BPTOR  UIUQS  NFRKR  ZNXDP  GMRLN
DEZAY  LPGDL  LPYMT  RXTHY  YNNOB
OHQGA  F
```

Fig. 6.3. A ciphertext created according to Vigenère with a four-letter keyword, arranged in five-letter groups.

This frequency smoothing becomes even more marked if I encode the same plaintext with a keyword that consists of ten different letters. This ciphertext is shown in figure 6.4. The greatest frequency is that of **B**, with 6.0%, while the least frequent letter, **C**, has 1.8%. We can see the trend: the longer the keyword, the more ironed out the frequencies.

```
IILUI   PPIAL   ADOWZ   XXYJB   ZVFFD
QFZVV   BHXHT   UJOPH   RKFGM   AHMPK
BFIJP   TYPNZ   AELHV   BPBXU   ISDBV
GXYFS   TYLKO   CZFII   PTGPN   QPMRG
XYJFM   FSQRM   AHJTP   IKZEQ   WBVGK
TPBML   SFOIE   XFPOC   FLAZO   IARXY
JBZUE   IWVQB   RWBQM   AHQUI   EXULJ
HXHNA   HLSTW   YJCGL   DSWUR   BRJPA
XZEOP   QBGWF   GHALC   MQVGK   CJVQA
HSFDM   FHYKI   OGKEM   OBONX   KIWLP
SFDMS   BVJUP   BNPGX   TVVGF   OHXZT
ABBUX   OZORB   UYQWZ   FTRUJ   HVYEM
OMFGS   CJHMS   EOKUZ   XRKBZ   HUGNN
WNWAR   Z
```

Fig. 6.4. A ciphertext created according to Vigenère with a ten-letter keyword. The same plaintext was used for figure 6.3.

DECODING WITH A SLEDGEHAMMER

One would think that in the age of the computer a Vigenère cipher would be easy to crack. After all, one need only guess the keyword. But keywords consist of the letters of the alphabet, and there are twenty-six of them. One could make the computer try out all possible keywords in turn—a universal library of keywords.

We may assume that no one will use a one-letter or two-letter keyword. One-letter keywords would result in a monalphabetic cipher; two-letter keywords would also produce a ciphertext that is easy to break. Let us try a three-letter keyword. In how many ways can I arrange the twenty-six letters of the alphabet in groups of three? The mathematicians have a simple rule: $26 \times 26 \times 26$ words can be formed; this makes 17,576 possible keywords. If the keyword really has only three letters, then one of these 17,576 will make sense. But I do not have to read all the results to see. I can teach the computer that in a meaningful English text one letter must appear with a frequency of about 12% and the next most frequent with 9%. If it offers me texts with only these frequency characteristics, my job will be a lot easier. Moreover, I can teach the computer further refinements of the English language, such as the frequency of *th*, *he*, *an*, and *in*. This will make my work easier still.

Decoding by this sledgehammer method, however, gets more difficult the longer the keyword is. If I do not get a solution with three-letter keywords, I will have to try four-letter ones—but of these there are 26 × 26 × 26 × 26, which makes more than 450,000. If I still get no result, I will have to resort to five-letter keywords, of which there are nearly twelve million. If I still get no meaningful text and if I therefore have to resort to six-letter keywords, I will have to look through 309 million possibilities. If my computer and I need only one second to examine each of these possible plaintexts for sense, then even if we work without a break day and night, the task will take us nearly ten years. The longer the keyword, the more tedious the task. If our keyword, like

DONAUDAMPFSCHIFFAHRTSGESELLSCHAFTSKAPITAENSWITWE

consists of forty-eight letters, then my computer and I will need a sixty-digit number of years of uninterrupted work. Astronomers estimate the age of the world as only a ten-digit number of years.

It is often stated, in connection with encoding methods, how many cases have to be examined in order to arrive at the correct solution. Mostly this means the sledgehammer approach. In World War II, the Germans believed that their Enigma machine supplied a cipher that was unbreakable. They believed the enormous number of possibilities that would have to be tested to arrive at a plaintext was sufficiently great to make the code secure. That was a big mistake. Even with a simple Vigenère, one does not have to examine all keywords. This was first realized by an East Prussian officer, long before anyone suspected that there would be such things as computers.

HOW A VIGENÈRE CIPHER IS CRACKED

At first glance it seems impossible to make any sense of a Vigenère cipher. In fact, Vigenère ciphers were long believed to be secure.

Basically, however, you already possess all the information you need to decipher the two secret texts of figures 6.3 and 6.4. You will find that you do not need the keyword. All you need to know is its length, and that I have revealed to you.

Let us take the ciphertext in figure 6.3. As the keyword is four letters long, the letters number 1, 5, 9, 13, . . . can be decoded with the first letter of the keyword. The letters number 2, 6, 10, 14, . . . can be decoded with the second letter of the keyword. The same applies to letters number 3, 7, 11, 15, . . . and letters number 4, 8, 12, 16, . . . From the text in figure 6.3 let us look for all ciphers that have been encoded with the same keyword letter. We obtain four strings of these ciphers, as shown in figure 6.5.

Encoded with the first key letter:

WORCDQRBOXXDDOPOBORDKCOXDDDFPBKQDCLWCDQKXDIAOOCXKXODC
REIRREXCDCRBSLMOPUSKXMDYDYXYBG

Encoded with the second key letter:

AYEOHOIEAGTTCSIWKNTHRURIEHYECSTCEAYEAHNNFTAUAHEMSSIOE
NSAETDTTIESGLOSTINRDRELLMTNOA

Encoded with the third key letter:

FVHTPMZHAJLOVVUFVPPLSTVULPZUVLPVZYUHUPLKHOYPUMKLVLVMJ
ABZZOLIOZMAWPUAOUFZPLZPLTHNHF

Encoded with the fourth key letter:

OHERAGTGVBFNZSABATARLZSRAERBHRAAGRBALAJVPRRGBNBTVPAGN
EPGBNNHVGVOHPGBRQRNGNAGPRYOQ

Fig. 6.5. Once we know that the keyword of the Vigenère cipher in figure 6.3 has a length of four, we can collect the ciphertext letters encoded with the same letter of the keyword into strings of letters.

Do you see that we have very nearly deciphered the text? Each of our four strings of letters is encoded by the same Caesar. For each plaintext letter the same letter of the keyword was used for encoding, that is, the same line of the Vigenère tableau, and each line represents one Caesar.

Any string of letters picked randomly from an English plaintext reveals the frequency distribution characteristic of the English language. Thus *e* will occur with a probability of about 12.5%. Hence the cipher corresponding to *e* must occur with that frequency. Let us therefore consider the string of letters encoded with the first key letter. The most frequent is **D** (16.9%). Next comes **O** (12.0%), followed by **X** (10.8%) and **C** (9.6%). Therefore **D** or **O** probably stands for *e*. Let us now look at the Vigenère tableau in figure 6.1 to find out in which line *e* is encoded with **D** or **O**. This could be the line starting with Z or K. Which of the two has the greater probability? In English plaintexts the next most frequent letter is *t*. If the Z line in the Vigenère tableau is the right one, then the *t* would have become **S**, which in our string appears only two times (2.1%). But if our string is encoded with the K line of the tableau, the abundant *t* in English texts would correspond to the abundant **D** in the string. It seems we are on the right track. On the assumption that the first string of letters is encoded with the K line, we get the corresponding plaintext letters.

This means that we have now decoded every fourth letter of the ciphertext. Moreover, we have discovered the first letter of the keyword, *K*. We proceed similarly with the other three strings of letters. Briefly, the most frequent letters are **E** (13.3%), **P** (13.3%), and **R** (13.4%) for strings 2, 3, and 4. For string 2, the assumption that **E** corresponds to *e*, that is, that these letters are encoded with the A line of the tableau, gives us the second letter of the keyword; we now have *KA*. With this assumption we can now decode half of all the letters. Doing this, we find that the frequency of the plaintext letters obtained roughly corresponds to the general frequencies of letters in the English language. The plaintext then begins: "ma--ey--he . . . " We encounter a problem with string 3. In it the most frequent cipher is **P**. Does it correspond to *e*? In that case the third string would have been encoded with the L line of the tableau, since it encodes *e* with **P**. But it would also encode the frequent *t* in English texts with **E**, which does not appear in string 3 at all. We had therefore better look for another line in the tableau. The next most frequent cipher in string 3 is **L**. If this corresponded to *e*, then string 3 would be encoded with the H line of the tableau. In this case the keyword would be *KAH* plus another letter. Assuming that this is so, we can decode string 3 and now have solved three-quarters of the ciphertext. It begins with "may-eyo-hea . . ." String 4 should be easy. The most frequent cipher is **R**. Assuming that it corresponds to *e*, we conclude that the string is encoded with the N line of the tableau. Indeed, trial immediately shows that this is the solution. I have in fact used the keyword *KAHN*. We now decode the letters **WAFOOYVHRE** . . . at the beginning of the ciphertext in accordance with the lines

KAHNKAHNKA of the Vigenère tableau. If we continue, the ciphertext turns into:

> maybeyouhearsomethingofthisgreateatingcontestthatcome
> soffinnewyorkonenightintheearlysummerofnineteenthirtysevenof
> courseeatingcontestsarebynomeansanythingnewandinfacttheyare
> quiteanoldfashionedgameinsomesectionsofthecountrysuchasthe
> southandeastbutthisisthefirstbigpubliccontestofthekindinyearsanditcre
> atesnolittlecommentalongbroadway

My keyword was intended as a tribute to David Kahn, the author of the famous book *The Codebreakers*. The plaintext comes from Damon Runyan's short story "A Piece of Pie."

In order to transform a Vigenère cipher into several easily decodable Caesar ciphers it is thus enough to know the length of the keyword. But do not forget, I revealed it to you. Without this help you would have faced a more difficult problem. How, then, does one discover the length of the keyword?

THE RHYTHM OF THE KEYWORD

Is there nothing we can discover in a Vigenère cipher if we do not know the length of the key or the keyword itself? Yes, there is — because in our example, encoded with *KAHN*, the rhythm produced by the keyword length is reflected also in the ciphertext. Every fourth letter is encoded with the same Caesar. In his classic work on cryptology, David Kahn says: "These repetitions betray the movements of the keyword below the surface of the cryptogram, just as the ducking of a fishing cork tells of a nibble."[1]

It was three centuries after Vigenère that an officer of the East Prussian 33rd Infantry Regiment wrote an instruction for determining the length of a key. Friedrich W. Kasiski (1805-1881) was born in Schlochau in West Prussia. He joined the regiment at the early age of seventeen and received his commission as an officer soon after. Retiring from his regiment with the rank of major, he found time to devote himself to cryptology. In 1863 his book *Die Geheimschriften und die Dechiffrierkunst*

(Secret Writings and the Art of Deciphering) was published in Berlin. It comprised a mere ninety-five pages and excited scarcely any attention. Kasiski soon gave up cryptology, became an amateur anthropologist, excavated prehistoric tombs and reported on them in specialized journals. He probably never knew that he had revolutionized cryptology. Let us retrace his arguments.

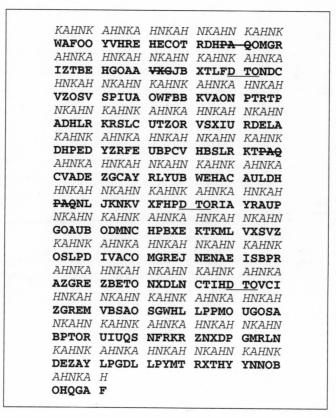

Fig. 6.6. Repetition of letter groups. Here the groups **PAQ** and **DTO**, in a ciphertext encoded by the Vigenère method, provide an indication of the length of the keyword.

There are letter combinations that occur with particular frequency in English, such as *the* and *ing*. In Vigenère ciphers they are mostly transformed into different letter combinations of the ciphertext. Thus in the plaintext taken from Damon Runyan the letter combination *ing* occurs four times. In figure 6.6 the corresponding letter triads are crossed out:

ing is three times encoded as **PAQ** and once as **VXG**. The key letters involved were *HNK* three times and *NKA* once. That *ing* is not always encoded in the same way is not surprising, as it is not always encoded with the same fragment of the keyword. But there are three instances when the letter triad is converted into the same sequence of ciphers, namely **PAQ**; in these instances *ing* happens to coincide with the same fragment of the keyword, *HNK*. This can happen only if the same letter sequences in the ciphertext are distant from each other by an exact multiple of the length of the keyword. We can see this in figure 6.6. It shows the ciphertext of figure 6.3 and, above it, the keyword in multiple repetition. The crossed-out identical letter triads **PAQ** have all been encoded with the key letters *HNK*. The distances between the identical cipher triads (more accurately: the distance from the beginning of one identical triad to the beginning of the next) for **PAQ** are 104 and 28, which is exactly twenty-six times and seven times the length of the keyword.

This gives us a chance to learn something about the length of the keyword. One looks for as many identical letter combinations as possible in the ciphertext and determines the distances between them. For the combinations that derive from the same letters of the plaintext, the distance will be a multiple of the keyword length.

Consider the combination **DTO** (fig. 6.6), which occurs three times in the ciphertext (underlined). The distances between the beginnings of the triad **DTO** are 80 and 120. All three **DTO**s happen to be an encryption of the plaintext combination *tth*, which, written without spaces, occurs three times in the Runyan passage. The keyword length must be a factor of 80 and 120. Also, the combination **VZOS** occurs twice, with a distance of 188. Let us factor all the differences we now have:

$$28 = 2 \times 2 \times 7$$
$$80 = 2 \times 2 \times 2 \times 2 \times 5$$
$$104 = 2 \times 2 \times 2 \times 13$$
$$120 = 2 \times 2 \times 2 \times 3 \times 5$$
$$188 = 2 \times 2 \times 47$$

The five differences have the factor 2×2 in common. The length of the keyword therefore must be 2 or 4. One can disregard the factor 2, since no one would choose such a short keyword. This leaves only the common factor 4, which is in fact the length of the keyword *KAHN*. We have taken just three recurring letter combinations to arrive at our answer. If you search the text again, you will find that **OMGR** occurs twice; it too can be used to determine the keyword length.

One must not think, however, that the distances between identical letter combinations of the ciphertext invariably are a multiple of the keyword. It is entirely possible that some identical letter combinations arise in the ciphertext accidentally, that such combinations do not go back to the same plaintext groups. Thus the plaintext letters *ypl* become **IPS** if encoded by the letters *KAH* of our keyword; but the same cipher combination is obtained by encoding *iif* with the *AHN* fragment of the keyword. The reader can easily convince himself of this by using the Vigenère tableau of figure 6.1. In this example, the same ciphertext combinations do not coincide with the same plaintext; the same ciphertext group has arisen by chance. The distance between the two identical ciphertext combinations therefore has nothing to do with the length of the keyword. So caution is needed, as well as a "nose" for codes, when you are trying to discover the length of the keyword.

```
DEFOGWSGHU  SRGZYKACXZ  DIPUCDAGLM
FSNQBSDIHP  LIFLLYEKHA  MTVYCSTGKC
DEKLLYTBQI  WNGXACYSLP  EOSEYALRBY
FDGRKCIAVQ  ZEUDBLHEHC  EERWGFGFVA
ZEQXJWDSRP  LHNWYXTRUL  GOAWFWFVUQ
LWVWFLHRNC  FTHFIQFRUR  ALVCCJCBPN
SNLZFGSRHV  WCHWGNEFZC  JERAAATRGY
TOHWRZEAHU  UAZSYAGAVF  WWNVUGRXLL
YUCIMJTUHK
```

Fig. 6.7. A ciphertext created by the Vigenère method with a keyword of unknown length.

For an illustration I have reproduced a new ciphertext in figure 6.7, broken up into groups of ten. In it the three-letter combination **LLY** occurs three times. The two distances from the beginning of one triad to the beginning of another are 20 and 175. This suggests that the keyword has a length of five, since that is the common factor of the two numbers. I have indeed used a keyword of that length. The plaintext comes from a short story by Sidney Sheldon.

In appendix A, I describe a simple Vigenère-like cipher machine that permits encoding with a finite keyword. Of course, the texts encoded with this machine have the same weaknesses as all polyalphabetic codes where key letters are periodically repeated. The machine, however, also makes it possible to work with infinitely long keywords. We will learn about their advantages and drawbacks in the next chapter.

NOTE

1. Kahn, *The Codebreakers* (New York: Macmillan, 1967) 208.

7. KEYWORDS WITHOUT END

> It may seem strange that numbers generated according
> to a rigid rule are described as "random numbers" . . .
> Although their generation is absolutely deterministic,
> these numbers have the characteristic of behaving like
> genuine random numbers, i.e., they behave as if they
> were drawn from a large lottery drum.
>
> —ROLF J. LORENZ, *Biometrie*

A TEXT ENCODED BY THE VIGENÈRE METHOD loses the typical letter frequency of its language the longer the keyword. We saw in the preceding chapter that a four-letter keyword reduces the maximum frequency of *e* from 12.7%t in the plaintext to 7.3% in the ciphertext. The longer the keyword, the more difficult any statistical analysis will be. The best encoding system, therefore, would use an infinitely long keyword or at least one that is no shorter than the plaintext. In that case the keyword will not create in the ciphertext any rhythm that might help decoding.

CARL SAGAN'S CONTACT AS A CODE WORM

If, however, we make the keyword as long as the plaintext, then transmitting the key becomes just as difficult as transmitting the text itself. We can make things easier for us by taking as the keyword a text that is known both to sender and receiver, such as the text of a generally accessible book. Let us take the late Carl Sagan's novel about extraterrestrial intelligences, *Contact*. The keyword in that case would be a well-nigh endless letter worm:

BYHUMANSTANDARDSITCOULDNOTPOSSIBLYHAVEBEENARTIFICIAL . . .

So it would continue without break throughout the 417 pages of the book to the conclusion:

. . . *THECIRCLEHADCLOSEDSHEFOUNDWHATSHEHADBEEN*
SEARCHINGFOR.

For communicating the key to the receiver we would not have to send him the complete text of the book. It would be enough to tell him: "*Contact*, Simon & Schuster edition, 1985." Then we could send him our message, for instance:

atthattimetheonlyknownabsolutelysafecypherwastheone

The first letter of the key is *B*. We take the B line of the Vigenère tableau (fig. 6.1) and under *a* we find **B**. The next key letter is *Y*. We take the Y line of the table: below the *t* we find **R**. Thus we continue, code letter by code letter, plaintext letter by plaintext letter. Finally we have the ciphertext:

BRABMTGAFEGKEFQDGDDCQYPOGHAILWTZDYMEX
CQLIEWRLZMMQVL

This ciphertext has no keyword rhythm in it—unless the text is longer than the 417 pages of the book, in which case the encoder, at the end of the book, would return to the beginning of the book.

Is this message really securely encoded? With lengthy secret messages we notice that not only the plaintext but also the ciphertext bears the characteristic of the English language. Little is gained by choosing a foreign-language book, such as a Jules Verne novel in the original French. In that case, too, the ciphertext will display a frequency pattern. For the moment, let us stay with an English key. Since in the key, just as in the plaintext, *e* is the most frequent letter, it will happen relatively often that *e* is encoded with the E line, which will result in an excessive frequency of the cipher **I**, as a glance at the table in figure 6.1 shows. Moreover, frequent letter pairs, such as *th* in the plaintext, will coincide with a frequent letter pair in the key. This pattern will then be reflected in frequent pair repetitions in the ciphertext. Conclusion: the frequency pattern of plaintext and key will be reflected in the frequency pattern of a sufficiently long ciphertext, facilitating unauthorized deciphering. Of course the deciphering will be more difficult than with a simple Vigenère.

For the next message, needless to say, we must not start with the same beginning of the code worm, that is, with *BYHUM* . . . Otherwise the opening letter of all these secret messages will be encoded with *B*, and the result will be a monalphabetic encoding of letters of the English alphabet. The same applies to the next ciphers. All second letters will be encoded with *Y*, all third letters with *H*, and so on. Given enough messages, a frequency analysis will make decoding possible. Suppose the unauthorized decoder always takes only the first letter of a hundred intercepted secret messages and determines their frequency; this will enable him to discover which of these messages begin with the plaintext letter *e*. Proceeding similarly with all the second letters of all the messages, and so on, he will then most probably find the plaintext letter *e* in all the messages. He will then search for the second most frequent plaintext letter, *t*. With some effort and some intuition he will succeed in deciphering all the secret texts.

The sender, therefore, should begin the next message at a different point of the key worm. He could, at regular intervals of time, use a new page of the key book. An instruction such as "each day a new page" would, of course, have to be communicated to the receiver together with the key. It would be dangerous to preface each message with an unencoded indication of the page to be used.

IT NEED NOT ALWAYS BE A CAESAR

Where our keyword is short or of book length, we have so far always used the Vigenère tableau of alphabets displaced against one another. This helped us a little with the decoding of the Runyan text, but was not crucial. What mattered was the length of the keyword. If that is known, one knows which letters were encoded in the same manner. Whether these individual encodings were done with Caesars or not is less important. In any case they are monalphabetic and can be cracked if the text is sufficiently long. We can make life more difficult for the unauthorized intruder if we use a table whose lines are not displaced but shuffled alphabets, as in the table in figure 7.1. If we wish to do that, we have to let the receiver have not only the keyword but the entire table. The great advantage of the Vigenère tableau with its displaced alphabets is that we can reconstruct it without

	a	b	c	d	e	f	g	h	i	j	k	l	m	n	o	p	q	r	s	t	u	v	w	x	y	z
A	E	N	A	M	O	F	L	P	D	K	Q	C	J	Z	R	Y	G	X	I	W	S	V	B	U	H	T
B	L	Y	F	Q	X	R	E	G	K	U	N	O	A	P	S	D	B	C	T	V	I	H	W	Z	M	J
C	S	C	R	T	A	H	U	Q	G	V	I	P	W	D	F	X	O	J	Y	N	B	Z	M	L	E	K
D	Q	G	P	R	A	O	S	F	N	Z	T	H	Y	B	X	U	W	M	E	V	L	I	C	K	D	J
E	R	G	Q	C	Z	P	F	O	T	B	N	H	U	L	E	S	M	K	V	Y	A	J	X	D	W	I
F	H	N	A	G	O	M	B	P	Z	I	L	Y	Q	X	F	W	C	V	R	U	K	T	E	S	J	D
G	S	I	A	R	T	H	J	Q	U	C	G	P	V	K	O	B	W	N	F	M	X	E	L	Y	D	Z
H	Z	L	Y	D	E	X	K	M	W	C	J	V	N	F	U	I	O	T	B	S	H	R	G	Q	P	A
I	L	I	P	K	M	O	Q	H	J	N	Z	R	A	Y	G	B	X	S	F	W	C	E	V	T	D	U
J	O	X	L	E	W	Y	N	K	V	Z	P	A	U	M	B	T	Q	J	S	F	I	R	C	H	D	G
K	Z	N	H	Y	A	M	X	O	J	W	B	L	V	P	I	U	C	K	T	Q	D	S	E	F	R	G
L	L	X	F	N	W	Y	K	A	V	Z	M	O	U	B	T	J	G	S	P	C	R	I	D	Q	H	E
M	O	G	N	A	P	B	M	Q	H	C	R	L	D	Z	S	I	K	Y	T	E	X	F	W	U	J	V
N	N	G	X	A	M	Y	O	F	W	Z	Q	L	V	S	H	U	P	R	T	K	E	J	B	I	C	D
O	Y	M	X	F	L	W	N	A	V	H	K	U	O	C	T	J	G	S	Z	P	I	R	B	E	Q	D
P	F	L	E	M	K	G	Z	N	Y	J	X	A	W	O	V	I	U	D	T	P	S	H	R	C	Q	B
Q	T	F	U	S	I	V	R	C	W	Q	H	Y	P	E	X	O	J	Z	N	G	M	B	L	D	K	A
R	W	B	E	H	I	R	K	N	P	Z	M	J	S	T	U	A	Q	O	V	X	L	C	Y	F	G	D
S	I	X	E	W	Y	H	V	Z	J	U	A	T	G	S	K	R	D	Q	F	P	L	O	B	N	C	M
T	A	X	L	W	Y	I	V	Z	K	E	U	M	H	T	J	S	D	R	N	Q	G	P	B	F	O	C
U	Z	C	E	Y	H	D	X	G	M	W	I	L	V	N	U	B	T	K	S	O	R	F	J	Q	A	P
V	Z	J	Y	G	X	F	W	K	V	I	U	A	T	L	S	H	R	E	Q	M	P	B	O	D	N	C
W	N	F	M	O	E	L	P	H	Z	K	Y	Q	X	D	W	J	V	R	U	G	T	I	S	C	B	A
X	A	N	B	M	O	C	L	P	D	Z	K	Y	Q	X	E	W	J	V	R	U	F	T	I	S	G	H
Y	I	R	B	H	Q	S	J	A	P	T	Z	G	Y	O	K	X	U	N	W	D	M	V	F	L	C	E
Z	K	T	J	B	S	U	A	L	R	V	I	D	Q	W	C	M	P	X	H	F	O	Y	E	N	G	Z

***Fig. 7.1.* A Vigenère tableau with different, shuffled alphabet lines. At the top we have the plaintext line, on the left, the key letters. If the keyword is *KAHN*, we begin again with the eleventh line. Then we use lines 1, 8, 14, 11, 1, 8, 14, 11, . . . in this order. Decoding is more difficult, because no Caesar displacements are used here. On the other hand, the secret transmission of the key is made more difficult.**

further aids. Even in a cell, existing just on bread and water, we could scratch a Vigenère tableau on the wall with a broken spoon. We could not do that with the table in figure 7.1.

In a Vigenère cipher with a finite key length, the rhythm of the keyword betrays itself in the ciphertext. No matter how long the keyword used, the ciphertext still reflects the regularities of the language in the plaintext and key. This can be avoided if we take a key text that has no rhythm and no preference for any letter, such as

AJKZFBIXRCBWWHF . . .

Of course we can no longer use books like Sagan's *Contact* for such key worms, but only such a text that from start to finish consists of arbitrarily arranged letters. Such a text will never become a bestseller.

In practice, people operate with numerals instead of letters. We have already seen that a Caesar displacement is readily expressed in numbers (see chapter 4), if for every letter, whether in the plaintext or in the key, a number is assigned in alphabetic order. But another method is often used in cryptology, one that is now more than two thousand years old.

POLYBIUS'S TABLE

The Greek author and historian Polybius was born about 200 B.C. and died about 120 B.C. He is the author of the first universal history. This comprised forty volumes, of which five have come down to us. He also concerned himself with ciphers. One system bears his name.

If you dispense with the distinction between the plaintext letters *i* and *j*, an encoding in figures offers itself with the aid of a kind of chessboard (fig. 7.2, top). Thus *g* becomes **22**, *p* becomes **35**, and so on.

We can make matters more difficult for the unauthorized decoder if we arrange the letters in the key table not in alphabetic order but in some other sequence. Thus we might first enter the letters of some keyword in the first few spaces of the table and fill the others with the rest of the alphabet (fig. 7.2, bottom). But, we will work here with the simpler table at the top. With it, *money* becomes **32, 34, 33, 15, 54**.

This kind of code was used by convicts in Tsarist Russia. By means of knocking signals through the walls of their cells, they could communicate. But instead of the five-row, five-column square they used one of six by six in order to accommodate the thirty-five letters of the old Cyrillic alphabet. The method described was called the *nihilistic* method, named for the Nihilists, the opponents of the Tsarist regime. For each letter of the alphabet there is one pair of numerals.

The method is not very secure. The unauthorized decoder soon notices that all messages consist of an even number of digits and that only the digits from 1 to 5—in the case of the Nihilists, from 1 to 6—occur. From that he concludes that each letter is represented by two digits. As the five numerals used can represent only twenty-five different number pairs, it seems reasonable to assume that each plaintext letter corresponds to one number pair. The decoder can then immediately establish whether or not he is dealing with a monalphabetic cipher. Of the twenty-five possible number pairs, given a sufficiently long text, the pair corresponding to *e* should be the most frequent. The decoder can therefore proceed as with any other monalphabetic cipher. He will soon reconstruct the Polybius table used, even in the case of shuffled alphabets as in figure 7.2, bottom. Nowadays the Polybius method is used chiefly for turning letter sequences into number sequences.

ENCODING WITH A NUMBER WORM

We will now encode a text with Sagan's *Contact*, this time using numbers. For a plaintext let us take:

atthattimetheonly . . .

With the help of the Polybius square (fig. 7.2, top) this becomes a *numerical plaintext*:

11 44 44 23 11 44 44 24 32 15 44 23 15 34 33 31 54 . . .

So far we have only a monalphabetic encoding. Let us therefore again take the keyword from Sagan's *Contact*, BYHUMANSTANDARDSIT . . . , and convert it with Polybius's help into a *numerical ciphertext*:

12 54 23 45 32 11 33 43 44 11 33 14 11 42 14 43 24 . . .

Now we have a little mathematics. We write our plaintext and keyword one under the other, both in numerical form. Then we add the two, as has been done in figure 7.3, top. This gives us the ciphertext in numerical form. Without some knowledge of the keyword, it is not easy to decipher.

Plate 1. Thomas Jefferson's wheel was used by the US Army as late as 1920. In 1920, it was no longer a case of wooden disks that had to be rotated against each other. (*Photo: Deutsches Museum, Munich*)

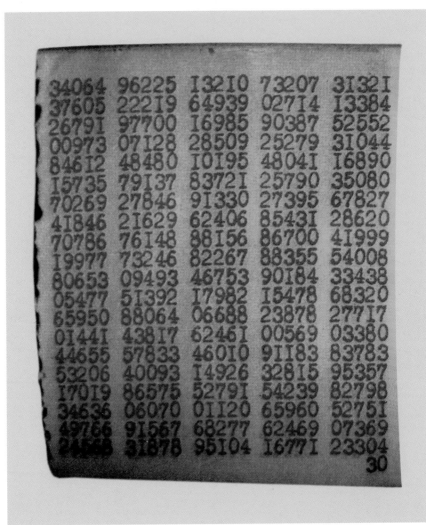

34064	96225	13210	73207	31321
37605	22219	64939	02714	13384
26791	97700	16985	90387	52552
00973	07128	28509	25279	31044
84612	48480	10195	48041	16890
15735	79137	83721	25790	35080
70269	27846	91330	27395	67827
41846	21629	62406	85431	28620
70786	76148	88156	86700	41999
19977	73246	82267	88355	54008
80653	09493	46753	90184	33438
05477	51392	17982	15478	68320
65950	88064	06688	23878	27717
01441	43817	62461	00569	03380
44655	57833	46010	91183	83783
53206	40093	14926	32815	95357
17019	86575	52791	54239	82798
34636	06070	01120	65960	52751
49766	91567	68277	62469	07369
24548	31878	95104	16771	23304

30

Plate 2. A list of random numbers of the Soviet secret service. Here the weaknesses described in chapter seven have evidently been avoided: there is no dearth of number duplication, even of triplication. (*Photo: Krypto AG, Zug, Switzerland*)

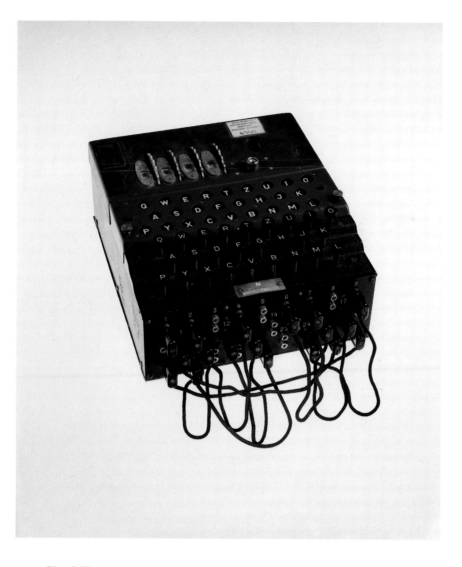

Plate 3. The naval Enigma with four rotors, 1944. The plaintext letters are typed out on the keyboard. For each typed letter a lightbulb comes on behind a glass screen bearing the ciphers. Decoding takes place in the same way. The cipher is keyed in, and the plaintext letter lights up. At the beginning of operation with Enigma, the key of the day has to be put in; this means that the encoder has to install the correct rotors in the correct order and with the correct position of the ring. He has to set up the rotors with the disks in such a way that the letters of the key of the day appear in the windows. Finally the correct connections have been made on the plugboard (front). (*Photo: Deutsches Museum, Munich*)

Plate 4. Two rotors of Enigma, Left: rotor 1, showing the letter disk and the cogwheel over which the disk can be rotated during encoding. The pins are contacts that touch the contact points on the neighboring rotor. Right: rotor 8 is so positioned that the twenty-six contact points are seen along with the letters on the setting ring. Also seen on the setting right are two notches. They ensure the movement of the next roller. The inner part with the electrical contacts and their wiring can be rotated against the outer part along with letter wheel, setting ring and notches. In this way the ring position demanded by the daily code is adjusted. (*Photo: Deutsches Museum, Munich*)

Fig. 7.2. Polybius tables. Top: filled out alphabetically; bottom: filled out with the aid of the mnemonic *newspaper* (keyword *NEWSPAR*). Each letter is represented by a pair of numerals. With the top table *e* becomes 15 and *m* becomes 32. The Polybius table provides a monalphabetic encoding—each letter has its precise pair of numerals assigned to it—but it offers a simple way of turning a text of letters into a numerical text that can be mathematically encrypted.

11	44	44	23	11	44	44	24	32	15	44	23	15	34	33	31	54	25	33	34	52
12	*54*	*23*	*45*	*32*	*11*	*33*	*43*	*44*	*11*	*33*	*14*	*11*	*42*	*14*	*43*	*24*	*44*	*13*	*34*	*45*
23	**98**	**67**	**68**	**43**	**55**	**77**	**67**	**76**	**26**	**77**	**37**	**26**	**76**	**47**	**74**	**78**	**69**	**46**	**68**	**97**

23	**98**	**67**	**68**	**43**	**55**	**77**	**67**	**76**	**26**	**77**	**37**	**26**	**76**	**47**	**74**	**78**	**69**	**46**	**68**	**97**
12	*54*	*23*	*45*	*32*	*11*	*33*	*43*	*44*	*11*	*33*	*14*	*11*	*42*	*14*	*43*	*24*	*44*	*13*	*34*	*45*
11	44	44	23	11	44	44	24	32	15	44	23	15	34	33	31	54	25	33	34	52

Fig. 7.3. Top: the plaintext sentence "atthattime . . . ," converted into a numerical plaintext with the Polybius table of figure 7.2, is encoded to numerical ciphertext by means of the keyword *BYHUMANST* . . . , which was likewise converted into a number worm. Bottom: the corresponding decoding.

What does the receiver now do with this message? Below the ciphertext he writes the numerical keyword and—as in figure 7.3, bottom—subtracts. (Though this does not occur in figure 7.3, do not carry or borrow any tens when adding and subtracting the two number strings.) This gives him the numerical plaintext he can convert into legible form with the Polybius table. The numerical method is not all that different from encoding with letters and a Vigenère tableau. As with the letter method, preferential number pairs of both the plaintext and the key text leave their traces on the ciphertext. To avoid this one should use a meaningless (randomly distributed) letter combination or a random sequence of numbers instead of a natural language.

CHANCE HAS NO MEMORY

After their defeat in World War I, the Germans faced the task of establishing a new state. On February 6, 1919, the National Assembly met in Weimar to set up what became known as the Weimar Republic. New diplomatic service was needed, and for it a new cipher system to enable embassies abroad to exchange encoded messages with the government back home. What cipher system was the new state to use? This problem was tackled by Werner Kunze and Rudolf Schauffler, the former a man with a mathematical bent of mind, the latter a cryptologist who had specialized mainly in languages and later earned a doctorate in mathematics. The two were brought together by Erich Langlotz, a research chemist. The codes then used for official purposes were simple: to the numerical sequence derived from the plaintext a numerical key was added without carrying the tens, in much the same way as we just did. The three men examined how secure such a cipher was. They soon convinced themselves that, provided there was enough text, even a key of forty or fifty-digit numerical sequences would not prevent deciphering by unauthorized persons. They believed that only a sequence of numbers that was random and did not repeat itself would ensure absolute security. The diplomatic service was therefore equipped with blocks of fifty pages, each page carrying eighty-five five-figure groups, the figures randomly chosen. No two pages were identical, and each was to be used only once. Once a message was encoded, the sheet used for encoding it had to be destroyed. This method was subsequently introduced also in other countries. In the English-speaking world it was known as a *one-time pad*.

The method is completely secure so long as its rules are strictly observed. No analysis of whatever quantities of text produces any hint of the key. The drawback of the method is that the key is rather voluminous—a whole pad of pages that the sender must get to the receiver by some secret route.

The Soviet secret service used this method even after World War II. On June 20, 1953, the American couple Ethel and Julius Rosenberg were executed at the Sing Sing state prison in New York. Two years earlier, they had been sentenced to death for the betrayal of atomic secrets to the Soviet Union. Their discovery was due to an operation failure: the Soviets had used the same key text more than once. The officer responsible for this mistake also had to pay with his life.[1]

The secret service of the former Soviet Union used randomly shuffled key texts or, more accurately, numerical sequences consisting of *random numbers*. Plate 2 illustrates such a key. When the Soviet spy Rudolf Abel was arrested in his New York hotel in June 1957, FBI agents found a pad whose postage-stamp-sized pages were covered with long sequences of numbers. These were numerical key worms. In the fifties and sixties other Soviet spies similarly failed to destroy their keys before being arrested. The Americans soon discovered that these were not truly random numbers. Far too often they contained sequences in which a numeral of the group 1, 2, 3, 4, 5 alternated with one from the group 6, 7, 8, 9, 0, as in the sequence 291738. Apparently these had been keyed into a typewriter by secretaries who, making up the numbers as they went, alternated the left hand with the right, the left hand pressing the keys of one group and the right hand the keys of the other. It was also very rare that a number was repeated, let alone that it appeared three times in a row. Whoever had produced the tables evidently believed—though possibly subconsciously—that duplication or even triplication offended against the rules of chance. As we shall see, real chance is not afraid of repetition.

These peculiarities of the Russian "random key texts" made history in August 1991. At that time, during the coup d'état against Mikhail Gorbachev, two of the conspirators, the KGB chief Vladimir Kryuchkov and the defense minister Dmitri Yazov, exchanged coded messages. But thanks to the regularities in the key text, the Americans were able to decipher the messages. President Bush then passed them on to Boris Yeltsin.

At first glance it seems easy enough to write down a sequence of numbers without giving preference to any of them, for instance, 08297321870134. But we have a predilection for certain numerals without being aware of it. Involuntarily, when choosing a new number, a person remembers the preceding one and tries to avoid repetitions. Chance, on the other hand, does not know what has already happened. Anyone seeking a secure key text should not rely on "human" random numbers.

Many gambling systems are based on the belief that chance has a memory. Anyone thinking that the 15 is "due" because the ball has avoided it a hundred times is mistaken. The fact that, with an ideal roulette table, the ball lands on all possible numbers equally often on average is not due to the fact that on its one hundredth run it tries to "make up" for what was irregular before.

Lottery numbers are also randomly generated. The numbers that will come up this week are independent of those of last week. Nevertheless a lot of players seem to be convinced that a number that has not been drawn for a long time has a better chance of coming up. Figure 7.4, taken from a German daily paper, shows a graphic designed to help readers with their next bet. Anyone seriously believing that 35 has a better chance of coming up among the next winning numbers because it has not come up for thirty-seven weeks thinks—if he thinks at all—wrongly.

Man cannot generate random numbers spontaneously. Only truly random events, such as drawing tickets from a hat, casting dice, or objective mathematical operations can do so.

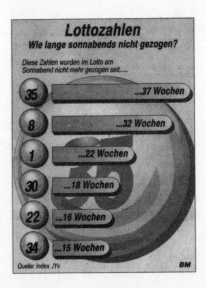

Fig. 7.4. A graphic in a German newspaper designed to help readers fill out their lottery tickets. It is suggested that a number, such as 35, that has not been drawn for a long time has a greater probability of coming up at the next drawing than one that was among the winning numbers the previous week.

CHANCE ARTIFICIALLY PRODUCED

There are different methods for generating a sequence of random numbers. I might, for instance, write down the numerals 0 to 9 on slips of paper, throw them into a hat, and then fish out one of them without looking. Having read the number and made a note of it, I throw the slip of paper back into the hat, shake the hat, and fish out another. If I continue this over a long period of time, I will obtain a sequence of random numbers that could serve as a key worm.

I send a copy of the worm to the receiver of my future secret messages. Whenever I want to send him a message, I convert the plaintext into a numerical sequence—using a Polybius table, for instance—and add the key worm number by number without carrying the tens. This gives me a numerical ciphertext. The receiver is in possession of my key worm and from that he subtracts the key text from the ciphertext (again without carrying tens) and thus gets the numerical plaintext, which he can reconvert to the alphabetical plaintext using the same Polybius table.

But the key text, which I must get to the receiver by some secret route, is just as long as the message to be transmitted.[2] Nothing much has thus been gained, because the probability of the key text falling into the wrong hands is as great as that of the plaintext falling into the wrong hands.

As we saw in chapter 1, instead of a prefabricated key table of random numbers, the spy ring that Richard Sorge was in used the figures of a statistical yearbook, which has the advantage of not being conspicuous in the event of a search, whereas an unexplained table of figures is bound to arouse suspicion. Instead of exchanging long lists of numerical sequences, one can transmit a brief reference, such as "book XYZ, page 12." It may even be sufficient if the receiver is sent a short number he can use to create a long keyword.

Let us take a brief example. We divide 1 by 7 and do not arrive at an end:

$$1/7 = 0.142857142857142857142857142857 \ldots$$

This is a periodic decimal fraction. We can use the regularly repeating six figures as random numbers for a short key worm. Let us take the plaintext word *boy*. With the help of the Polybius table (figure 7.2, top) it is transformed into the numerical plaintext 12 34 54. Let us therefore write the beginning of our numerical keywords underneath and add

$$
\begin{array}{ccc}
12 & 34 & 54 \\
14 & 28 & 57 \\
\hline
\mathbf{26} & \mathbf{52} & \mathbf{01}
\end{array}
$$

This is the ciphertext that the receiver can turn back into the numerical plaintext by subtracting the key. Our keyword is not much good, because it is too short. But there are other numbers that, on division, produce longer numerical sequences. Let us take the number 499. Division of 1 by 499 results in a sequence of 498 nonperiodic figures that begin to repeat periodically only from the 499th. With this number, quite long messages might be encoded. All the receiver has to get as a key is the number 499; with that he can create the numerical key.

More suitable still would be decimal numbers whose sequence of numerals never repeats itself. The best known of these is the number π, the ratio between the circumference and the diameter of a circle:

$$\pi = 3.141592653 \ldots$$

Mathematicians know that no period is concealed in this numerical sequence (figure 7.5). Even though there are number groups that recur, there are always other numbers between them. In 1995 mathematicians of Tokyo University determined π to 3.22 billion digits, beating the earlier world record of 67 million. Their big computer took thirty six hours and fifty one minutes for the calculation. With the numerical sequence of π, texts of any length can be encoded. As far as is known, no number enjoys a preferential status, and no regularities have so far been discovered. The numerical sequence of π offers a secure key. You merely have to tell the receiver to take the numerical sequence from this or that position after the decimal point. Then he will be able to decipher your message. You could also take 2π or 7π. Mathematicians know many such numbers with infinitely long sequences; all these are suitable for encoding.

Random numerical sequences are important also for other purposes. Mathematicians have therefore developed methods for generating random numbers, that is, sequences that do not repeat themselves and in which no number occupies a privileged position. The principle is to take an initial number, known as the *seed*, and by an algorithm derive from it a new number. This number then becomes the seed for the next number,

Volume 7   Number 3   1985 $4.95

The Mathematical
Intelligencer

```
1415926535  8979323846  2643383279  5028841971  6939937510
5820974944  5923078164  0628620899  8628034825  3421170679
8214808651  3282306647  0938446095  5058223172  5359408128
4811174502  8410270193  8521105559  6446229489  5493038196
4428810975  6659334461  2847564823  3786783165  2712019091
4564856692  3460348610  4543266482  1339360726  0249141273
7245870066  0631558817  4881520920  9628292540  9171536436
7892590360  0113305305  4882046652  1384146951  9415116094
3305727036  5759591953  0921861173  8193261179  3105118548
0744623799  6274956735  1885752724  8912279381  8301194912
9833673362  4406566430  8602139494  6395224737  1907021798
6094370277  0539217176  2931767523  8467481846  7669405132
0005681271  4526356082  7785771342  7577896091  7363717872
1468440901  2249534301  4654958537  1050792279  6892589235
4201995611  2129021960  8640344181  5981362977  4771309960
5187072113  4999999837  2978049951  0597317328  1609631859
5024459455  3469083026  4252230825  3344685035  2619311881
7101000313  7838752886  5875332083  8142061717  7669147303
5982534904  2875546873  1159562863  8823537875  9375195778
1857780532  1712268066  1300192787  6611195909  2164201989
```

Fig. 7.5. **The first one thousand decimal places of the number** π **on the cover of a periodical published by Springer Verlag, Berlin/Heidelberg.**

which in turn is the seed for the one that follows, and so on indefinitely, without the numbers ever getting into a periodic sequence. Whether the numbers are evenly distributed depends on the nature of the mathematical operation. Such programs are known as *random generators*; nowadays they are stored in nearly all computers. Many computer games make use of random numbers. But even those numbers are not truly random. Since they have a finite length in the computer, the computer can produce only a finite—though very large—total of random numbers. At some point the random generator may generate a seed that it generated before. From that point onward the sequence of seeds will be periodically repeated. With poor random generators these periods are rather short; with good ones they are very long. In a good program, the sequence will be repeated only after many billions of steps. Figure 7.6 shows a numerical sequence that I produced on my PC with a random generator.[3] More accurately: I generated random numbers that I used to make a number worm. For my seed I chose zero. The first number pair was 39. With the procedure explained in the endnote, my random generator continually supplies new number pairs.

```
39076369288052309110900508077 6
92303634558703996263006974217 5
43289560122824453496461649747 9
48234051408592135062785819779 4
98011858749599643181714174264 0
26548175318027013494976717548 3
43996406843246979690781794383 1
10334762794852880971660086995 1
22665559076114238281739436247 2
72465557103212707646160762613 3
16503495844696937800137518459 2
73781604318342760969724277963 3
48070301748301870476053608678 6
15029497392011411483981727870 5
51243196901858763455023767179 7
11219109154371222343998052439 7
12870149971389297229137876054 9
56089495292807468382393482239 8
17274593337818448764292852869 6
51664055872172864175048643707 8
56096929579503990703569215453 6
90364788836720853456471904489 4
```

Fig. 7.6. **Random numbers produced by a random generator.**

Now we can newly encode our plaintext from Sagan's *Contact* once again. In figure 7.7, top, we proceed from the alphabetic plaintext, write our numerical random key below, and add, again without carrying ten. This gives us the numerical ciphertext. The receiver, in figure 7.7, bottom, writes the numerical key text below and subtracts. This gives him the numerical plaintext, which, using the Polybius table, he translates into an alphabetical plaintext.

```
1144442311444424321544231534333315425333452
39076369288052309110900508077692303634558 7. . .
4041078239249654232534281331092384516789 3 9. . .
```

```
4041078239249654232534281331092384516789 3 9. . .
39076369288052309110900508077692303634558 7. . .
1144442311444424321544231534333315425333452. . .
```

Fig. 7.7. **Top: encoding with the beginning of the key worm of random numbers of figure 7.6. Bottom: the corresponding decoding.**

The receiver of course must possess the same random generator. I also have to give him the seed for the start, in this case zero, and if necessary the mnemonic for the Polybius table. With these he can decode my message. We therefore need send only a very little key information to transmit ciphertexts of any length we wish. In practice I would not have chosen zero as a seed number. I also used the ten-digit number 4562183170 as a seed number and got another key worm. There exist ten billion different numbers of ten digits. Anyone trying to test all possible seed numbers by the sledgehammer method in the hope of hitting on a legible plaintext, if he took only one second for each test, would have to work for about three thousand years nonstop.

KEY WORMS IN THE TELEPHONE BOOK

A simple method for finding a worm of random figures was proposed by the English journalist Robert Matthews.[4] Matthews took the London telephone directory with its roughly 1.2 million seven-digit numbers. These are arranged alphabetically by the names of the subscribers. The first seven digits refer to the nodal points in the London network, in other words, they depend on the district of the city. If all people with the name Patel lived in the same neighborhood, for instance, then many numbers starting identically would follow one another in the directory. The first few digits of the numbers are therefore not randomly distributed. Things are different with the final digits. Matthews, examining the last two digits in every way on his PC, considers them to be genuine random numbers. A number worm can easily be produced from them.

Take the telephone book of a sizable town, start with a certain subscriber, and write down the final two numerals of his telephone number. Proceed to the next listing and do the same. In this manner you get a number worm that the receiver, too, can create so long as he knows the name of the town and of the subscriber with whom he should start.

(Matthews has also set out directions for the do-it-yourself construction of a simple encoding machine. This can operate either with finite keywords as in the Vigenère tableau or with key worms of any length, such as those derived from the telephone bok. The machine is described in appendix A.)

NOTES

1. "It's a Lottery," *New Scientist* (July 22, 1995) 42.

2. If I use a Polybius table as in figure 7.2, bottom, I have to make sure that the receiver also gets the keyword or the mnemonic.

3. I multiplied the seed by 5 and add the number 123456789. From the result I took the remainder modulo 2^{20}, which gave me the number S. The next to last and third to last numerals of S was my first number pair. This pair now serves as the seed to generate the next pair.

4. "A Rotation Device for Periodic and Random-Key Encryption," *Cryptologia* (July 1989) 266.

8. SHUFFLED TEXTS

A popular schoolboy cipher is the "rail fence," in which the plaintext is staggered between rows and the rows are then read sequentially to give the cipher. In a depth-two rail fence (two rows) the message

we are discovered save yourself

becomes

```
W A E I C V R D A E O R E F
  E R D S O E E S V Y U S L
```

or

WAEICVRDAEOREFERDSOEESVYUSL

—Encyclopaedia Britannica

N THE WINTER OF 1609-1610, the Italian astronomer Galileo Galilei turned his telescope toward the sky and discovered that the foggy band of the Milky Way actually consisted of countless weak stars. He saw that the planet Jupiter had moons orbiting it, that on the moon mountains cast their shadows far into plains, and that the disk of the sun exhibited dark spots. The planet Saturn seemed to consist of three stars. These were exciting new pieces of knowledge. Just as scientists do to this day, Galileo wanted to make sure that people knew he had made these discoveries first.

ANAGRAMS

Scientists in those days used a trick to secure for themselves the fame of discovery without letting the cat out of the bag. They summed up their results in a concise sentence, usually in Latin, and encoded it by changing the order of all the letters occurring in the sentence. For instance, they would arrange them simply in alphabetical order. It is easy to encode a sentence in this way. Let us take the plaintext "Sirius has an inhabited planet." Arranged alphabetically, the letters produce the ciphertext **AAAABDEE-HHIIIILNNNPRSSSTTU**. It is practically impossible to reconstruct the plaintext from this. But if someone else discovers the planet, you can prove, by rearranging the letter combination, that you discovered it first. No one could then challenge your glory of being the first discoverer.

Ciphers of this type are called *anagrams*. The letters need not be arranged in alphabetical order: any shuffling of the plaintext letters will do. Thus Galileo recorded his discovery about Saturn in the following Latin plaintext:

altissimvm planetam tergeminvm observavi

In English: "I observed the highest planet in threefold shape." By "highest planet" he meant Saturn. In the picture of the universe of Galileo's day, Saturn was the planet circling the sun at the greatest distance. He encrypted the Latin sentence by shuffling the letters, and published his result as the anagram

SMAISMRMILMEPOETALEVMIBVNENVGTTAVIRAS

No one could see any sense in this. But if another astronomer had appeared on the scene and claimed that he had seen Saturn in threefold shape, Galileo would have been able to point out, triumphantly, that he had recorded the discovery in his anagram some time earlier. That would have been convincing proof. Galileo encrypted many of his discoveries in this manner. The sentence above, while perfectly encrypted, was wrong in itself. Less than a half century later, the Dutch astronomer Christiaan Huygens realized the truth. He too summed up his result in a Latin sentence, meaning, "It is surrounded by a thin flat ring that does not touch it and is inclined against the ecliptic." Huygens simply arranged the letters of his sentence in alphabetical order. It wasn't until three years later that he made the solution public.

SHUFFLED TEXT AGAINST SHUFFLED ALPHABET

The practice, or malpractice, of encrypting by anagram differs fundamentally from the monalphabetic ciphers of chapter 4. There the alphabet was shuffled and a cipher alphabet created that was confronted with a normally arranged plaintext alphabet, as shown, for instance, in figure 4.6 (page 74). The letter *e* became **F**, *k* became **G**, and so on. Examining the frequency distribution of the ciphers made it possible to spot the *e* of the plaintext. Here it is not the alphabet that is shuffled but the plaintext itself. Consider the plaintext:

icouldnthelpiticanresistanythingexcepttemptation

Let us, like Galileo, turn this into an anagram:

AAACCCDEEEEEGHHIIIIIILLMNNNNNOOPPPRSSTTTTTTTTUXY

In both the plaintext and in the anagram created by reshuffling the order of the letters, *e* remains **E**. Anagrams are used not for transmitting secret messages but for safeguarding someone's priority.

The letters of the plaintext are merely placed in another spot. This is a transposition, like Count Sandorf's cipher in chapter 1. In the methods described in chapters 4 through 7, however, and also in chapter 9 and subsequently, the letters remain in place but are replaced by other letters or symbols. Mathematicians who study ciphers call this substitution. Put simply: in a transposition, the plaintext is shuffled; in a substitution, the alphabet is shuffled.

Since in a transposition the letters are not replaced by others, **E** remains the most frequent letter in the ciphertext, followed by **T**, though this knowledge does not help the unauthorized decoder. But there is some information he can extract from a text encoded by transposition. If he finds that the occurrence of the letters corresponds to the frequency distribution of the English language, he can conclude that he is dealing with the transposition of an English plaintext. If not **E** but **A** is the most frequent letter, he could be dealing with a Portuguese plaintext. If **E** is the most frequent letter and **N** the second most frequent one, he can assume, with a high degree of probability, that his plaintext is German.

If we intend to encode secret messages by transposition, we must choose a pattern that will also make decoding easy. Count Sandorf's code provides an example.

THE TEMPLATE OF THE AUSTRIAN COLONEL

Jules Verne wrote his *Mathias Sandorf* in 1885, four years after the Austrian Colonel Eduard Fleissner von Wostrowitz published an essay entitled "New Secret Writing Template." The template described by Fleissner is, as the one in figure 1.3, a square with a number of fields cut out. It has an even number of rows and columns, so that the total number of fields is divisible by four. A quarter of them must be cut out. The template is used for encoding as well as decoding a text. For deciphering, the text must be written into squares the size of the template.

For encoding, the template is placed on a clean sheet of paper, and the plaintext, letter by letter, is written into the windows (fields) of the template. When all these fields have been used, the template is rotated ninety degrees clockwise, and the next letters are entered. This process is continued until the template has been used in all four positions. The template is so arranged that eventually all the fields of a square will be filled in without any being used twice. In the event that the text is longer than the number of fields, a second square of the same size is constructed. Spare fields of the square are filled with random letters. The final ciphertext consists of all the rows of the square, just as in the Sandorf ciphertext (figure 1.4).

For decoding, the template is placed on the first square of the ciphertext, and the visible letters are read and noted down. The template is next rotated ninety degrees, and the same thing is done. Not every template is suitable for this method. In its four positions it must not expose any field twice, nor must it leave a field covered.

Fleissner's templates do not offer a very secure cipher. The total number of letters provides a clue to the number of fields in the coding square. Thus if the ciphertext consists of one hundred and eight symbols, it seems reasonable to assume that it derives from three squares of size six by six. But even if one knows the size of the squares and has a lot of text at one's disposal, it is not easy to discover which fields of the template were cut out. Whichever way the letters were arranged by the template, it produces only a transposition: *e* remains **E** and *n* remains **N**. What helps the decoder are the letter pairs. The pair *th* is the most frequent twin group in English, and *h* and *e* often occur paired, and as *a* and *n*.

In point of fact the first ciphertext square in figure 1.4 shows a **T** in the fourth line, followed shortly afterward by an **H**. Anyone attempting to decode the message could now try to discover if this actually represents a *th* in the plaintext. In that case the Fleissner template would, in one position, have to be open in spots 2 and 5 in the fourth line, while spots 3 and 4 would have to be closed. In the next position of the template, the symbols **G** and **A** would have to be open; in the next, an **H** and an **E**. The fourth position finally reveals an **N** and a **U**, possibly with other letters in

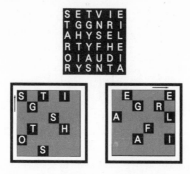

Fig. 8.1. A ciphertext produced with a Fleissner template can be encrypted a second time. One writes the ciphertext down again into a square, as in figure 1.4 (top). Then one uses the same template, but this time back to front. Now the apertures are mirror-inverted compared with the template used for the first encrypting. The template is again rotated around on the letter square through four positions. The first square supplies a new ciphertext: STIGSTHOS (bottom left). After a clockwise rotation by ninety degrees, we get EEGRALFAI (bottom right).

between. In this way the decoder can feel his way forward. He might try, for instance, whether the **TH** from which he proceeded belongs to a *the*. We know that this is not the case. He simply has to experiment, to play a hunch. He might also try the **T** in spot 1 of line 2 and the **H** in spot 2 of line 3. In fact these two letters do belong together. In this way, with the help of letter pairs from the ciphertext, the characteristics of the template used for encoding may be guessed. It is then only a question of time, given a sufficient quantity of ciphertexts, before all the windows of the template have been discovered.

Decoding becomes more difficult if the template is also reversed, so that it presents a mirror image of its normal position. This makes it possible to encode our ciphertext with the template once again, as shown in figure 8.1. A second encrypting of an encrypted text is called a *superencryption*. But *e* remains **E** no matter how often we turn or reverse the template.

How do I make a Fleissner template? Which fields must I cut out to make sure that after four rotations all fields will be open once and none twice? There is a simple instruction for designing the template, which I will demonstrate for a square of six by six fields. Of the thirty-six fields nine must be cut out. For this the template is divided into four subsquares of three by three fields, as in figure 8.2, left. We number the nine fields of the first subsquare sequentially from 1 through 9. Then we rotate three

1	2	3	7	4	1
4	5	6	8	5	2
7	8	9	9	6	3
3	9	6	6	8	7
2	5	8	9	5	4
1	4	7	3	2	1

		3	4		
		6			2
8					
		6			7
			5		
1					

Fig. 8.2. How to make your own Fleissner table. Left: into the top left sub-square of a square of six by six fields you write the numbers 1 to 9 in sequential order. You rotate the square by ninety degrees clockwise and again enter the numbers 1 to 9 into the top left subsquare. Continue in this manner until all thirty-six fields are filled and the square looks like the left half of the figure. The text explains how you discover which fields you have to cut out (right half of the figure).

times by ninety degrees, and each time number the top left squares in the same way, so that 1 through 9 appear in the big square four times. Now we choose nine fields for cutting out. We mark one of the four fields containing the 1, then one containing the 2, then one with the 3, and continue in this way until we have marked nine fields. In all, we have 262,144 possibilities of marking. The marked fields are then cut out. With every one of these possible templates, each field is exposed with the four rotations, and each only once. If we want to make a template of size eight by eight, we proceed analogously. The four small squares will then have a size of four by four. From this template we will need to cut out sixteen fields.

This *turning-grille method* presents scarcely any problems to the unauthorized decoder. We have seen that the length of the ciphertext allows conclusions as to the size of the template, and we have seen how clues are obtained for the position of the windows. But despite their weaknesses, templates were used as recently as World War II between German spies in South America and German Intelligence.

TRANSPOSITION WITH KEYWORD

The example of Count Sandorf makes us realize that the problems of the turning-grille method is that the template must be passed on and can easily fall into the wrong hands. There are other methods by which a plaintext can be encoded by transposition without the possession of a compromising template.

We once more encode the text from Hemingway's "The Killers" (see fig. 5.18).

t	w	o	o	t	h	e	r	p	e	o	p	l	e	h
a	d	b	e	e	n	i	n	t	h	e	l	u	n	c
h	r	o	o	m	o	n	c	e	g	e	o	r	g	e
h	a	d	g	o	n	e	o	u	t	t	o	t	h	e
k	i	t	c	h	e	n	a	n	d	m	a	d	e	a
h	a	m	a	n	d	e	g	g	s	a	n	d	w	i
c	h	t	h	a	t	a	m	a	n	w	a	n	t	e
d	t	o	t	a	k	e	w	i	t	h	h	i	m	x

Fig. 8.3. **A plaintext brought into rectangular form.**

To that end we write it down, without spaces between the words, into a rectangle, in rows of fifteen letters (fig. 8.3). Since at the end of the message there is an empty space, we fill it in with a random letter. A simple encoding would be to rearrange the columns according to some rule, then read each column from top to bottom and write the letters down in groups. But what rule are we to apply for the rearrangement? The rearranging rule is the key to the method, and both sender and receiver must know it. But a rule such as "Exchange the first column for the fifth, the second with the twelfth . . ." would soon be longer than the message itself. But there is a simple aid. We take a sentence that is easy to remember, like "The bear went over the mountain." It must contain at least as many letters as our rectangle has columns. We then write down our mnemonic sentence without spaces: *THEBEARWENTOVERTHEMOUNTAIN.* We now start counting off the letters in alphabetic order. Occurrences more than once in the first fifteen letters of the sentence are numbered left to right: *A* is 1; *B* becomes 2; *C* and *D* do not occur; the four *E*s are numbered 3, 4, 5, 6; and so on. Finally we have

T	*H*	*E*	*B*	*E*	*A*	*R*	*W*	*E*	*N*	*T*	*O*	*V*	*E*	*R*
12	7	3	2	4	1	10	15	5	8	13	9	14	6	11

Below this we place our rectangle, as shown in figure 8.4, top. Next we order the columns according to the sequence of numbers, which gives us the arrangement of figure 8.4, center. Now we write down the letters column by column as groups of eight. This gives us the ciphertext shown in figure 8.4, bottom.

The receiver knows the key, that is, the sentence about the bear and the mountain, and by counting off he creates the sequence

$$12 \quad 7 \quad 3 \quad 2 \quad 4 \quad 1 \quad 10 \quad 15 \quad 5 \quad 8 \quad 13 \quad 9 \quad 14 \quad 6 \quad 11$$

He now writes down the first group of eight as a column under the number 1, the second under 2, and so on, and the plaintext emerges before him. For this method all that had to be exchanged was the key about the bear and the mountain, not the template.

T	*H*	*E*	*B*	*E*	*A*	*R*	*W*	*E*	*N*	*T*	*O*	*V*	*E*	*R*
12	7	3	2	4	1	10	15	5	8	13	9	14	6	11
t	w	o	o	t	h	e	r	p	e	o	p	l	e	h
a	d	b	e	e	n	i	n	t	h	e	l	u	n	c
h	r	o	o	m	o	n	c	e	g	e	o	r	g	e
h	a	d	g	o	n	e	o	u	t	t	o	t	h	e
k	i	t	c	h	e	n	a	n	d	m	a	d	e	a
h	a	m	a	n	d	e	g	g	s	a	n	d	w	i
c	h	t	h	a	t	a	m	a	n	w	a	n	t	e
d	t	o	t	a	k	e	w	i	t	h	h	i	m	x
h	o	o	t	p	e	w	e	p	e	h	t	o	l	r
n	e	b	e	t	n	d	h	l	i	c	a	e	u	n
o	o	o	m	e	g	r	g	o	n	e	h	e	r	c
n	g	d	o	u	h	a	t	o	e	e	h	t	t	o
e	c	t	h	n	e	i	d	a	n	a	k	m	d	a
d	a	m	n	g	w	a	s	n	e	i	h	a	d	g
t	h	t	a	a	t	h	n	a	a	e	c	w	n	m
k	t	o	a	i	m	t	t	h	e	x	d	h	i	w

HNONEDTK OEOGCAHT OBODTMTO TEMOHNAA PTEUNGAI ENGHEWTM
WDRAIAHT EHGTDSNT PLOOANAH EINENEAE HCEEAIEX TAHHKHCD
OEETMAWH LURTDDNI RNCOAGMW

Fig. 8.4. Encoding of the plaintext of figure 8.3. By means of the key *THEBEAR-WENTOVER* (top), the columns are numbered and accordingly rearranged (center). The ciphertext is produced by reading column by column (bottom). It is fairly easy to break.

This method, too, is not particularly secure. From the number of letters and their grouping the unauthorized decoder can get an idea of the length and width of the rectangle and set up the pattern of the bottom rectangle in figure 8.4. The letters *t* and *h* occur in most of the lines. Do they derive from the frequent plaintext combination *th*? Let us take the first line. The letter *t* occurs in columns 4 and 12. If one of the *t*s were to be followed by *h*, then the columns would have to be rearranged so that either columns 4 and 1 or 4 and 11 are consecutive, or else columns 12 and 1 or 12 and 11. Each of these exchanges has an effect upon the other lines, and the decoder must examine which exchange helps him forward. He might also experiment with the *t* and *h* symbols in other lines. He could save himself trouble by writing each column down on a strip of paper and trying out various rearrangements for meaningful text fragments.

The advantage of the method is that the key can be easily changed. Thus Josef Starziczny, head of the German spy network in Brazil during World War II, used the cipher method just described to communicate with the Intelligence center in Hamburg. He took the key from a Spanish book. By a rule agreed on with Hamburg, he calculated the page number of the book according to a particular day from the actual date of that day, opened the page, and used the initial letters of the first twenty lines as his key text, just as we used the sentence of the bear and the mountain. Like us, he created a number sequence from it and used that sequence to reposition the columns of a plaintext fitted into a rectangle. The receiver, of course, had the same book. He too calculated the page number from the date and was able to determine the twenty key letters. Although the key was changed every day, the Americans had no difficulty in reading these messages.[1]

We can go one step further and rearrange not only the columns but also the rows, in other words perform a superencryption. But we will need a mnemonic, in our case one of at least eight letters, such as *NEW JERSEY*. We number the first eight letters:

NEWJERSE
51842673

and accordingly rearrange the rows of the text encoded with the bear and the mountain (fig. 8.5). Next, column by column, we create groups of eight: **NEKNHDT ECTGOAH BTODOMT**. In addition to the bear and the mountain, the mnemonic *NEW JERSEY* would have to be transmitted from sender to receiver. But we do not gain a lot with the second keyword. By our using frequent letter pairs, the columns of the ciphertext can again be brought into the correct position. Then each row will supply part of the plaintext, and one only has to rearrange the rows—which is no problem. We could, however, make life more difficult for an unauthorized decoder by superencrypting a substitution-encoded text with a subsequent transposition. In other words: first a shuffled alphabet (substitution) and then a shuffled text (transposition).

A Polybius substitution suggests itself, one that assigns a number pair to each plaintext letter. Admittedly, this is only a monalphabetic encoding and easily cracked by frequency analysis. But if we reshuffle a text obtained by a Polybius cipher in such a way that the number pairs are also torn apart, the possibility of frequency analysis is lost—because now the pair corresponding to e, let us say 51, stands in two columns and is separated by the subsequent transposition.

N	5	h	o	o	t	p	e	w	e	p	e	h	t	o	l	r
E	1	n	e	b	e	t	n	d	h	l	i	c	a	e	u	n
W	8	o	o	o	m	e	g	r	g	o	n	e	h	e	r	c
J	4	n	g	d	o	u	h	a	t	o	e	e	h	t	t	o
E	2	e	c	t	h	n	e	i	d	a	n	a	k	m	d	a
R	6	d	a	m	n	g	w	a	s	n	e	i	h	a	d	g
S	7	t	h	t	a	a	t	h	n	a	a	e	c	w	n	m
E	3	k	t	o	a	i	m	t	t	h	e	x	d	h	i	w
E	1	n	e	b	e	t	n	d	h	l	i	c	a	e	u	n
E	2	e	c	t	h	n	e	i	d	a	n	a	k	m	d	a
E	3	k	t	o	a	i	m	t	t	h	e	x	d	h	i	w
J	4	n	g	d	o	u	h	a	t	o	e	e	h	t	t	o
N	5	h	o	o	t	p	e	w	e	p	e	h	t	o	l	r
R	6	d	a	m	n	g	w	a	s	n	e	i	h	a	d	g
S	7	t	h	t	a	a	t	h	n	a	a	e	c	w	n	m

NEKNHDT ECTGOAH BTODOMT EHAOTNA TNIUPGA NEMHEWT DITAWAH HDTTESN LAHOPNA INEEEEA CAXEHIE AKDHTHC EMHTOAW UDITLND NAWORGM

Fig. 8.5. In the pattern obtained in the middle part of figure 8.4, the rows are renumbered with the mnemonic New Jersey and rearranged (center). The ciphertext is then produced by column-by-column reading (bottom).

We can for example arrange into squares a text that has been converted into number pairs with one of the key tables in figure 7.2, then choose a mnemonic, exchange the columns, and write down column by column as a ciphertext.

POLYBIUS IN WORLD WAR I

The French radio operators who on March 5, 1918, were monitoring the signal traffic of the Germans became excited. Suddenly all the signals consisted of strings of only five different letters. The Morse dots and dashes gave only the letters **A**, **D**, **F**, **G**, and **X**. They were strings like **AGXXDD AGGFD AADXFX AGFGXD AAXAG**, which the men with the headphones wrote down. They understood very well why these letters kept recurring: they were the ones that in Morse code could best be distinguished from one another. The operators also noticed that the number of letters in each transmission was even.

The sudden introduction of a new cipher system along the entire Western front suggested that a long-planned major attack by the Germans was imminent. In actual fact, the Battle of the Somme was to begin on March 21, 1918. It was a matter of urgency therefore to discover what system the German operators were using.

It was a Polybius cipher with subsequent transposition. It was based on the following pattern. The twenty-five letters of the alphabet (no distinction being made between *i* and *j*) are entered into a Polybius table of the kind shown in figure 7.2. But in this table, unlike the earlier table, we label the rows and columns with the letters **A**, **D**, **F**, **G**, and **X** (fig. 8.6). We need not fill the table in alphabetic order; we can use a keyword, as in figure 7.2, bottom. For simplicity's sake let us keep to the table without the keyword. Let us next take a simple plaintext and write it down in groups of five, as in figure 8.7, top. Using the table in figure 8.6, we obtain a new (monalphabetic) ciphertext (fig. 8.7, bottom left). By omit-

	A	D	F	G	X
A	a	b	c	d	e
D	f	g	h	i/j	k
F	l	m	n	o	p
G	q	r	s	t	u
X	v	w	x	y	z

***Fig. 8.6.* A Polybius table as used in World War I for the ADFGX system.**

```
            T   O   T   H   E
            H   I   G   H   C
            O   M   M   A   N
            D   S   I   T   U
            A   T   I   O   N
            R   E   P   O   R
            T
```

GG	FG	GG	DF	AX		GGFGGGDFAX
DF	DG	DD	DF	AF		DFDGDDDFAF
FG	FD	FD	AA	FF		FGFDFDAAFF
AG	GF	DG	GG	GX		AGGFDGGGGX
AA	GG	DG	FG	FF		AAGGDGFGFF
GD	AX	FX	FG	GD		GDAXFXFGGD
GG						GG

Fig. 8.7. Top: a plaintext arranged in lines of five letters. Bottom, left: the letters of the plaintext replaced, with the cipher table of figure 8.6, by letter pairs of the ADFGX system. Bottom, right: the same without spaces.

S	*H*	*A*	*K*	*E*	*S*	*P*	*E*	*A*	*R*
9	5	1	6	3	10	7	4	2	8
G	G	F	G	G	G	D	F	A	X
D	F	D	G	D	D	D	F	A	F
F	G	F	D	F	D	A	A	F	F
A	G	G	F	D	G	G	G	G	X
A	A	G	G	D	G	F	G	F	F
G	D	A	X	F	X	F	G	G	D
G	G								

1	2	3	4	5	6	7	8	9	10
F	A	G	F	G	G	D	X	G	G
D	A	D	F	F	G	D	F	D	D
F	F	F	A	G	D	A	F	F	D
G	G	D	G	G	F	G	X	A	G
G	F	D	G	A	G	F	F	A	G
A	G	F	G	D	X	F	D	G	X
				G					G

FDFGGA AAFGFG GDFDDF FFAGGG
GFGGADG GGDFGX DDAGFF XFFXFD
GDFAAGG GDDGGX

Fig. 8.8. The columns obtained by substitution in figure 8.7 are rearranged, as in figure 8.4, with the help of a mnemonic. The ciphertext is again created by column-by-column reading.

ting the spaces we are left with a block (fig. 8.7, bottom right). We super-encrypt the block once more by again rearranging the columns in figure 8.8 by means of the keyword *SHAKESPEARE* (top and center). This produces the ciphertext (bottom).

The decoder follows the reverse procedure. He writes down the rows as columns, and since he knows that they were rearranged with *SHAKESPEARE*, he can undo the rearrangement. After that he uses the Polybius table to proceed from letter pairs to plaintext letters. He therefore needs to know only one keyword, *SHAKESPEARE*, or two, if the Polybius table was created with a keyword.

While the French master cryptologist Georges Painvin was still pondering over the incomprehensible radio signals, the Germans had approached to within thirty miles of Paris. Then Painvin solved the riddle of the ADFGX signals, and the French were once more able to read the German radio traffic. At that point, however, the Germans came up with a new code, in which, in addition to the earlier five letters, V now also occurred.

With six letters a Polybius table of thirty-six fields can be created. In point of fact, the Germans then had such a table, which now differentiated between *i* and *j* and also contained the numerals 0 to 9. On June 1, 1918, Painvin had before him the first message encoded with the new system. By the evening of June 3, he had deciphered it. He was an indefatigable worker. During the nine months that he struggled to keep abreast of the German cryptologists, he is reputed to have lost thirty-three pounds. It is probably thanks to Painvin that German soldiers did not stroll down the Champs-Élysées in World War I.

Not all cryptologists who were successful in the two world wars were as successful as Painvin in civilian life. After 1918, he became an important businessman, heading France's largest chemical company. But even in old age he regarded his solution of the riddle of the ADFGVX code as the greatest achievement of his life.

In recent times, transpositions, attractive though they seem at first glance, have been eclipsed by substitutions. After World War I, machines increasingly took over encoding and decoding. But whenever it is a matter of encoding with pencil and paper alone, transpositions combined with substitutions are still used. When the Soviet spy Reino Hayhanen defected to the Americans in 1957, in the middle of the Cold War, he revealed to them the cipher system he had used for correspondence with

Moscow. The system bore the same cover name as the spy: VIC. It consisted of three steps. First the plaintext was encoded with a monalphabetic Polybius substitution. Then it was superencrypted twice more by complicated transpositions.

NOTE

1. F. Bratzel and L. B. Rout, "Abwehr Ciphers in South America," *Cryptologia* (April 1983) 132.

9. FROM CODING DISK TO ENIGMA

Coding procedure is the law governing encoding.

Key denotes the changing documents according to which, in the various procedures, the coding tool is prepared for encoding.

Cipher table is the assembly of individual keys for a longer period of time.

Coding tool is the aid required for encoding, e.g., a coding machine (hitherto described as cipher machine).

Identification group serves as the identification of the key used in a phrase.

—*from the secret* Encrypting Instructions for the Enigma Cipher Machine, *Berlin, 1940*

THE DAY IS May 11, 1943. The pressurized steel body of the German U-boat U-528 has sprung a leak. The depth charges of the *Fleetwood* and the bombs of the aircraft detonated too close. As the air escapes and buoyancy diminishes, the submarine begins to sink. The commander, Lieutenant Georg von Rabenau, twenty-five, gives the order to open the blow-in valves. In the ballast tanks, the air forces out the water, and the vessel rises again to the surface. The commander orders the radio operator to send out an encoded signal: "Boat cannot dive." The British corvettes have dropped their depth charges and left the scene of action. The *Fleetwood* is again following its convoy OS47. Just then its crew notices the surfaced submarine, turns about, and opens fire. Von Rabenau decides to scuttle the U-boat. A dinghy is launched, a few men jump overboard. For this contingency provision has been made to do everything to prevent the cipher system from falling into enemy hands. The lists of daily codes are written in water-soluble ink on a kind of blotting paper.

But that is not enough. A further secret is how the rotors of the cipher machine Enigma are wired. The rotors, too, must disappear. The radio operator has already taken them out and put them in a pouch.

Reimar Lüst, engineer-lieutenant of the reserve and only nineteen, flings the pouch overboard in a wide arc. With a splash it lands in the water, and he watches it until it can no longer be made out in the depths. The key drums of the Enigma of U-528 have since been lying at the bottom of the Atlantic at a depth of 320 meters, southwest of Ireland at 46°55' northern latitude and 14°44' western longitude.

Of the crew of fifty-six, forty-five succeeded in reaching the British ship.[1]

THE INVENTION OF THE WHEEL

In cryptology, wheels have always played an important role. The cipher disk of figure 4.2 with its twenty-six sectors possesses two disks, or wheels. By rotating them one against the other, you can produce Caesar displacements.

Let us take another look at our electrical coding machine in figure 4.10. We bend the strip with its wiring so that the short top and bottom edges touch. The strip is thus made into a cylinder, which we can turn into a pillbox by adding two flat sides, as in figure 9.1, center. The illustration shows where the contacts now are. The wiring, which has remained unchanged, is taken through the interior of the pillbox. The strip has become a *key rotor*. The contacts that lead to the switches and lightbulbs of the machine must be accordingly arranged in circular disks. Each left-hand contact of the rotor must be connected to a lightbulb; each right-hand contact of the rotor must be connected to a switch. The fact that the contacts are now arranged in disks has changed nothing about the coding. So far the new machine offers no more than the old one did. The advantage is that the drum in the machine can be rotated. After a quarter turn, the switch contacts are connected to different lightbulb contacts, though the wiring inside the rotor has not been changed (fig. 9.2).

I have described here a machine for an alphabet of only four letters. For the normal alphabet we would need twenty-six switches, twenty-six lightbulbs, and on each side of the drum twenty-six contacts. Each con-

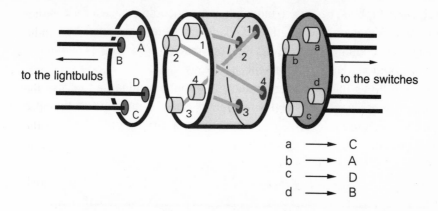

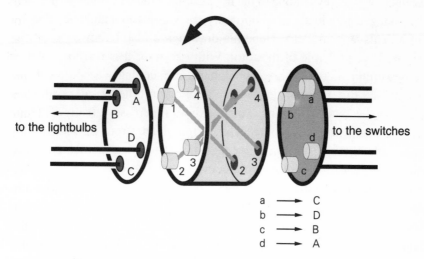

Fig. 9.1. The connections as in figure 4.10. The wiring is no longer on a flat strip but inside a round pillbox, the key rotor. The connections to the battery are not shown here. Two disks carry the contacts leading to switches and lightbulbs. The wiring produces the same transformation of plaintext letters into ciphers as the wiring in figure 4.10, top.

Fig. 9.2. Compared with figure 9.1, the key rotor is has been rotated a quarter turn in the direction of the arrow. Now switches and lightbulbs are connected differently; the plaintext letters are converted into different ciphers.

tact on the left must be connected to a contact on the right. But no matter what position the rotor occupies, it cannot avoid monalphabetic encoding. We can arrange, for instance, that after each letter typed in, the rotor turns 1/26 of a full rotation. The ciphers produced in this way are essentially

Vigenère ciphers, because a monalphabetic encoding is used for each letter. With Vigenère, the length of the keyword determines after how many letters the coding repeats itself; with our machine, this comes about after a full rotation, that is, after twenty-six steps.

It follows that a cipher produced by our machine can be cracked in the same way as a Vigenère cipher. Such a machine is therefore not of much use. Nevertheless, drums were a turning point in the art of encryption.

THREE INVENTORS—BUT ONLY ONE BECAME RICH

The technical realization of the rotor principle was first accomplished by the American Eduard Hugo Hebern (1869-1952). He wired up two electric typewriters (the first models had just then come on the market), connecting the keys of one to the levers of the other. That the wiring could be changed provided the opportunity for various monalphabetic encodings. This was in 1915. Hebern's drawings of 1917, however, already showed the principle of the rotor. With one rotor it is possible to effect a maximum of twenty-six monalphabetic encodings, according to the twenty-six different positions of the rotor against the (fixed) positions of the switches and lightbulbs. This maximum increases greatly if we put two drums next to each other. The current enters from a contact on the right side of the first rotor, is conducted by the wiring to a left contact of that rotor, and flows into a right contact of the second rotor. Figure 9.3 shows a switching diagram for the simple case of a four-letter alphabet. If the drums are not moved, they supply just a monalphabetic encoding. But each rotor can be turned in twenty-six different ways with regard to the other, and the two drums again in twenty-six different ways with regard to the fixed outer contacts, so we have $26 \times 26 = 676$ positions. If rotor W1 turns by one step after each letter and if rotor W2 turns by one step after each complete rotation of rotor W1, the ciphers will repeat themselves after 676 symbols. This corresponds to a Vigenère code with a worm of length 676.

An unauthorized decoder need not wait for the repetition of the worm. All he needs is a sufficiently large number of messages. So long as the encoding of each message starts from the same initial position of the

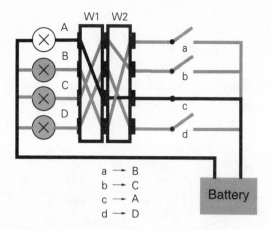

Fig. 9.3. An arrangement of two drums that can be rotated against each other and against the switch and lightbulb contacts. The drums are here drawn from the side, unlike those in figures 9.1 and 9.2. By different positions of the drums with regard to each other and with regard to the fixed contacts of the switches and lightbulbs, sixteen different encodings can be achieved with a four-letter alphabet.

rotors, the first letters of all messages (just as all second letters by themselves, and all third ones, etc.) will be encoded monalphabetically in the same way. And monalphabetic encodings can be broken by a frequency analysis of the ciphers. With a sufficiently large number of secret signals, one can discover not only the plaintexts but also the wiring pattern of the two drums. Only if the initial position of the drums in relation to each other and in relation to the fixed contacts of the casing is continually changed, ideally from signal to signal, will decoding fail.

Hebern's first machine contained five drums. In consequence there were $26 \times 26 \times 26 \times 26 \times 26 = 11,881,376$ different possible settings of the mechanism (fig. 9.4).

As an inventor Hebern was a genius; as a businessman he was unlucky. In 1921 he founded the first firm in America that manufactured cipher machines. He was convinced that his invention would herald a new era in coding. In this he was right. He sold shares and built a large factory in Oakland, California. The U.S. Navy was interested in his machines, and he expected it to purchase large quantities. That was a mistake. Between 1924 and 1926, the navy bought exactly two machines. A private firm and the Italian and British admiralties purchased nine

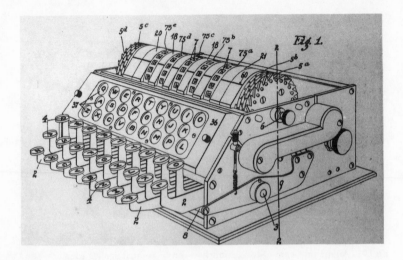

Fig. 9.4. **Eduard Hugo Hebern's electrical cipher machine (about 1921).**

altogether. The machine's price tag was only a few hundred dollars. The shares, issued at five dollars each, dropped to one dollar. Hebern's firm went bankrupt.

During World War II and subsequently in the Cold War, the American forces used hundreds of thousands of cipher machines, all of them working according to the principle of Hebern's drums. After a long-drawn-out lawsuit, Hebern was offered thirty thousand dollars, not what he had demanded but a settlement to bring about a quick conclusion of the case, since there was a danger that cryptological secrets of the armed forces might leak out to the public. But by then Hebern had been dead for eight years.

Hebern was not the only inventor of the cipher rotor. In Holland, Hugo Alexander Koch, a native of Delft, took out a patent in October 1919 for a "secret writing machine." In 1927 he sold the patent rights to the German engineer Artur Scherbius (1878-1929), who had taken out a patent for a cipher machine on the rotor principle in Germany as early as 1918. Scherbius not only had his ideas for cipher machines patented; he also built them. Details of his machine emerge from the patent application he submitted in the United States (fig. 9.5). This machine had something new: the *reflecting cylinder*. In the illustration, this is the cylinder on the right, marked 11.

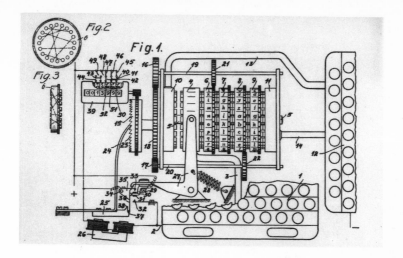

Fig. 9.5. Diagram of the Scherbius machine (about 1923). Top left: a cipher rotor with its wiring.

In the Scherbius machine not only is a rotor advanced by one step after each letter, and the next rotor one step after every complete rotation, but also, by means of a gear with various ratios, other drums are moved a specific number of steps after every letter. Figure 9.6 shows the principle of the switching. We have two movable drums and, to their left, the (fixed) reflecting cylinder. In the position of the rotors illustrated, depression of the *c* key causes lightbulb B to come on. Depression of the *b* key turns on lightbulb C. The advantage of the reflecting cylinder is that the same machine can be used for encoding and decoding. If we start from a certain position of the drums and key in the letters of the plaintext one by one, such as the word "adac," then, as step by step the drums are rotated against each other, the lightbulbs DCBA should light up. If, in the same initial position of the drums, we key in "dcba," the lightbulbs ADAC come on, and the plaintext is restored, since the drums at each letter typed in during decoding have the same position in relation to each other as they had during encoding. As can be seen from figure 9.6, with such a wiring scheme, plaintext letter and cipher can never be the same.

Anyone trying to decode messages encoded with the machine must know not only the wiring inside the individual drums but also the order in which they are arranged next to one another in the machine. In addi-

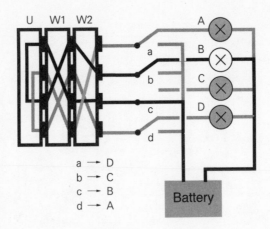

Fig. 9.6. **The two-rotor machine of figure 9.3 amplified by a reflecting cylinder (U). During encoding, drums W1 and W2 move while the reflecting cylinder is fixed. When a plaintext letter is typed in, the lightbulb of the same letter can never come on. The closing of a switch, such as switch *c* in the illustration, simultaneously breaks the circuit to lightbulb C.**

tion he must know the wiring in the reflecting cylinder and the rules by which the drums are rotated in relation to one another.

Scherbius thought up a name for his machine, one he hoped would promote sales: Enigma, the Greek word for riddle. He constructed several models, each different, and in 1923 founded a joint-stock company. In August of that year, his firm on Berlin's Steglitzer Strasse started production. Scherbius gave demonstrations of his machine at conventions, but the expected business failed to materialize.

However, the machine aroused the interest of the Reichswehr, the one-hundred-thousand-man army that the Allies had conceded to Germany in the Treaty of Versailles. Soon afterward the machine was being manufactured not for the public but solely for the armed forces.

In 1934, three years after Scherbius lost his life in an accident, the firm dissolved. But there was a comeback for Enigma after Hitler rose to power and began rearming Germany. I will deal later in greater detail with Enigma's role in World War II.

There was a third inventor who made use of the rotor principle. In October 1919, three days after Koch applied for his patent in Holland, the Swede Arvid Gerhard Damm applied for a patent in Stockholm. Damm was an eccentric. Originally he worked as an engineer in a textile mill in Finland. He was responsible for several improvements to the looms there. At home he opened doors and switched on lights by pressing a button. In his private life, too, Damm did not always follow conventional ways. He was reputed to have gained the favors of a virtuous circus equestrienne by going through a pretend marriage in which one of his friends, disguised as a priest, performed the ceremony.

After the outbreak of World War I, Damm, along with a British textile manufacturer, applied for three patents for a cipher machine in Germany—which was surprising, since his partner was considered an enemy. Later Damm started a company. He quickly found investors, including the nephew of Alfred Nobel, the inventor of dynamite and founder of the prizes named for him. The investor with the famous name attracted a further provider of capital, a man named Hagelin.

Damm constructed several machines and demonstrated them to potential customers. They did not exactly sell like hotcakes. Figure 9.7

AKTIEBOLAGET

CRYPTOGRAPH

STOCKHOLM · SWEDEN
TELEGRAMS: CRYPTO. STOCKHOLM

MAKERS OF
CIPHERING MACHINES OF ALL KINDS
(DAMM'S SYSTEM)
FOR DIPLOMATIC, MILITARY AND MARINE SERVICE AND
TELEGRAPHIC AND COMMERCIAL CORRESPONDENCE

CONSULTANTS FOR
ALL CRYPTOGRAPHIC MATTERS

Fig. 9.7. **Title page of the catalog of the Swedish cipher-machine company, 1922. The proprietor at the time was the inventor Arvid Gerhard Damm. Ten years later, Boris Hagelin took it over.**

shows the title page of the company's catalog of 1922. Then a new man appeared on the scene: Boris Caesar Wilhelm Hagelin, the son of the above-mentioned partner. Young Hagelin was an engineer and had gathered experience in Russia, Sweden, and the United States. He now simplified one of Damm's machines, equipped it with a keyboard, and fitted it with lightbulbs, rather like Hebern's machine. In 1929 he managed to sell a substantial number of these. When Damm died in 1927, Hagelin took control of the firm and continued to improve its models. He replaced the lightbulbs with a printer in 1934. Admittedly his machine still weighed thirty-seven pounds, but it fitted into a briefcase and could transpose two hundred letters per minute. The French general staff inquired if Hagelin could build a machine, complete with printer, that would fit into a small case. Printing was important, because the lightbulbs required the presence of a second person if the encoding-decoding process was to be fast. Hagelin succeeded in building a machine that weighed less than three pounds and was smaller than the telephone instruments used at the time. Subsequently he sold five thousand of these to the French.

When the Germans invaded Norway in 1940, Hagelin feared that even Sweden was no longer safe and decided to move to the United States. In the meantime, Hitler had conquered France, Holland, and Belgium. There were no more ships sailing from Sweden to the United States. The Hagelins thereupon conceived the adventurous plan of leaving from Genoa. They traveled from Trelleborg via Berlin, right through Hitler's Germany. Three days later, they were in Genoa. They got to New York on board the *Conte di Savoia*, the construction plans for their machines in their baggage. From America, Hagelin managed to import fifty machines from Stockholm to New York. In the United States he immediately began production. The advantage of his machines was that their five drums turned forward in an irregular manner, so that the cipher repeated itself only after about one hundred million letters. In all, he sold some 140,000 machines during the war. This made him a millionaire.

One year before the end of the war, Hagelin, now enormously wealthy, returned to Sweden and established a factory south of Stockholm. After World War II, the business continued to flourish. The states that emerged during the political reorganization of the postwar years all needed a great number of cipher machines for their armies and for communication with their embassies. But Hagelin knew that Swedish law allowed the state to appropriate inventions considered useful to the defense of the country. This law, together with Swedish tax regulations, induced him to move his research and development department to Switzerland in 1948, where he eventually employed a staff of one hundred and seventy for the manufacture of his cipher machines. Boris Hagelin died in 1959, the only inventor to have struck it rich through cipher machines. His company, Krypto AG, still has its registered address in Zug, Switzerland. In its prospectus it states that it supplies customers in one hundred and thirty countries, including Iraq, Iran, and Libya.

THE CURSE OF THE REFLECTING CYLINDER

Because of its reflecting cylinder, the Scherbius machine could be used both for encoding and decoding. But the German users of this machine in World War II did not realize its great drawback. We will see that it was this reflecting cylinder that enabled Polish and British cryptologists to decode the signals encrypted with Enigma.

If you wish to use the same machine for encoding and decoding, you greatly restrict the possibilities of encryption. We know that each position of the drums connects every switch with one lightbulb. Since switches and lightbulbs are marked with letters, the machine ensures that each switch letter corresponds to one lightbulb letter. We therefore have a substitution, a shuffling or permutation of the alphabet. A machine with a reflecting cylinder, however, greatly reduces the number of possible encodings. It uses only permutations that, when applied twice to the alphabet, restore the original arrangement. This is illustrated by the example of the four-letter alphabet in the box on the next page.

What do things look like if we use the complete twenty-six-letter alphabet? We saw in chapter 4 that the number of permutations of the alphabet has twenty-seven digits. If the machine is used in the same position twice on the same plaintext, again supplying that plaintext, the number of possible permutations has only thirteen digits. Although this is still a very large number, it is many billion times less than before. The advantage of using the same machine for both encoding and decoding therefore dramatically reduces its possibilities.

PERMUTATIONS THAT ANNUL THEMSELVES

In the simple case of our four-letter alphabet, there are twenty-four permutations. However, among

ABCD ABCD ABCD ABCD ABCD ABCD
ABCD ABDC ACBD ACDB ADBC ADCB

ABCD ABCD ABCD ABCD ABCD ABCD
BACD BADC BCAD BCDA BDAC BDCA

ABCD ABCD ABCD ABCD ABCD ABCD
CBAD CBDA CABD CADB CDBA CDAB

ABCD ABCD ABCD ABCD ABCD ABCD
DBCA DBAC DCBA DCAB DABC DACB

there are only three that, as Enigma, transpose *no* letter into themselves or, after double application, transpose *every* letter into themselves. These are the permutations

ABCD   ABCD   ABCD
DCBA   CDAB   BADC

Let us test these out. Take the first: A becomes D, D becomes A. In the second, A becomes C and C becomes A. But B also becomes D, and D becomes B. Matters are much the same with the third. We can encode entire texts with one of the permutations, for instance with the first. Let us encode ADAC. This gives us DADB. If we encode this word once more with the first permutation, we find that DADB becomes ADAC—back to the beginning. Double encoding therefore results in the plaintext. In permutation language we can state: Permutations produced by Enigma with its reflecting cylinder have the characteristic that each is its own reciprocal. What it accomplishes in the first step it annuls in the second. Such permutations are called *involutory* by mathematicians.

THE RADIO SIGNAL WITHOUT L

The advantage of the reflecting cylinder—that one can use the same machine for encoding and decoding—has another consequence. Whatever letter is typed in, the lightbulb of that letter never lights up. We can easily convince ourselves from figure 9.6 that at the moment the switch of a particular letter is depressed—in the illustration, it is the c switch—no current can flow simultaneously to lightbulb C. No plaintext letter can therefore be converted into the same cipher. This made it possible, in World War II, to decipher a signal that had no content whatever, and the deciphering cost the Italian navy its command of the eastern Mediterranean.

Mavis Lever was a student of German at London University. At the age of eighteen, she joined the British decoders at Bletchley Park, the headquarters of British cryptology in World War II. The young student was struck by the fact that a lengthy signal of the Italian navy did not contain the letter **L**. In a ciphertext encoded not monalphabetically or not according to Vigenère, all letters of the alphabet should occur with more or less the same frequency. Why was there no **L** in this signal? Lever's suspicion was aroused. Could this be a blind of the Italian encoders? On their Enigma, had they chosen as a plaintext a string of ls in order to confound the Allies? In that case, no **L** would appear in the ciphertext since l is never transformed into **L**. If her assumption was correct, the signal might throw some light on the inner workings of the Italian Enigma. As she followed up her idea, she soon realized that she was on the right track. The ciphertext revealed to her what the machine, in consecutive rotor positions, had made of the letter l. From that emerged indications concerning the wiring, and the cipher was eventually broken. The signals of the Italian navy enabled the British in March 1941, in the battle of Cape Matapan at the southern tip of Corinth, to annihilate three Italian cruisers and two destroyers—a blow from which the Italian navy never recovered.[2]

The weakness of Enigma with its reflecting cylinder, however, emerged also with signals that carried meaning and normal texts. The great many permutations that, if used twice, produce the initial arrangement, reveal other regularities. Even though these do not immediately permit decoding, the marked reduction of possibilities, together with mistakes and carelessness in operation, enabled Polish mathematicians to read Enigma-encrypted signals as early as the thirties. The Allies later profited from that knowledge. Hagelin's machines, thousands of which were used by the Americans in World War II, had no reflecting cylinders.

HITLER'S ENIGMA

Following Hitler's seizure of power in 1933, the Scherbius cipher machine was further improved. It was used in several variants. The army, navy, and diplomatic service used different models. But ultimately all the models resembled the Scherbius machine, which as early as 1928 was equipped with a *plugboard*, a board of twenty-six double jack plugs, by which the connections were made from the keys to the rotors and back to the lightbulbs. This made it possible once more to shuffle some of the twenty-six letters of the alphabet. The German army's Enigma had three movable rotors, a reflecting cylinder, and a plugboard. Figure 9.8 shows its arrangement for a four-letter alphabet.

The plugboard could, for instance, be connected to produce the following shuffling:

```
ABCDEFGHIJKLMNOPQRSTUVWXYZ
EYCFADHGOKJMLNIWQSRUTZPXBV
```

Notice that this is a permutation in which A becomes E and, at the same time, E becomes A. If applied to the plaintext and thereafter to the permutated text, the plaintext reappears. The permutation is an *involution*.

A model of the Scherbius machine is shown in plate 3. This four-rotor machine was used by the German navy toward the end of the war. Two rotors removed from it are shown in plate 4. Each consists of an inner part that carries the electric contacts on both sides; within it, the contacts of one side are wired to the contacts of the other side. A ring, clearly visible in the right-hand rotor in plate 4, encloses the inner part. On its outside, the ring shows the twenty-six letters of the alphabet. In addition it has one or two notches that ensure the transfer of the motion to the next rotor. When the drum is installed in the machine, a window in the casing reveals one letter of the ring, from which the position of the rotor can be read off. A knurled wheel fitted to the rotor projects from the casing and makes it possible to turn the drum in the machine from outside. At a suitable position, a notch on the ring releases a mechanism that, at the next pressing of a key, advances the next rotor by one letter. With the rotor pictured in plate 4, right, the neighboring rotor is moved when the letter Z or M appears in the window.

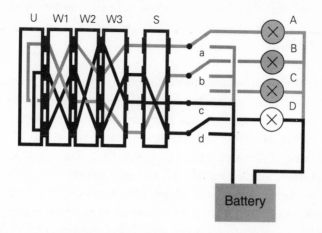

Fig. 9.8. **The arrangement of Enigma for the simple case of a four-letter alphabet. Switches *a*, *b*, *c*, *d* are linked to lightbulbs A, B, C, D. The connections run from the switches via plugboard S through three rotors, marked W1, W2, W3; through reflecting cylinder U; then back again through the three rotors and the plugboard to the lightbulbs. In the illustration, the *c* switch has been pressed, and lightbulb D lights up. With each encoded letter, the drums rotate, changing their encoding. We can see that this encoding is involutory. Just as cipher D lights up in the illustration as *c* is depressed, so C lights up when *d* is pressed. The plaintext *adac* therefore becomes BCBD, and *bcbd* becomes ADAC. It can also be seen that plaintext and ciphertext letters can never be the same—a great weakness of Enigma.**

But matters are more complicated still. The ring with the notches and the inner part of the rotor, which contains the wiring and the contacts, can be rotated with respect to each other. This makes it possible to change the *ring position*, which makes deciphering even more difficult for the adversary.

At the beginning of World War II, there were eight rotors available, bearing the numbers I, II, . . . VIII. Each rotor had its letter ring with notches and inside that the rotor's characteristic wiring. Plate 4 left, shows rotor I; rotor VIII is on the right.

The encoder had several ways to adjust his machine. He could

1. choose three from several drums (four, if he had a four-rotor Enigma)
2. bring each drum into a particular ring position
3. use the drums in a particular sequence (with three drums, he had six sequences; with four, twenty-four)

4. bring the three drums into an initial position so that three particular letters showed in the three windows (with four drums, analogously)

5. plug in the jacks

All these steps had to be performed according to a *daily key* available to him. He could then be sure that his colleague, who was to decode his signal, had brought his Enigma into the identical starting position. Figure 9.9 shows the operational use of Enigma in World War II.

Since changing the rotors was a cumbersome business, their order, the *rotor position*, was left unchanged for three months until 1935. Later they were changed every month, and after October 1936 every day. During World War II, the rotor position was changed every eight hours.

The daily key, which determined the choice of drums, their sequence, the ring positions, the initial positions of the drums and the plugboard arrangement, was laid down in the *Army Cipher Manual*. Once the encoder had prepared his Enigma in all these respects, he could type in his plaintext. So he keyed in the first letter of the message. He had to press the key hard, because force was needed to set the first drum moving. And quite possibly this would be a position where the second drum would advance a step with the first, and sometimes maybe even the third. The typing of each letter closed an electrical circuit that ran from the switch via the plugboard through the three rotors and into the reflecting cylinder, and back through the three rotors and again through the plugboard to a lightbulb, which would light up. When the encoder pressed a second letter key, a lightbulb again lit up. He had to learn to press the plaintext keys with his left hand and use his right for noting down the ciphers, as indicated by the lightbulbs. He would then have to pass the ciphertext to the radio operator for transmission. The receiver, having received the ciphertext from his radio operator, had to key in the ciphers with one hand and with the other write down the plaintext letters according to the lightbulbs that came on.

In February 1942, the German navy introduced an additional rotor; this was identified by the Greek letter beta and referred to as the *Greek drum*. In order to fit it into the casing, both it and the reflecting cylinder had to be made thinner. The thin reflecting cylinder came in two versions, known as A and B. The cylinder connected thirteen letters (ABCDE-FGIJKMTV) to the rest of the alphabet (YRUHQSLPXNOZW).

Fig. 9.9. Enigma in operational use in World War II. Panzergrenadier General Guderian waiting for a signal to be decoded.   *Photo archive Preussischer Kulturbesitz.*

One might think that an unauthorized decoder would find it impossible to decipher such elaborately encoded messages. The decoder would know neither the selection of drums nor their sequential order, neither the ring position nor the initial position, nor would he have any information about the plugboard connections, let alone the internal wiring of the drums.

It was not quite as hopeless as it might first seem. However cunning the daily key, however many notches there were on a drum to move its neighbor—with the same daily key the first letter of every signal would be encoded with the same setting of the machine. Provided there was a sufficiently large number of intercepted messages, there were many clues. All the first ciphers were monalphabetically encoded, just as all the second, even though differently from the first. The same was true of all letters that, in different signals, stood in the same places. Letter chains monalphabetically encoded can be decoded by means of frequency analysis. Thus even the most sophisticated Enigma with the most ingenious daily key would be ultimately useless.

It was necessary therefore to modify the setting from signal to signal. For that, the sender of a signal had to think up a *signal key*. This consisted of three letters and would, independently of the daily key, lay down the initial position of the drums. But the receiver also had to know that signal key. How was it to be communicated without the listening enemy discovering it? The receiver was informed about the new initial position of the drums by three letters transmitted at the beginning of the signal. They were still sent according to the daily key. Once the receiver had translated these three letters with the daily key, he would then set the drums in the position necessary for the impending signal. Thus he could decode the ciphertext that followed. To make sure these three letters were safely transmitted—after all, the messages were sent by radio and often in bad atmospheric conditions—they were sent twice, so that the beginning of each signal consisted of six letters, whose plaintext consisted of two nonidentical groups of three. Since with every letter the rotors adopted a different position, what was transmitted were not identical groups of three but just six letters. The receiver had to set the drums according to the daily key and with it decipher the six letters. If everything worked all right, the plaintext before him would consist of the group of three twice. Next he had to set his three drums according to this group of three—to make sure, that is, that those letters appeared in the windows of his

Enigma. Proceeding from this setting, he would then have to key in the rest of the ciphertext.

It is estimated that two hundred thousand Enigmas were built in Germany. Few survive to this day. After the war, the Allies destroyed them in large numbers. Nowadays an Enigma has become a collector's item. In the twenties, their price was about 600 Reichsmark. It is said that the market value of an original machine is now around $150,000. In its "Informatik und Automatik" section, the Deutsches Museum in Munich possesses numerous instruments that were used for encrypting in the past. The four-rotor naval Enigma in plate 3 belongs to that collection.

In appendix B, I describe a program that simulates on a computer the operation of Enigma. The PC becomes a virtual Enigma. You can change rotors, ring settings, and drum arrangement, as well as lay down your plugboard pattern and the initial situation of the rotors. Having selected those settings, you can encode and decode at will.

NOTES

1. After the war, Lieutenant Georg von Rabenau became commander of the Federal German Navy. Lieutenant Reimar Lüst was later president of the Max Planck Society and is now president of the Alexander von Humboldt Foundation. Between these two posts he was in charge, for six years, of the destiny of ESA, the European Space Agency.

2. D. Kahn, *Seizing the Enigma* (Boston: Souvenir Press, 1991) 86 and 139.

10. ENIGMA'S SECRET IS UNVEILED

> Historians . . . are cautious. At any rate, there seems to be unanimity that without radio intelligence—especially successful on the Allied side—the war might have gone on for another two years. But that, in all probability, would have meant the dropping of the atom bomb on Germany.
> —HERBERT W. FRANKE, *Die geheime Nachricht*

IN THE SUMMER OF 1929, a Polish student of twenty-four, Marian Rejewski, matriculated at the University of Göttingen to study mathematics. He came from Bydgoszcz, the city that at the time of his birth was called Bromberg but after World War I had been assigned to Poland. After graduating from school, he studied mathematics in Poznań. There he came across a discipline on the margin of mathematics. The Cipher Bureau of the Polish general staff had organized a course on cryptology for some twenty hand-picked students of the university. The secret service people had chosen Poznań for this special class because the city had been part of Germany from 1793 to 1918 and most of the students had a command of German. The idea was to nurture a young generation of cryptologists who would be capable of decoding the signals of the German army. While Rejewski was still in Göttingen, his university in Poland offered him the post of assistant professor. He turned his back on Germany and for the next two years worked at the University of Poznań. There the earlier cryptology class had borne fruit: indeed a cipher bureau had been set up. Two younger students were working in it—Henryk Zygalski and Jerzy Różycki. At that point Rejewski began to concern himself with cryptology in all seriousness.

WANTED: YOUNG MATHEMATICIANS WITH AN INTEREST IN CRYPTOLOGY

Before long the three young mathematicians were offered posts in the Cipher Bureau in Warsaw, the Biuro szyfrów. They were assigned to Section BS4, the section responsible for Germany. The Warsaw bureau had already scored a major success. When in 1920 Polish forces under Marshal Pilsudski halted the Bolsheviks at the gates of Warsaw, the Biuro szyfrów had played a major part by cracking the Russian cipher. The cipher of the German Reichswehr had similarly presented no problem to BS4, until 1928. But then the Germans introduced a new system: Enigma. The Poles assumed correctly that behind the new codes was a machine like Scherbius's.

The war against Enigma began in peacetime. At some point, using a Swedish intermediary, the bureau had acquired a civilian Enigma. The machine had been commercially available for a long time and was therefore familiar to the Poles, but the drums of the Reichswehr Enigma and later the Wehrmacht Enigma were wired differently. The BS4 group assumed correctly that the machine now being used had a reflecting cylinder, and that therefore it would also have the weaknesses of such a system.

Then the Polish Cipher Bureau had a lucky break.[1] On a Friday in 1928, an official of the German legation in Warsaw turned up at the railway parcel customs office, urgently inquiring about a packing case consigned to his legation by the foreign office in Berlin. The German insisted that the case be immediately released by customs. His excitement made the Polish customs officials suspicious and obstinate. They suspected that the diplomatic package had by mistake been handled by the post office as normal freight. Customs was not allowed to open diplomatic packages, only ordinary freight. Shrugging their shoulders, they declared that the item had not yet arrived. As soon as the German left, the customs officials informed Polish military intelligence. Intelligence people opened the crate and found, carefully packed in straw, a brand-new Enigma. Over the weekend the men from BS4 thoroughly examined the machine. On Monday the German embassy received the crate, which bore no traces of having been improperly opened. The Poles had gained a lot, but by no means everything, because to study the inner workings of a commercial Enigma is one thing, to read messages encrypted with an army Enigma quite another.

THE FIRST SIX LETTERS OF THE ENIGMA SIGNALS

That, more or less, was the situation when the three young mathematicians arrived in Warsaw from Poznań. As we said in the last chapter, each message to be encrypted with Enigma was prefaced, in the plaintext, by a repeated group of three: the signal key. The signal key was encrypted by the machine in its basic position as required by the daily key.

Let us recall how Enigma operates. Each position of the wheels assigns to every plaintext letter a lightbulb and thereby a cipher. Each new setting gives rise to a new permutation of the alphabet. Was the plaintext really as efficiently hidden by this method as it would have been if encoded with an infinitely long key worm of random numbers (see chapter 7)? Enigma's rigid pattern had three weak points.

1. Encoding of the first six letters was always done in accordance with the daily key, which meant that the machine was kept in the same initial setting for a whole day.

2. The first group of six of each intercepted signal had two identical groups of three in plaintext. Thus if a signal began with the group of six **DMQVBN**, then the first and fourth letter represented the same plaintext letter; they were merely encoded by different permutations. The same applied to the second and fifth letters and to the third and sixth letters.

3. The reflecting cylinder dramatically reduced the number of possible permutations. Because of the cylinder, they were all involutary.

In consequence the machine was far more predictable than the German army command believed. The weaknesses of Enigma eventually enabled the Poles to read the German signals. Provided the men of BS4 had a large enough number of signals from the same day, these yielded a wealth of information on the given daily key's first six permutations of Enigma. Even during peacetime exercises the Polish cryptologists had at their disposal about a hundred signals each day, encoded in the same initial setting of Enigma. That was enough to discover the signal key and the daily key, and in the course of time the wiring of the drums and the cabling of the plugboard.

But the men of BS4 had their work made even easier for them. Out of laziness the encoders often chose signal codes made up of three identical letters or of three letters adjacent to each other or diagonal to each other on the Enigma keyboard. In *Decrypted Secrets*, the Munich mathematician Friedrich L. Bauer gives a list of sixty-five ciphertext groups of six that were sent on the same day in World War II.[2] Among these the combination **SYXSCW** occurs six times. It turned out that the encoders had chosen the signal key *AAA*, which, along with the daily key, always provided the same group of six. **RJLPWX** occurs four times; this is based on the equally lazy signal code *BBB*. Thanks to such behavior, the three Polish mathematicians on some days had no shortage of messages that used the same signal key.

Another weakness in the method of choosing signal codes was the fact that during the encoding of the extremely important first six letters of a message usually only one drum was being moved while the others were still stationary. In December 1932, the Warsaw team got hold of some material that was to make things easier still for them.

THE GERMAN SPY AND THE MURDERED CHIEF OF STAFF

At the beginning of 1931, an official of the German Reichswehr ministry, a young man named Hans Thilo Schmidt, made contact with French Intelligence and supplied information on ciphers, including the Enigma machine (needless to say, for a sum of money). His cover name was the letter combination HE. The two letters, pronounced individually in French, sound like the German word *Asche* (ashes). Initially the French were suspicious of agent Asche. Were the Germans trying to insinuate him into French Intelligence as a double agent? But the director of the Cipher Bureau, Captain Gustave Bertrand, of whom we will hear more soon, interrogated Schmidt and came to the conclusion that Asche could really supply important material. At various meetings in different European towns, Asche handed over, among other things, a copy of the German service instructions on the use of Enigma and the daily keys for September and October 1932—that is, the initial settings of the rotors for every day, the ring settings, and the wiring in the plugboard. Present at some of these meetings was also a French agent with the cover name Rex. Rex interpreted, since Asche did not speak French.[3] As early as December 1932, Bertrand sent the information on to Warsaw. There a sufficient number of signals had been collected from the months before; not only were these belatedly decoded, but further details were learned, from the comparison of ciphertext and plaintext, about the wiring of the Enigma drums. By 1934, the Poles had solved the Enigma secrets. They were now able to read the signals of the German armed forces and the German SS Security Service.

A signal intercepted on June 30, 1934, resulted in the plaintext "an alle flugplätze ernst roehm abliefern tot oder lebend" (to all airports ernst roehm to be delivered dead or alive). That was the order for the Night of the Long Knives. That day Hitler, together with his minister Goebbels, from Munich launched the bloody massacre of his old followers from the SA Brownshirts. The most prominent victim was the SA chief of staff Röhm, one of Hitler's friends from the days when he was still struggling for power. Not only Röhm and his followers were murdered. Hitler made use of this opportunity to rid himself also of other persons he disliked. But back to the decoders of Warsaw.

A BOMBE AGAINST ENIGMA

The Germans never ceased worrying about the security of their Enigma—rightly so, as we know. That is why they did everything to prevent decoding. The Poles, naturally, tried to keep pace with them. Even when the wiring was known, it was still a long way from the first six symbols to drawing conclusions about rotor sequence, ring setting, initial position, and plugboard cabling. To obtain this information required a great many messages encoded with the same daily key.

With every new daily setting of Enigma, the Polish cryptologists had to start over. This was a cumbersome albeit mechanical task. It could be performed by a machine. So the three mathematicians designed an instrument, as shown in figure 10.1. It contained two sets of three rotors each. These were wired as Enigma was wired and could be individually set. In addition there were twenty-six lightbulbs and the same number of

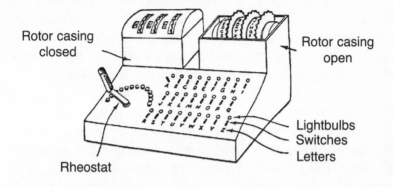

Fig. 10.1. The *cyclometer* of the Polish cryptologists contained drums that simulated the drums in Enigma. With it the characteristics of ciphers obtainable by Enigma were examined and cataloged.

switches. The gadget, however, was intended neither for encoding nor decoding; its one and only task was to identify certain characteristics of the shuffled alphabets produced by different rotor positions. The Poles ran through all possible settings in order to observe the characteristics of the ciphers created from the number of lightbulbs that came on. They were able to run through all $26 \times 26 \times 26 = 17{,}576$ rotor positions and spot a few characteristics of the permutations created. The machine was called a *cyclometer*. With it the men of BS4 produced a catalog that made it possible, even after only a few intercepted signals, to determine the daily key within a few minutes. That was in the autumn of 1938. Hitler meanwhile had occupied Austria and moved into the German-speaking part of Czechoslovakia, the Sudetenland.

Section BS4 in Warsaw could not rest on the laurels of their cyclometer. On November 1, 1937, the Germans had introduced a new reflecting cylinder, and on December 15, 1938, the number of available rotors was increased from three to five, with only three being used at any one time. Three drums can be arranged in the machine in six different ways. There were sixty ways of selecting three drums out of five and arranging them in different sequences. The Polish decoders now had to run through ten times the former number of cases. The cyclometer was no longer sufficient: The Poles therefore built a more sophisticated machine, which they named *bomba*, the bomb. But, strangely enough, they were thinking not of an aerial bomb—even though the town of Guernica had been destroyed by German and Italian airmen in the Spanish Civil War the previous year—but of an ice-cream bombe. With this device they simulated six Enigmas. Six bombes (in Polish, *bomby*) were built, but none has survived. Nobody now knows precisely how they worked.

The situation in Europe was getting worse. In March 1939, Hitler occupied the rest of Bohemia and Moravia. It was more than likely that his next target would be Poland. Indeed, he made no secret of his ambition to reconquer the territories Germany had lost in the Treaty of Versailles. This applied to Polish cities such as Poznań and Cracow, and to the region that separated East Prussia from the German Reich, known as the "Polish corridor." It became urgently necessary for the secret services of all the threatened countries to get together.

On July 25, 1939, representatives of the Polish, British, and French intelligence services met at Pyry near Warsaw. The French delegation included Captain Gustave Bertrand, who had worked with the German spy Asche. The Poles handed the Allies the results of their investigations of Enigma. At that time the ciphers made possible by five rotors had not yet been broken. It was decided to share this task. The Poles were to carry on with their mathematical and theoretical work, and the French were to try to use contact people to gain information from Germany on the extension of the rotor positions. The British decided to build a large number of bombes in order to crack the five-rotor codes. In addition, the Poles gave the French two of the copies they had built of Enigma.

Shortly afterward Hitler declared war on Poland. World War II had begun.

THREE MATHEMATICIANS ESCAPE

A week after Hitler's troops crossed the Polish frontier, the Cipher Bureau in Warsaw was dissolved. Its staff traveled by special train to Brest-Litovsk and from there by car to the Polish-Romanian frontier. While the cryptologists fled from the German Wehrmacht advancing from the west, the Red Army crossed Poland's eastern frontier. Hitler and Stalin had agreed to divide Poland between them. Many people fled Poland in the direction of Romania, including the Polish government. En route the trains were time and again strafed by German planes. The BS4 men found themselves compelled to destroy the bombes they had brought with them. Of the three mathematicians only Rejewski was to see his homeland again.

Refugees are not welcome anywhere. The Romanians were putting the Poles in an internment camp. But the three mathematicians succeeded in boarding the next train to the Romanian capital, in the hope that the British embassy in Bucharest would help them get to England. After all, the British had been cooperative at the Warsaw meeting. But when the three approached the British embassy, they were fobbed off with the words "Come back in a few days." As the fugitives had evaded the Romanian internment regulations, they were in fear of being picked up at any moment by the Romanian police. In their distress they called on the French embassy. There they were cordially received and immediately given entry visas to France. The French were most anxious to enlist the Poles to work with the French Cipher Bureau. Bertrand had specially traveled to Romania to look for his Polish colleagues. He had also located several technicians from Warsaw who had been involved in the construction of a copy of Enigma and had built the cyclometer and several bombes.

Bertrand put them all up at the Château de Vignolles, a manor at Gretz-Armainvilliers southeast of Paris. The château was given the cover name Bruno. The group immediately set about rebuilding Enigma. Parts of it were commissioned from workshops scattered far outside Paris—nobody was to guess the real purpose of the individual components—which were then assembled at Bruno. So far the cipher created with the five drums had not been broken. Bruno cooperated with the British cipher service, which had itself begun to build bombes.

The Polish group at Bruno maintained close contact with Britain. In mid-January 1940, they had a visit from a twenty-eight-year-old mathematician from Cambridge, Alan Turing, who was later to wage war against Enigma with great success. Bruno exchanged messages with England by teleprinter, the cables running over four hundred miles through French and British territory. There was a risk that the line had been tapped. To make sure that their teletypes could not be read by the Germans, the cryptologists encoded their messages, using for that purpose the Enigma copies they had built. After all, they knew how difficult decoding an Enigma message was. Sometimes they tried to imitate the style of those messages and concluded with "Heil Hitler!" From June 1940 on, the group was able to send decoded German Enigma signals to England.

By then the Germans had marched into France, Holland, and Belgium and were within a few miles of Gretz-Armainvilliers. The Bruno bureau had to be hurriedly evacuated. For a short while the team was in Paris, where they worked around the clock on the signals of the advancing German army. Then they had to flee. Even during their escape to the south, they worked on intercepted radio signals. When France capitulated, Bertrand, along with fifteen Poles and seven Spaniards, went to Algeria. (The Spaniards were involved with deciphering Italian radio traffic.) On October 1, the group set up a new bureau at Uzès, northeast of Nîmes, at the Château de Fouzes, which received the camouflage name Cadix. The team itself had the code name Group 300. Now the decoders were on the territory of the Vichy government, which cooperated with the Germans. It was their task to pass on deciphered signals to the British. Group 300 had decoded over six hundred signals intended for the German troops under Field Marshal Rommel's command in North Africa.

Toward the end of 1941, Różycki, the youngest of the three Polish mathematicians, was working in Algeria at a field station of the French Cipher Bureau. For his return to Vichy France, he boarded the French liner *Lamorcière*. It has never been established whether the ship ran aground on a reef or struck a mine. Różycki was among the dead.

In September 1942, Bertrand learned that a German special unit had arrived at Montpellier to find secret radio transmitters. For transmitting to London the decoded messages intended for the German Africa Corps, Cadix used a transmitter smuggled in from England. It was only a matter of time before the Germans would find it. In point of fact, power was switched off in various districts at irregular hours of the day and night in order to discover the location of the transmitter by the interruption of its transmissions. On November 6, the German direction-finding team searched two farmsteads in the neighborhood. Cadix was hurriedly evacuated. A few days later, Hitler's army marched into the part of France that until then had been unoccupied. Thus the château fell into their hands.

Rejewski and Zygalski tried to reach England. They had to take a roundabout route via Spain, Portugal, and Gibraltar, and they were repeatedly arrested. After more than eight months, they reached their destination, joined the Polish army in exile, and were instructed to decode the Playfair ciphers of the SS.

It is not clear why these two outstanding cipher experts were not employed on the really difficult problems. Somehow the British would not accept that the Poles had made so much progress with the Enigma deciphering. The newly established British Ultra project now had the task of working on Enigma-encoded signals, and the Poles were never included in that enterprise. From August 1939 on, there was a large establishment at Bletchley Park, an estate north of London, with a staff of thousands, all of them busy deciphering Enigma signals. But it was thirty years after the war before Rejewski learned of this activity.

At the end of World War II, there were some twenty thousand Polish soldiers in the West. Only ten percent of them were willing to return to Communist Poland; these included Rejewski. Back in Poland, he looked in vain for the position of mathematics teacher at a high school. Little is known about how he spent the next few years. In his official obituary of 1980, issued by the Polish government, it is stated rather mysteriously that he had worked for twenty years in various branches of the administration in Bydgoszcz and had retired in 1967.

REJEWSKI'S LAST DECODING

In the summer of 1976, Marian Rejewski was asked by a Polish friend from World War II, then living in England, to have a look at an encoded letter dating back to 1904. At that time part of Poland had belonged to Russia and part to Germany, and Josef Pilsudski, the leader of the Polish Socialist Party, was seeking international help in the establishment of an independent Poland. Pilsudski had also approached Japan, which was just then at war with Russia. There exist a lot of coded documents from those days, documents that no one managed to decipher. Hence this appeal to Rejewski's skill. But he declined. The copy shown him was poor; some symbols were missing at the edge and others were illegible. But reading the account of a Warsaw friend of how Rejewski, almost against his will, nevertheless solved the problem, one is reminded of Sir Arthur Conan Doyle's description of the work of Sherlock Holmes.

Rejewski really wanted to have a vacation with his family. But Mrs. Rejewski told the friend that her husband was behaving oddly. He would walk up and down in his room for hours. Then suddenly he told his family to take their vacation without him and leave him behind in Warsaw. Some time later, the friend received a telephone call: Rejewski asked him to visit. When the friend arrived, he found an exhausted and totally changed Rejewski. Brusquely Rejewski held out a sheet of paper, the result of his work over the past few months.

He had deciphered the secret text of 1904. As the solution was sent to his wartime friend in England, Rejewski informed him that he wished to receive no further texts.[4]

While the military men were showered with medals after the war, the service of the intelligence people remained unacknowledged. At the end of the war, Rejewski and Zygalski were made lieutenants. Zygalski remained in England, taught at a college, and died in 1978. In that same year, Rejewski was offered an honorary degree in Poland, but he showed no interest. Not until some thirty years after the war was his achievement made known in France, by Bertrand. Film and television took up the story of his life. Rejewski died in 1980, at the age of seventy-four. The conqueror of the German Enigma machine was one of the men who had a major share in the Allied victory over Nazi Germany.

But the name of another of the three Polish cryptologists was to make international headlines, in 1964. At the Olympic Games in Tokyo, an art student won a silver medal for the Polish fencing team. He was the son of Jerzy Różycki, who had lost his life in a shipwreck in January of 1942.

THE BLETCHLEY PARK CROWD

One of the members of the British delegation at the 1939 Warsaw meeting was Commander Alistair Denniston, head of the Government Code and Cypher School, who had worked for the Admiralty as a cryptologist, a member of the famous Room 40 in World War I. He is described as a quiet, slightly reserved man; he was about fifty at the time.

The British government, realizing the importance of the cipher department, requisitioned an aristocratic country mansion in a secluded neighborhood near the village of Bletchley, some forty miles north of

London, and Denniston's Cypher School—this was its official spelling—
moved there in August 1939. The cryptologists began their work in what
used to be the stables. In addition to Denniston, the group included other
veterans of Room 40, such as William F. Clarke and Nigel de Grey. De
Grey had been one of the first to hold the ciphertext of Zimmermann's
telegram in his hands. More experts needed to be hired. Mathematicians
were to be found mainly at Cambridge University.

Just then the young English mathematician Alan Mathison Turing had
returned to Cambridge from the United States. Turing, born in London in
1912, entered King's College, Cambridge, at age nineteen. A mere four
years later, his doctoral thesis won him a prize. In 1936, he went to
Princeton for a couple of years. There he concerned himself with mathematical logic and the theory of electrical computers. Although these did
not then exist, their way of working was already a subject of theoretical
study. After the war, Turing was to play an important role in the development of the first computers. At Bletchley Park he made the acquaintance
of Enigma and also learned some details about the Polish bombe.

This, in short, was the situation at the time. The Poles were able to read
the signals of the three-rotor Enigma that had a choice of five rotors. To
these five rotors two more had been added, and subsequently rotor VIII. All
this made decoding an ever more complicated and lengthy process. And
then the Germans changed the transmission of the signal key. In May 1940,
the helpful six symbols at the beginning of the signal disappeared. It became
more and more laborious to try out all the possible settings of the machine.

Turing now constructed bombes that were more efficient than the
Polish *bomby*. The sophisticated machines required technicians for their
maintenance and repair. Radio operators were needed to lie in wait for
signals, around the clock and on all relevant frequencies, and to record the
countless messages. Only then could the most important people, the
decoders, get down to their job. Together with the auxiliary staff, some
ten thousand people were working at Bletchley Park.

The English bombe scanned the thousands of signals intercepted
every day for words frequent in military jargon, such as *oberkommando*
(high command), *fuehrerhauptquartier* (the Führer's headquarters), or
kommandeur (commanding officer). In this the decoders were helped by
the fact that with Enigma the plaintext letter and the ciphertext letter can
never be the same: the curse of the reflecting cylinder. If therefore the letter **F** occurred at some place in the ciphertext, they could be certain that

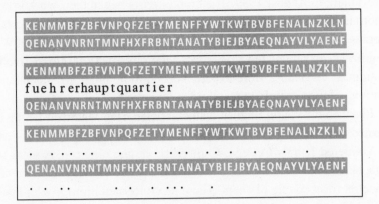

Fig. 10.2. Top: a ciphertext obtained by substitution. As with an Enigma encoding, no letter in the German plaintext has been transposed into the same ciphertext letter. In this text, the word *fuehrerhauptquartier* is suspected to be present. Center: a possible position of the plaintext word *fuehrerhauptquartier* in the ciphertext. In this position there are no identical letters aligned with each other. Bottom: dots under the ciphertext indicate the places where the suspected plaintext word *fuehrerhauptquartier* might begin.

the plaintext word *fuehrerhauptquartier* could not begin at that spot. One only had to write down the plaintext word *fuehrerhauptquartier* on a slip of paper and place this below the ciphertext: if two identical letters were aligned with each other, then this was not the position for the plaintext word.

Let us look at the simple cipher of eighty-seven symbols in figure 10.2, top. If it has been so encoded that the same plaintext and ciphertext letter can never stand one above the other, then there are only twenty-eight places in the text where the word can start. The word can start, for instance, when it stands under the ciphertext at the very beginning (fig. 10.2, center). The plaintext and ciphertext letters above each other are all different. But this is no longer the case if the plaintext word is moved one letter to the right: then a **T** stands above a *t*. Dots under the ciphertext in figure 10.2, bottom, indicate the twenty-eight possible beginnings of the plaintext word. For each of these, you can in principle try out all rotor positions to establish if one of them transposes the plaintext word into the cipher group in question. Naturally, if *fuehrerhauptquartier* does not occur in the text at all, the procedure fails.[5]

At times the British even tried to get certain words into the German radio signals. If, for example, they ordered a light buoy marking an important channel to be destroyed from the air, they could expect German shipping to be notified by radio of the failure of that buoy. That meant that the encoded word *leuchtboje* (light buoy) would very probably occur in the signals. Thus a shot-up buoy could show the way to the correct rotor position.

Plaintext words assumed to be contained in a signal were called *cribs* in Bletchley Park parlance. The bombes needed cribs in order to encode them with the largest possible number of applicable rotor selections, rotor sequences, ring settings, and cabling options and to discover if the resulting letter combinations occurred in the intercepted signal. If a letter combination occurred, then a bombe setting might indicate the daily key used for the signal. Useful cribs were provided also by stereotype forms of address, such as an officer's rank and service branch, all of which occurred frequently in the plaintexts. There was a catalog in Bletchley Park that contained the ciphers of the word *eins* (one) for various possible daily keys. As Enigma could not encode numerals, they had to be spelled out. It paid off, therefore, to search Enigma signals for the plaintext word *eins*.

But the Bletchley Park decoders did not always need to get their bombes to test all possible rotor settings. During the war, the Germans were not allowed to use the same rotor selection and sequence twice in the same month. As the month advanced, the bombes, instead of running through sixty possible settings, therefore had to try out fewer and fewer of them. Another aid to the Bletchley Park experts were signals that were encoded both by Enigma and by some other, more easily breakable, system. Thus if a waterway was mined, this warning had to be transmitted not only to the German U-boats by the Enigma system, but also to the minesweepers that used simpler ciphers—and with these the Allies were familiar.

In effect the British bombe was a computer. It contained about thirty-three rotor instruments. The rotors were electrically driven. It could take many hours for the bombe to discover a particular word in a ciphertext. But at other times the correct rotor position was hit on after a mere ten minutes. The first bombe designed by Turing went into operation in January 1940. Later the mathematician Gordon Welchman succeeded in introducing improvements. At the end of 1941, Bletchley Park had twelve such machines at its disposal; by March 1943, there were sixty. But even then the computers sometimes needed up to three days, working around the clock, to find a daily key. The first successful decipherings were made at Bletchley Park in the spring of 1940, during the German campaign in Norway. A year later, the British were able to read a substantial portion of the Enigma radio traffic. In a German aircraft shot down off Norway, an Enigma machine was found and sent on to Bletchley Park along with the codebook. In the campaign in France, a German reconnaissance unit, ventured too far ahead with its tanks. When they were captured, the Allies found more useful material. In May 1941, the Royal Navy captured a German U-boat, again complete with Enigma and codebook. All the information thus gained was utilized in the further development of the bombe.

THE TRAGIC STORY OF ALAN TURING

On September 4, 1939, three days after Hitler's attack on Poland, Alan Turing, aged twenty-seven, began his employment at Bletchley Park. While still at Princeton, he had concerned himself with cryptology, speculating on how symbols could be replaced by numbers, then multiplied by a secret number, with the result to be transmitted as a ciphertext. When it first occurred to him, sometime in 1937, that Britain might be involved in a war with Germany, he concluded that this secret number would have to be long enough to ensure that a hundred Germans working eight hours a day would need a hundred years to discover it by systematic trial and error. Turing had also given some thought to the problem of how multiplications could be performed by electrical circuits, and he had himself constructed a small electronic calculating machine that did just that.

In Bletchley Park, Turing was the right man in the right place. As early as January 1940, he traveled to France to visit the Polish mathematicians at Bruno; he was keenly interested in their bombes. What he learned from them and his own earlier reflections probably provided the concept of the *Turing Bombe*. British sources contain little information on this meeting of mathematicians—further proof of British efforts to downplay the contribution of the Polish cryptologists.

After the end of the war, Turing worked at the National Laboratory of

Physics, and from 1948 on he directed work on the development of a computing center at the University of Manchester. Time and again he reflected on the extent to which a machine could think, that is, the extent to which what we now call artificial intelligence could be accomplished.

The mathematical genius was also a homosexual. As nature had made him that way, he found it perfectly natural, made no secret of it, and experienced no sense of guilt. He hoped that homosexuality would soon be legitimized in Britain. But at the time it was still regarded as "gross indecency contrary to Section 11 of the Criminal Law Amendment Act 1885."[6] His sexual orientation eventually became his downfall. In December 1951, he met Arnold Murray in the street; Murray was nineteen and unemployed. Between the unequal partners a sexual relationship quickly developed. Soon, however, Turing had reason to mistrust Murray, who kept borrowing money from him without ever paying it back. Murray probably also stole from him.

On January 23, Turing's apartment was broken into. Only a few things were missing, of a total value of about fifty pounds. When Turing challenged his partner, Murray assured him that he had had no part in the theft but admitted having told an unemployed friend about Turing's apartment, whereupon that friend suggested Murray should burgle it. Murray had refused, but he was convinced that his acquaintance had done the burglary.

Turing reported the incident to the police. But in his statements he tied himself up in such knots that the police found it easy to discover the truth about his partner and the unknown third man. Thus the mathematician became a criminal. The case *Regina v. Murray and Turing* came up on March 32, 1952. Both men pleaded guilty to all counts of the indictment (acts of gross indecency with a male person), but Murray's counsel succeeded in shifting the bulk of guilt on Turing, the older man, whom he accused of having seduced his client. Turing was sentenced to one year's imprisonment, with the choice of probation on condition he undergo chemical treatment. Instead of prison Turing chose "organotherapy," which was to make him impotent for the duration of the treatment. He kept his post at the university, and in May 1951 it was even decided to create for him a special department of computer theory in Manchester. But although British public opinion had become more liberal with regard to homosexuality, Turing suffered from the disgrace of the therapy and his public exposure.

On June 8, his housekeeper found him dead in his bed, foam at his mouth. The cause of death was cyanide poisoning. In the house the police found a container of potassium cyanide and a glass with cyanide solution. By the bed lay an apple that had been bitten into; Turing presumably had dipped it into the cyanide. The coroner concluded that it was suicide. In his book *Alan Turing*, Rolf Hochhuth points out that in the editions of the *Encyclopaedia Britannica* published prior to 1963, the mathematician was not even mentioned, but in later editions he was given prominence both as a logician and creator of the Turing Machine, a precursor of the modern computer. Hochhuth refers to Turing's merits in the war:

> But his most significant achievement, that presumably made him the savior, more than any other except Churchill, that is not mentioned by a single syllable! Furthermore . . . they write that though he took the poison himself, it was probably not with suicidal intent but as an experiment. They make no mention of his homosexuality trial. . . . But not to mention by a single word that Turing broke Enigma, that is the peak of infamy.[7]

Let us return to Bletchley Park, where Turing's bombes were deciphering the German Enigma signals during World War II. Anyone employed there had to sign the Official Secrets Act, binding him or her to lifelong silence about the work done there. Thus it happened that the work of the cryptologists around Turing remained hidden from the public during the first three postwar decades. But then Gustave Bertrand's wartime recollections appeared in France.[8] The secret of the struggle with Enigma was no longer secret. In Britain, Frederick W. Winterbotham in 1974 published his memoirs under the title *The Ultra Secret*.[9] Ultra was the code name for the deciphering of the Enigma signals at Bletchley Park.

THE SPY TO WHOM HITLER DISCLOSED HIS SECRETS

The deciphered Enigma signals were immediately passed on to the proper quarters, including Prime Minister Winston Churchill. One of the liaison people between Bletchley Park and the government was Winterbotham.

On July 13, 1917, during World War I, a German fighter shot down a British aircraft of the Nieuport type far behind the German lines in Belgium. After a crash landing, a German officer dragged the injured

British pilot, Winterbotham, out of the wreckage. The Englishman spent eighteen months in German captivity. Over that period he had time not only to get his broken nose healed but also to acquire the fundamentals of the German language. The impression he formed of the Germans then was to determine his whole future life. Remarks by officers of the defeated German army left no doubt in Winterbotham that sooner or later Germany would avenge the defeat suffered in World War I.

Back in England, he studied law, tried his hand as a farmer, and after 1930 worked for the air force division of the British secret service. At that time the Germans were not permitted to have an air force of their own. News, however, filtered to London that Russia was training German pilots. To gain information on this point was part of Winterbotham's duties. By 1930, Hitler's National Socialist German Workers' Party, the NSDAP, was a major force. Winterbotham traveled to Germany, where through the mediation of a correspondent of the London *Times* he succeeded in making contact with Alfred Rosenberg. Rosenberg was the chief ideologist of the NSDAP and, following Hitler's seizure of power in 1933, became head of the party's foreign policy department. In World War II, Rosenberg was Reich minister for the occupied eastern territories. In 1946, he was sentenced to death in the Nuremberg trial of the principal war criminals and executed. Contact between the British spy Winterbotham and the German minister Rosenberg continued over a period of nearly eight years.

Even before 1933, Rosenberg invited Winterbotham to Germany and introduced him to many influential figures, including Hitler. At the time the Nazis were anxious to maintain good relations with Britain—as Hitler, by then in power, very clearly stated to the Englishman in a conversation in 1934: "There should be only three major powers in the world—the British Empire, the Americas, and the German Empire of the future." He continued: "All we ask is that Britain should be content to look after her Empire and not interfere with Germany's plans of expansion."[10] Winterbotham also arranged a visit by Rosenberg to England.

Over the years, Winterbotham was a welcome guest not only among Hitler's leadership clique but also among the generals. What he learned on those occasions he combined with the reports that other agents sent to London. Frederick Winterbotham was no James Bond; he did not secretly photograph documents, did not send his reports back to England in code, did not try to gain unauthorized access to information. He did not have to listen surreptitiously; he simply listened when others chatted.

Above all, he was horrified at the rapid rearmament of the German air force—that was something he understood. In his memoirs he complains time and again that his warnings to England fell on deaf ears.[11]

His relations with those in power in the Third Reich came to an end in the fall of 1938. His interlocutors were becoming increasingly reserved: they were disappointed that they were apparently unable to influence British politicians through him. When, after the Reich Party Rally in Nuremberg, Winterbotham took his leave of Rosenberg, both men probably realized that they would not meet again.

Back in England, Winterbotham turned to another form of reconnaissance, aerial photography. This was then still in its infancy. He succeeded in installing concealed cameras in a Lockheed passenger aircraft. During ostensibly civilian flights, these were able to confirm the construction of new airfields in Germany.

According to Winterbotham, the Lockheed plane was exhibited at an air show in Frankfurt with the secret cameras well concealed. Albert Kesselring, then chief of the Luftwaffe general staff, was particularly interested in this plane and asked the pilot if he might test-fly it. The pilot who normally performed the espionage flights made this possible for him. Kesselring was delighted as they flew over the Rhine. Just then the pilot noticed below them certain construction sites that he had not yet photographed. Surreptitiously he turned on the cameras. Thus the chief of the German Luftwaffe general staff unwittingly participated in British secret service espionage photographs.

ULTRA'S SUCCESSFUL ADVANCE

During World War II, Winterbotham was responsible, with others, for the evaluation of the Enigma radio traffic deciphered at Bletchley Park. He was one of the first to break the thirty years' silence about the work done there.

The British penetrated the German traffic in the very first year of the war. Thus, on August 8, 1940, Bletchley Park decoded Hermann Göring's Order of the Day proclaiming Operation *Adler* (Eagle), the air battle over England, later to be known as the Battle of Britain. Churchill immediately received a copy of the text.

vonreichsmarschallgoeringanalleeinheitenderluftflottendreiundzwanzi-
gundfuenfoperationadlerinkuerzesterzeitwerdensiediebritischeair-
forcevomhimmelfegenheilhitler

(From Reich Marshal Goering to all units of air fleets 23 and 5.
Operation Eagle very shortly. You will sweep the British air force from
the sky. Heil Hitler.)

Further messages on Operation Eagle came in. Ultra was able to observe
the preparations. When the attack came, the British were ready for it.
The first wave of German bombers was intercepted while still over the
Channel, and only a few got through. In their second attack also the
Germans suffered heavy losses.

Göring's plan ran like this: first bomb all airfields and destroy as
many bombers as possible, next involve the British fighters in engage-
ments with German fighters, which the British were bound to lose.
Thanks to Ultra, the British knew about the plan. They dispersed their aircraft, camouflaged, between many airfields, and their fighters did not
accept combat with the Germans. This counterstrategy led to differences
of opinion within the Royal Air Force, since Göring's intentions were not
known to many officers. Ultra was so secret that only a handful of initi-
ates were allowed to know that Enigma signals could be read.

When his plan failed, Göring changed strategy and concentrated his
forces on the bombing of London. It is said that this was his greatest mistake. On September 5, he ordered the annihilation of London's docks by
three hundred bombers. The bombers were to be escorted by fighters.
Within minutes the order was communicated to Winston Churchill.
Admittedly it was a heavy raid, but the British, having been forewarned,
were able to make sure that their fighters remained intact. On September
17, 1940, the Germans came again. But thanks to Ultra, they were expected,
and the attack was warded off. Two days later, Ultra learned that the war
material assembled in Holland for the invasion of the British Isles was
being removed by the Wehrmacht. Hitler's operation SEELÖWE, the
conquest of Britain, had been canceled.

The terror was not over. According to Winterbotham, in November
1940 Ultra learned of an imminent air raid on Coventry. Churchill, he
reports, from that moment faced a difficult decision. If the city was evacuated, the Germans would know that their Enigma signals were being

read by the British, and the Allies would give away a vast advantage in the conduct of the war. Churchill was confronted with the choice between saving some human lives in Coventry during the next few days and saving many more lives in the long run by not revealing the secret of Ultra. He chose the latter course. In order to keep the damage in Coventry as small as possible, he ordered the fire trucks and ambulances there to be reinforced and put on alert. This story has been challenged.[12] Winterbotham's book, published in 1974, also caused irritation in broad circles because it mentioned neither Rejewski nor Turing and because it conveyed the impression that Ultra was the reason Hitler gave up his plan to invade England. Historians regard this as an exaggeration.[13]

On the other hand, the contribution of Ultra to the Battle of the Atlantic was unquestionably crucial.

THE BATTLE OF THE ATLANTIC

On September 28, 1941, the German U-boats U-67 and U-111 tried to torpedo HMS *Clyde* off the Cape Verde Islands. Just then, unexpectedly, a British submarine appeared and drove off the attackers. Admiral Dönitz, the commander-in-chief of the German U-boat fleet, became suspicious. It could hardly be by accident that in such unfrequented waters an enemy submarine should show up at the right moment. Either the attack itself had been betrayed or the German signals were being read by the enemy.

Four months later, the German U-boats began to operate with a new type of Enigma, which now had four rotors—the "Greek drum" had been added, also called the beta drum, which was thinner than the others. In addition, the new Enigmas were equipped with a thinner and differently wired reflecting cylinder. The Greek drum, the thin reflecting cylinder, and the three rotors of the older type all fitted into the casing of the three-rotor Enigmas. Unlike the old rotors, the new rotor was not rotated in operation. It always remained in the position in which it had been installed. If it was installed so that the letter A showed in the window, then its wiring, along with that of the thin reflecting cylinder, worked just as the old, thick, reflecting cylinder. In this position, the new four-rotor Enigma behaved just like the old three-rotor machine, which made it possible for messages to be exchanged between a new-type and an old-type Enigma. This was done for unimportant messages, such as weather reports.

The fourth rotor provided Enigma with twenty-six times as many possible settings as the earlier version. Anyone trying to run them through a bombe now had twenty-six times the former work.

From February 1, 1942, on, the new machine was used for signal traffic with the U-boats in the Atlantic. The British now no longer knew where the German U-boats were—with the result that convoys from America could no longer be guided along secure routes. The consequences were disastrous. American shipyards were feverishly building new ships, but most of them crossed the Atlantic only three times before they were sunk. The number of available ships dropped: the German U-boat fleet grew.

The Bletchley Park group called for a greater number of high-speed bombes, but then they had a stroke of luck. The weather reports became the Germans' doom.

Toward the end of October 1942, four British destroyers near the harbor of Haifa, Israel, tracked down U-559, a German U-boat based at Messina in Sicily. With a total of 288 depth charges, they forced Kommandant Heidtmann to surface. No sooner was the heavily damaged U-boat on the surface than it was fired at from all sides. The crew tried to save themselves by jumping overboard. A few British sailors swam across to the U-boat to salvage secret material. As more and more water entered the hull, they seized a signal book and the key then used for weather reports. Two of the British sailors were unable to find their way out of the sinking vessel.

The weather key helped the Bletchley Park experts understand how the German navy operated the four-rotor Enigma. The weather reports were transmitted in three-drum encoding, in other words, with the Greek drum in the A position. Not only were the Bletchley Park people able to read these signals, but thanks to the weather key of U-559 they were also able to determine the positions of the three movable rotors. For subsequent important signals the German encoders left the three movable rotors in their previous positions and changed only the setting of the Greek drum. But the positions of the movable rotors were known to the British from the weather reports. All they had to find out was in which of the twenty-six positions the Greek drum was set—a much simpler problem.

After December 13, 1942, the signals of the German navy were no longer secret to Bletchley Park. Up to three thousand deciphered signals about operations in the Atlantic would arrive there each day.[14] A week later, the Admiralty once more knew the locations of the German U-boats in the Atlantic. The convoys were now able to avoid them. At last more ships were being built than sunk. A page had been turned in the Battle of the Atlantic.

JAPANESE RADIO SIGNALS FROM BURNING BERLIN

In March 1945, the Soviet troops sweeping in from the east were once more temporarily halted along the Oder-Neisse line and in the Giant Mountains. The German western front, however, had collapsed, and the Allies were approaching the Elbe. On March 8, the Allies intercepted a radio signal from Berlin and immediately passed it on to the U.S. Army Cipher Section near Washington, DC. There was no difficulty in deciphering it. Its sender was the Japanese ambassador, Oshima Hiroshi, who had already sent several coded reports to Tokyo from bomb-shattered Berlin. On October 9, 1942, for instance, he had reported on a visit to Hitler's east Prussian headquarters, where Hitler told him that he suspected that the Allies, coming from Africa, would land in the Balkans and not in Italy. In the fall of 1943, Oshima visited the Western Wall, the defense system that Hitler had ordered to be set up against an attack from the west. On this Oshima reported to Tokyo in great detail, in thousands of words.

Then, in the spring of 1945, his report was addressed to Foreign Minister Shigemitsu Mamoru. The report contained no military secrets; it merely described conditions in a dying Berlin. Gas had become exceedingly scarce and could be bought only on the black market, in exchange for coffee. Traffic across the city was impeded by barricades set up everywhere, especially in the government quarter. They were two-to-three meters high and one-to-two meters thick. Prisoners of war, convicts, *Volkssturm** men and women built from rubble and bricks.[15]

The Allies were able to read the Japanese signals, since they were

---

*A paramilitary troop made up of those too young, too old, or too weak for the regular army.

encoded with a machine the Americans called Purple. This was the Japanese counterpart to Enigma, with plugboard, four-step switches as used in telephony, and two typewriters. The plaintext was typed into one typewriter, and the other produced the ciphertext. The Japanese words were printed in Latin script. Certain groups of three were used for punctuation. Decoding initially proved very difficult. Only when garbled signals were repeated did it become slowly possible to penetrate the secrets of Purple. A major part in this success was played by William Friedman.

Enigma and Purple, just as the Hagelin machines used by the Americans in World War II, represented a peak in mechanical encrypting. Yet a new era had been initiated with the Polish *bomby* and the bombes of Bletchley Park: encrypting with electronic machines. The computer was moving into cryptology.

NOTES

1. Brian Johnson, *The Secret War* (London: British Broadcasting Corporation, 1978) 311ff.

2. Friedrich L. Bauer, *Decrypted Secrets: Methods and Maxims of Cryptology* (New York: Springer Verlag, 1997) 376.

3. Subsequently, after the German occupation of France, Rex was to betray the spy Asche. In July 1943, Asche was executed.

4. Wladislaw Kozaczuk, "A New Challenge for the Old Enigma Buster," *Cryptologia* (July 1990) 204.

5. Here I have taken a text that contains the plaintext word *fuehrerhauptquartier*, but have not encoded it according to the Enigma principle, choosing a simple monalphabetic code instead. The code, however, is such that, as with Enigma, it will not substitute a letter for itself.

6. Andrew Hodges, *Alan Turing: The Enigma* (London: Burnett Books, 1983) 458.

7. Rolf Hochhuth, *Alan Turing* (Reinbek: Rowohlt Verlag, 1987) 165.

8. Gustave Bernard, *Enigma ou la plus grande enigme de la guerre, 1939-1945* (Paris: Pion, 1973).

9. Frederick W. Winterbotham, *The Ultra Secret* (London: Weidenfeld and Nicolson, 1974).

10. Frederick W. Winterbotham, *The Nazi Connection* (New York: Dell, 1978) 53.

11. I do not know how reliable Winterbotham's later reports to his superiors were. In his memoirs he states that he called the German escort assigned to him Charlie, because he believed there was a German phrase "guter Karl": evidently he confused Karl with Kerl. He also refers to a port city Wannemünde, evidently Warnemünde,and refers to the "Danziger Geldwasser" instead of Goldwasser, and the "Tegelsee" near Munich instead of Tegernsee.

12. The American historian Forrest Pogue and others regard the story of Churchill's tolerating the bombing of Coventry as an invention (see, e.g., David Kahn, *Kahn on Codes* [New York: Macmillan, 1983] 96). Whatever the background of the tragedy of Coventry, the Allies could not fully utilize the information they had from Ultra without revealing that they could read the German signals. Winterbotham's version is contradicted also by Stuart Milner-Barry, who was working then in the section responsible for the rough translation of the signals, known as Hut 6. He recalls that a planned attack was indeed announced in an Enigma signal but that the target was not identified by name—it was identified by a number that the decoders were unable to interpret. Milner-Barry believes he remembers that the attack was expected to be on London (F. Harry Hinsley and Alan Stripp, *Code Breakers* [Oxford: Oxford Universtiy Press, 1993] 95).

13. Kahn, *Kahn on Codes*, 110.

14. Andrew Hodges, *Alan Turing: The Enigma* (London: Burnett Books, 1983) 244.

15. Carl Boyd, "Anguish under Siege: High-Grade Japanese Signal Intelligence and the Fall of Berlin," *Cryptologia* (July 1989) 194.

11. THE ARRIVAL OF THE COMPUTER

> Governments keep a lot of secrets from their people. . . .
> Why aren't the people in return allowed to keep secrets
> from the government?
>
> —PHILIP ZIMMERMANN, *Der Spiegel*

> The uncontrolled use of cryptography by criminals and
> terrorists represents an unacceptable risk.
>
> —LOUIS FREEH, FBI Director

LETTERS AND NUMERALS ARE GREAT for writing and calculating. But when, in 1833, the Göttingen mathematician Carl Friedrich Gauss and his colleague, the physicist Wilhelm Weber, constructed the first telegraph, they realized that an electric wire could carry only pulses of current. At about that same time, the American artist and inventor Samuel Finlay Morse was facing the same problem. He encoded letters and numerals into long and short pulses. This is how the Morse alphabet originated: *a* is short-long, *b* is long-short-short-short, . . . *z* is long-long-short-short. Even the most moving poems or plays can be converted into a sequence of long and short beeps and broadcast as radio signals.

The Morse symbols can also be expressed as numerical sequences: long is one, and short is zero. In that case *a* becomes 01, *b* becomes 1000, . . . *z* becomes 1100. Unlike alphabetic numbering (a = 1, b = 2, . . . z = 26), the only numbers used here are 0 and 1. This is something we are not accustomed to, since we calculate in a decimal system that uses, in addition to 0 and 1, the numbers 2 to 9. We do this because we have ten fingers. But one can also envisage numerical systems for people with six fingers or with only two. Such systems are in no way inferior to ours.

OTHER NUMERICAL SYSTEMS

Who wastes any time reflecting about a number he writes down—such as 1997? Of course the writer is aware that these symbols represent one thousand plus another nine hundred years, to which are added nine times ten years and finally another seven. The ancient Romans would have written the figure differently: MCMXCVII. For an educated Roman, this notation was easily grasped; reading the figure, he would have a sense of its magnitude. But if he were to add two numbers, say MDCCXLVI and MMCXXVI, he would have difficulty doing so. In our system we write them as 1746 and 2126, and addition is easy, the sum being 3872.

In the decimal system, a numeral has different meanings according to where it appears in a number—such as the 9 in 1997. Reading from the right, we first have the number of units, then the number of tens; the next digit tells us the number of hundreds ($100 = 10 \times 10 = 10^2$). Next comes the number of thousands ($1000 = 10^3$), and so on. For addition, we combine the numbers of the same order of digits. If the result exceeds nine, we put down only the amount exceeding ten and increase the sum of the next higher digit (to the left) by 1. In our way of notation, every number is written as a sum of powers of ten, and we put down only the number of each power of ten:

$$1746 = 1 \times 10^3 + 7 \times 10^2 + 4 \times 10^1 + 6$$

We call this presentation of numbers the *decimal system*. In our long history we have on occasion also used our toes and calculated in a system of twenty. Traces of this are found to this day in the French language, where 80 is not eight times ten but four times twenty, *quatre-vingt*. An eye clinic in Paris, built in the thirteenth century for three hundred blinded war veterans, is to this day called Hôpital des Quinze-Vingt, literally, Hospital of the Fifteen Twenties. The Maya and Aztecs also had a system of twenty. But since Donald Duck and his other cartoon friends have a thumb and only three fingers on each hand, logically they would use a system of eight the same way we use the decimal system. They would therefore count: 1, 2, 3, 4, 5, 6, 7, 10, 11, ... 16, 17, 20, 21, . . . In the Ducksville system, the number that we write as 1746 would have to be composed of powers of 8, that is:

$$1746 = 3 \times 8^3 + 3 \times 8^2 + 2 \times 8^1 + 2$$

Our 1746 would be 3322 to Donald Duck. Note that this is the same number but in a different notation.

Addition in the system of eight is the same as in ours, except that the carrying of ten is replaced by the carrying of eight. Let us take the abovementioned calculation 1746 + 2126 = 3872 in the decimal system. In the system of eight, the three numbers 1746, 2126, and 3872 become 3322, 4116, and 7440. Just as 3872 is the sum in the decimal system, 7440 is the sum in the system of eight. Donald Duck and his friends add like this:

$$\begin{array}{r} 3322 \\ 4116 \\ \hline 7440 \end{array}$$

The result is the same in both systems, though it is written differently, because different numerical systems are merely different languages in which a number is expressed. Relations between numbers are independent of numerical systems. The even number 10 is divisible by 2 also in a system of three, where it is written as 101, because in a ternary system $101 = 12 + 12 = 2 \times 12$.

One could envisage other numerical systems, such as one with a base of 13 for the inhabitants of a planet with six fingers on one hand and seven on the other.

HOW MANY FINGERS DO VENUSIANS HAVE?

Martin Gardner, well known for his many mathematical brainteasers in the journal *Scientific American,* came up with the following puzzle.[1] A space capsule, after a soft landing on the surface of Venus, radios back to Earth the picture of a rock face into which the following symbols are scratched:

$$\begin{array}{r} \square\ @ \\ \square\ @ \\ \hline \square\ \ast\ \square \end{array}$$

Evidently this is an addition noted down by the Venusians. It appears that they are using a numerical system similar to ours. If the basis of their system is determined by the number of fingers on one hand, how many fingers do the Venusians have on each hand?

MATHEMATICS IN A TWO-FINGER WORLD

The binary system is important if numbers are to be sent down electrical lines. We already know that the Morse alphabet knows only two symbols, long and short.

Creatures with only two fingers do not count $0, 1, 2, 3, \ldots 9, 10, 11$, 12, but 0, 1, 10, 11, 100, 101, 110, 111, 1000, 1001, 1010, 1011, $\ldots$ Instead of 8, the two-finger world writes 1000, because $1000 = 2^3 = 8$. This is no different from our practice; we write 1000 for one thousand, because 1000 is 10^3. What, then, does our number 1764 look like in the binary system? Let us remember that $2^1 = 2, 2^2 = 4, 2^3 = 8, 2^4 = 16, 2^5 = 32, 2^6 = 64, 2^7 = 128, 2^8 = 256, 2^9 = 512,$ and $2^{10} = 1024$.

It follows therefore that $1764 = 1 \times 2^{10} + 1 \times 2^9 + 0 \times 2^8 + 1 \times 2^7 + 1 \times 2^6 + 1 \times 2^5 + 0 \times 2^4 + 0 \times 2^3 + 1 \times 2^2 + 0 \times 2^1 + 0$.

In the binary system this is 11011100100. Compared to our traditional notation it seems rather cumbersome, but 11011100100 can be sent down a wire in no time. Let us, for practice, calculate another example in the binary system. Let us take $7 + 13 = 20$. In the binary system the 7 becomes $1 \times 2^2 + 1 \times 2^1 + 1$, the number 111, and the 13 becomes 1101. We add these up, remembering that $1 + 1 = 10$:

$$
\begin{array}{r}
111 \\
\underline{1101} \\
10100
\end{array}
$$

The last number means $1 \times 2^4 + 1 \times 2^2$, which is $16 + 4 = 20$. It does not matter which system we work in.

The procedure of adding two *binary* numbers, as numbers formulated in the binary system are called, is the same as adding in the decimal system. As soon as the sum of two numerals reaches or exceeds the ten, we carry the ten in the decimal system. Analogously, in the binary system we carry the two whenever the sum of two numerals reaches 2. The inhabitants of Ducksville in their system of eight carry the 8.

However, in the decimal system we have already come across addition that does not carry the ten. Admittedly this does not give us a correct result, but from two numbers—a plaintext number and a key number—it produces a third number, the ciphertext number. Richard Sorge's radio operator added like that, and we did the same on page 17. Accordingly we now add numbers in the binary system without carrying the two. In the example above, we thus obtain

$$
\begin{array}{r}
111 \\
\underline{1101} \\
1010
\end{array}
$$

That is, 10 in the decimal system. This strange way of addition without carrying the two does not therefore give us the mathematical sum, which would be 20. It does, however, turn two numbers into a third. This was noticed by a young American engineer as early as 1917.

CIPHERS IN THE TELEX SYSTEM

Gilbert S. Vernam worked in a team of the American Telephone and Telegraph Company, AT&T. The great novelty at that time was a telegraph apparatus that could print. No longer did a long strip of paper with a series of dots and dashes come out of the machine, but a finished text printed by an electric typewriter. The principle is still used in telex operations. The electric machine was governed by a strip of paper into which holes had been punched in groups of five (fig. 11.1)

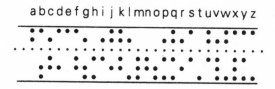

abcdefghi j klmnopqr stuvwxyz

Fig. 11.1. Letters, numerals, and punctuation marks are represented in the telex system by punched holes and unpunched spaces on a paper strip. The continuous horizontal line of small holes serves the movement of the strip through the machine. As the strip passes through the telex machine over a metal base, five electrically conductive sensors probe the paper strip. When a hole passes a sensor, a circuit is closed.

The code goes back to the French inventor J. M. E. Baudot. Each sign corresponds to a combination of five punched holes and nonpunched spaces in the strip, separated by a row of smaller sprocket holes for feeding the strip through the machine. In this manner all letters, numerals, and punctuation marks can be represented in a binary system. Thus a is expressed in the strip as hole, hole, sprocket hole, vacant, vacant, vacant, or as the binary number 11 000. The letter z is 10 001.

This makes encoding in the Baudot system possible. Let us take the word *rose*, that is, 01010 00011 10100 10000. As a keyword we again choose *KAHN*, in the code of the telex strip 11110 11000 00101 00110. If, as in figure 11.2, we add these two numbers without carrying the two, we obtain a ciphertext. To reconstruct the plaintext, the decoder merely subtracts the key from the ciphertext.

plaintext:	01 010	00 011	10 100	10 000
key:	*11 110*	*11 000*	*00 101*	*00 110*
ciphertext:	**10 100**	**11 011**	**10 001**	**10 110**

Fig. 11.2

Vernam constructed a device that was able to read two paper strips simultaneously, symbol by symbol. Both made holes and left unpunched vacant spots in the code of five described above. One strip contained the plaintext, the other the key. While the machine probed both strips simultaneously, it punched out the ciphertext on a third strip. In this operation, a hole was punched whenever the plaintext showed a hole and the key none, or the other way around, and no hole was punched whenever the two strips both had a hole or no hole in the same spot.

This corresponds exactly to addition in the binary system without the carrying of two, since $0 + 1$ and $1 + 0$ give 1, while $0 + 0$ and $1 + 1$ give 0. For decoding, the machine subtracted the key from the ciphertext according to the rules $0 - 1 = 1$, $1 - 0 = 1$, $0 - 0 = 0$, and $1 - 1 = 0$. By means of wiring that either punched holes or left vacant spaces according to these rules, the plaintext was recovered in binary form and could be printed out on a typewriter.

Sender and receiver had to be in possession of the same key strip. Initially the AT&T engineers glued the beginnings and the ends of their key strips together into loops. This gave them a self-repeating key. The code could be broken by the same method as a Vigenère cipher according to Kasiski. While machine encoding made encrypting and deciphering easier, it did not enhance security unless very long loops were used. About the same time as the one-time pad, the method of infinitely long key words, was invented in Europe, Vernam's team also worked with extremely long paper strips as keys. The loop method did not catch on, and Vernam is one of the many inventors in the cipher field who died without amassing a fortune.

Vernam's principle was resurrected in Germany shortly before World War II and during the years that followed it. In 1941, a new cipher machine came into use, the Schlüsselzusatz, built by the firm Lorenz in versions SZ-40 and SZ-42. The plaintext was punched on a strip in Baudot code. As the strip was fed in, each of the five holes of the Baudot code was probed. The signal "hole" (1) or "nonhole" (0) of each of these rows was passed on to two rotors and encoded once. There were ten rotors. Encoding was performed in such a way that each of the ten rotors carried a certain number of pins on its outside—one of them, for instance, twenty-three, another fifty-nine. The pins could remain in their original position, which meant 1, or they could be depressed, which meant 0. In the Vernam method, each spot of the five rows of holes was electrically probed and the result (hole or nonhole, i.e., 1 or 0) was compared with the corresponding place of the key strip and linked to the position of the rotors at the time. The result for all five rows of holes of the plaintext strip was recorded, on a newly punched strip, as hole or nonhole. The new strip thus contained the ciphertext. Once a group of five of the plaintext had been read and punched out as ciphertext, the ten rotors moved on in a definite but irregular manner.

Ciphers produced by the Lorenz Schlüsselzusatz were used for top-level communication, for instance between Hitler's headquarters and the general staffs scattered all over Europe.

Alongside its work on Enigma, Bletchley Park was also concerned with this German cipher technique. Sophisticated though the system was, the British cracked it. For this, however, the normal bombes were no longer sufficient. New and more efficient machines were built, such as the Colossus computer. Whereas the bombes were electromechanical machines—with electromagnets driving the rotors, testing the relays as to whether a crib led to a possible daily key, and, if it did, stopping the rotors—the Colossus machines operated electronically. This means that circuits stored data, controlled the pace of calculation, and examined whether numbers stored in the binary system agreed with others or not. The first Colossus machine contained 1,500 valves—the transistor was not invented until 1948—and later models were equipped with 2,500.

Of course we need not depend on a paper strip with a hole-nonhole code in order to characterize numbers in the binary system. Electric pulses in a rhythmic sequence, that is, pulse and nonpulse, are equally suitable for the transmission of texts. They can be stored, moreover, in the form of magnetic patterns on a magnetic tape or on the hard disk of a computer. Strings of electronic switches can be put into on and off positions and binary numbers thus stored. The art of encrypting was given a new direction by the computer.

DES, THE AMERICAN STANDARD SYSTEM

In 1977, the American government introduced its new Data Encryption Standard, DES for short. It is probably the most frequently used system today. In its complete version this American invention may be used only with the permission of the American government. DES was initially developed by IBM. No one has so far succeeded in decoding a message encoded by DES, unless he knows the key.[2]

Readers interested in the details of this rather complicated method are referred to the simplified description in the box that follows.

Computers have made it possible to encode large quantities of data. In principle anyone with a PC can effortlessly encode his letters. This involves the state. It is an ancient tradition that states spy not only on their enemies but also on their allies; that citizens can keep their affairs secret from the state is something new. We increasingly move money along telecommunication channels. In order to allow such transactions to take place without interference, the instructions must be encoded. Anyone ordering merchandise over the Internet does not want his credit card number, let alone his PIN, to become known to a third party. Anyone wishing to read the balance of his account on his PC screen does not want an unauthorized person to gain this knowledge. As more and more information is exchanged electronically, the demand for encryption grows. But how does the state react to private encryption?

THE DES SCHEME

In the DES system, the plaintext is written in the form of binary numbers and divided into blocks of sixty-four numerals, that is, into chains of the form 0110011010100011010001 ... In computer parlance these are blocks of sixty-four *bits*. Each block undergoes a complicated procedure. A few hints are given below.

Sender and receiver possess a key—a block of fifty-six bits. From this the DES procedure produces sixteen partial keys of a length of forty-eight bits each. The method has a subprogram capable of combining a block of thirty-two bits with one of the partial keys mentioned, so that a new block of thirty-two is created. But this is only the preparatory stage.

First, each plaintext block is split into a left and a right block of thirty-two bits each. Next, in sixteen consecutive steps, the right and left blocks are exchanged and each time linked with one of the partial keys of forty-eight bits. Finally the two halves, shuffled beyond recognition and combined with partial keys, are reunited into a block of sixty-four bits. This is the ciphertext block. Only with a knowledge of the key can the decoder retrace the individual steps and thus arrive at the original block.

But even this method is still too simple. As every block of sixty-four is encrypted in the same way, identical plaintext blocks result in identical ciphertext blocks. In a sense, therefore, this method is monalphabetic. If several plaintexts begin with the same lengthy text, say an address or allocution, the ciphertexts will also begin with the same block. That is why the blocks of sixty-four are individually encrypted only in the simplest version of the DES method, the so-called ECB mode. In the more sophisticated modes, the blocks, during encrypting, are additionally so linked with one another that the same plaintext blocks never produce the same ciphertext blocks. Many DES users in the United States content themselves with the primitive ECB mode despite its weakness.[3]

ENCRYPTION AND AUTHORITY

The powerful people of this world have always used ciphers. They have exchanged coded messages among one another and decoded the messages of others for their own advantage.

In 1628, the Huguenots were holding the town of Réalmont in southern France, but it was besieged and cut off by the Catholic troops of the king. The defenders had a canon firing from a tower, and it seemed that they were not about to surrender the town. But then the besiegers managed to capture a man who was carrying a coded message to Huguenot troops in the neighborhood. A hurriedly summoned amateur cryptologist had no problem decoding the secret writing. It was a request for ammunition, as the canon of the defenders had virtually spent all its missiles. Without commentary the besiegers sent the plaintext back to the senders, who shortly afterward surrendered.

The decoder was quite young. His name was M. Antoine Rossignol, and he was to become the greatest cryptologist of his day. When Cardinal Richelieu besieged the Huguenots in La Rochelle and again intercepted a coded message, he called for Rossignol, who decoded this message as well. Thus the besiegers learned that there was great hunger in the town and that food, expected to be brought in by English ships, was needed urgently. All Richelieu had to do was close the harbor. A month later, the town surrendered.

King Louis XIII thereupon took Rossignol into his service. The court communicated with its agencies in cipher, and for this exchange of information Rossignol introduced two-part nomenclators—the first person to do so. These were the precursor of codebooks. The king was so impressed by his cryptologist that on his deathbed he recommended him to his court officials. Louis XIV, the Sun King, likewise made use of Rossignol's talents, and Rossignol's fame, influence, and fortune rapidly increased. He was the first to know what went on in the state; and he even knew, sooner than anyone else, what new mistress was enjoying the king's favors. Louis XV, too, repeatedly called on Rossignol's assistance.

But cryptology was practiced not only at the French court. Louis XV was surprised when he received a packet of deciphered letters from Vienna that European rulers had sent to their ambassadors there. He even found some of his own letters in plaintext. All these documents had been deciphered by the Austrian secret service.

All the countries of Europe then had their cipher departments, the so-called black chambers. The Austrians had the best and most efficient, the Secret Cabinet Chancery. At seven o'clock in the morning the sacks with the mail for the foreign embassies in Vienna would be delivered there. The officials carefully removed the seals and noted the sequence of the sheets in the letter, so that these could later be slipped back into their envelopes in the same way. The contents were read aloud, with shorthand writers taking notes. Then the letters were sealed again. By nine thirty, the diplomatic mail was back at the post office, and at ten it was delivered to the embassies. The same happened to the afternoon mail. Coded messages were decoded in the Cipher Department. The secret service worked so perfectly that only once or twice did a letter end up in the wrong envelope. Not only the diplomatic mail but also correspondence between suspect persons was treated in this way.

There is the story of a man who told a friend in his letter that he was enclosing a live flea to test whether anyone had tampered with his mail. In reality he did not put a flea into his letter. But when his friend opened it, a flea jumped out. So perfectly did the Viennese black chamber operate.

Even in our own day, governments attempt to read encrypted messages not only of enemy states but also of friendly ones. A temporary exception was made in the United States. "A gentleman does not read other people's letters," exclaimed Henry L. Stimson, the newly appointed secretary of defense in 1929 as he withdrew financial support from America's black chamber. The United States Army thereupon established its own cipher section under the directorship of William Friedman, the greatest cryptologist of his day.

Nowadays the United States has its powerful National Security Agency, whose seal we saw in figure 4.3. The NSA was created in 1952 by President Harry S. Truman, but its existence remained a secret for many years. It monitors the information services of states that might endanger the nation's security and decodes coded communications. Its roughly forty thousand employees include more mathematicians than any other organization in the world.

The NSA also controls the export of cipher systems. According to the American cryptologist Philip Zimmermann, American companies manufacturing cipher systems are visited by the NSA. It is suggested to the company executives, confidentially, that they weaken the security of these programs.[4] American export regulations used to prohibit the exportation of cipher systems to foreign countries if the keys of those systems were more than forty bits long. Since September 1998, the Commerce Department has permitted the export of cryptological software with key lengths of up to 56 bits to any nation, except to any of the seven so-called terrorist countries (Libya, North Korea, Sudan, Syria, Iran, Iraq, and Cuba). It may be assumed that the NSA, with its computers and cryptologists, is confident that it can crack such ciphers.

In February 1997, a story made the rounds of the press that a young information scientist in Zurich had succeeded in cracking a system based on a 48-bit key. To do this, a greatly many computers had been used over the Internet.

The secret services of many western countries are suspected of deliberately doctoring cipher systems before exporting them to other countries, like those in the Middle East. A well-known company that, among other things, supplies equipment for the cipher services of Iran, Iraq, and Libya, is believed to have built into its machines little tricks that provide in the ciphertexts produced, certain hints as to the key used. In many political situations the United States has possessed knowledge that it could have obtained only by unauthorized deciphering. There is some evidence that the NSA also has access to the data flow between the world banks. It may be a good thing to be able to trace the routes of drug money—but can we be sure that American business is not also gaining for itself advantages by penetrating encrypted European information traffic? Even the EU states do not always trust one another. When South Korea invited bids for a high-speed train system, *Der Spiegel* observed: "The debacle of the failed ICE high-speed train deals is still a painful memory for the managers. During the negotiations in South Korea, the French competitors had underbid everyone with clairvoyant assurance. Now the technicians are searching the company's computers for information leaks."[5]

As early as 1987, Richard J. Polis, the founder of a Geneva firm for the protection of electronic data banks, discovered that the government was frequently logging into bank networks illegally to gain customer data. The American government in particular, he stated, was repeatedly trying to break into European banks.[6] This deplorable state of affairs can be opposed only by sufficiently secure encryption.

Encryption, however, not only prevents somebody from illegally getting hold of data, it also enables every citizen to exchange secret messages with every other. That is a citizen's privilege, some might say—as Philip Zimmermann does in the epigraph to this chapter. Zimmermann is the inventor of the PGP cipher program. But just as a married man can exchange messages with his mistress—which may possibly do damage to his marriage but not to society as a whole—so can criminal and subversive organizations use encryption. Over the Internet, the drug mafia can control the transport route of the next consignment from Colombia, and terrorists, whether on the right or on the left, can use the Internet to determine where and when the next attack is to take place.

Toward the end of 1996, Peter Frisch, president of the German Federal Office for the Protection of the Constitution, in an interview warned that in the international computer networks "propaganda by neo-

Nazis and instructions on the construction of weapons by right-wing or left-wing extremists are available for downloading by anyone."[7] Frisch advocates a cryptolaw that would enable security authorities to read encoded messages in electronic data networks.

This is opposed by all champions of data protection, as well as by those who regarded even the last census in Germany as an attack on the citizen's private sphere. I cannot agree. I have lived altogether ten years under two dictatorships and value the democracy under which I have now lived nearly fifty years—despite some of its drawbacks. That is why I would grant our government the right to control encrypted data traffic in justified cases —possibly in such a way that everybody who has to send encoded data over the Internet, such as banks, would deposit the key with a state authority, while a private group would make sure that the state does not abuse this privilege.

Opinions are divided on this issue. The two epigraphs to this chapter show that there is no agreement on it even in the United States.

In Germany, the exchange of encoded messages is not forbidden at present. In France, cryptography is considered a weapon and requires a special license.[8] In the United States anyone is allowed to encrypt, but the export of cipher programs is restricted. In Russia, no private encryption is allowed, at least not without a license from Big Brother.

Discussion about encrypted messages became acute toward the end of the seventies, when a totally new principle of encryption was discovered.

NOTES

1. Martin Garner, *Mathematical Magic Show* (New York: Knopf, 1988).

2. Simplified program versions in the programmer languages FORTRAN and PASCAL can be found in W. W. Press, B. P. Flannery, S. A. Taukolsky, and W. T. Vetterling, *Numerical Recipes* (Cambridge: Cambridge University Press, 1986).

3. Philip Zimmermann, *The Official PGP™ User's Guide*, Vol. 1. (Cambridge, MA: MIT Press, 1995).

4. *Der Spiegel* (36/1996) 201.

5. *Der Spiegel* (36/1996) 195.

6. "European Needs and Attitudes toward Information Security," *Cryptologia* (October 1988) 134.

7. *Göttinger Tageblatt* (December 18, 1996) 13.

8. Claus Schönleber, *Verschlüsselungsverfahren für PC-Daten* (Poing: Franzis Verlag, 1995) 181.

12. ENCRYPTION QUITE PUBLICLY

> We live in one of the few countries on earth where one's
> social status may be improved by the confession that
> one has no talent for mathematics.
> — WALTER KRÄMER in his book *Denkste!*,
>   complaining about the situation in Germany

> One thing one keeps hearing . . . is certainly wrong.
> Because mathematicians have for centuries been search-
> ing for factorization algorithms without to date finding
> a really rapid one, the problem must be regarded as dif-
> ficult. Only since computers have been around are algo-
> rithms being invented that make use of the computers'
> advantages; previously there were only procedures for
> speeding up calculations with pencil and paper.
> — JOHANNES BUCHMANN, *Faktorisierung grosser Zahlen*

WE HAVE GOTTEN USED TO THE IDEA: when Mr. White and Mrs. Black want to send each other coded messages, they first have to exchange a key. Even Caesar had to tell his correspondent by how many places it was necessary to displace the alphabet in order to get from the ciphertext to the plaintext. Anyone encoding with Vigenère has to make sure the receiver knows the keyword. Systems with keywords as long as the entire plaintext, for instance the one-time pad system (chapter 7), may guarantee that no unauthorized person can penetrate the text—but only so long as that person does not get hold of the key. With all the cipher systems we have encountered so far, the sender and receiver must be in possession of the key. The same applies to the steganography example in chapter 2 and also to the Jules Verne-type transposition discussed in chapter 1. Both sender and receiver need the same template.

Even if they use almost endlessly long key worms, they still must start with the same seed numbers. In every case it is necessary to agree on a key prior to the transmission of a message.

A SHORT LESSON ON KEYS

Let us consider, by a simple illustration, the problem of depositing a coding key with sender and receiver. Coding keys are much like the keys we use in our daily lives. Encrypting is similar to hiding a message in a locked box (fig. 12.1). Mr. White has a key to its lock. With it he can open the box and place a plaintext in it, such as a letter. As soon as he has locked the box, the message is no longer generally accessible; it has become a ciphertext.

The receiver, Mrs. Black, who also has a key to the lock, can open the box. At the moment of opening, the letter is no longer secret, it is plaintext. Mrs. Black, thanks to her key, can read it. Sender and receiver are equal partners, each having a copy of the same key. Because sender and receiver are thus equally equipped, this arrangement is called *symmetrical key management*. It is a feature of all cipher methods we have encoun-

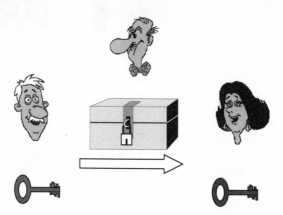

Fig. 12.1. Diagram of symmetrical encryption. Mr. White and Mrs. Black each possess a key to the lock on the box. When Mr. White has locked the box with his key, Mrs. Black can unlock it with hers. At some time in the past, one of the two must have received a copy of the key from the other.

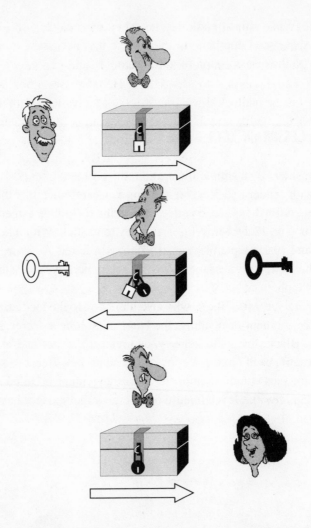

Fig. 12.2. **Diagram of symmetrical encryption without an exchange of keys. Mrs. Black and Mr. White each possess a lock and a key to it. Mr. White locks the box with his lock and sends it to Mrs. Black. She appends her lock, locks it, and returns the box to him. Mr. White removes his lock and sends the box back to Mrs. Black. She can now open the box with her key. No key had to be exchanged between the two.**

tered so far. Sender and receiver always use the same tools. That is why Mrs. Black can send and Mr. White can receive. But at some time in the past, there had to have been a passing of a copy of the key—and that is and remains a weak spot.

It might seem to be the rule that whoever wants to encode must also have the key that is needed to decode. This is not so. It can be done differently, if more cumbersomely.

Take our simple example of a box, a lock, and two keys. Mr. White wishes to send a message to Mrs. Black. He possesses a box, a padlock, and a key for the padlock. Mrs. Black, too, has a padlock with a key to it. Neither key of one fits into the padlock of the other. Mr. White now writes his letter to Mrs. Black, places it in the box, attaches his lock to it, and locks the lock. The locked box goes to Mrs. Black (fig. 12.2). She does not even try to open Mr. White's lock, as her key does not fit it. Instead she takes her own padlock, fits it to the box as well, and likewise locks it. The doubly locked box now goes back to Mr. White. He opens his lock, removes it, and returns the box to Mrs. Black. The box now makes its third journey, this time protected only by Mrs. Black's padlock. And she can now open her own lock with her key and finally get the letter. Radiantly happy, she reads, "Tomorrow at three." For such a brief message this was a rather complicated procedure—but he did not have to part with his key, and she did not have to part with hers. On its journeys the box was always secured by at least one lock. The unauthorized Mr. Gray got no chance to open the box.

All this may be possible with a box, two padlocks, and two keys—but what is the situation in cryptology? Let us assume that Mr. White's key is the opening of Sagan's *Contact*: *BYHUMANSTANDARDSITCOU* . . . , or, in numbers, if we replace each letter by its number in the alphabet:

B	Y	H	U	M	A	N	S	T	A	N	D	A	R	D	S	I	T	C	O	U
20	25	08	21	13	01	14	19	20	01	14	04	01	18	04	19	09	20	03	15	21

Mrs. Black has her own key, the beginning of R. V. Jones's *Most Secret War*: "This book tells of the rise of scientific intelligence in warfare." The keyword as a number worm is therefore:

T	H	I	S	B	O	O	K	T	E	L	L	S	O	F	T	H	E	R	I	S
20	08	09	19	02	15	15	11	20	05	12	12	19	15	06	20	08	05	18	09	19

Mr. White takes his plaintext and converts it into numbers by the same principle:

s	e	e	y	o	u	t	o	m	o	r	r	o	w
19	05	05	25	15	21	20	15	13	15	18	18	15	23

He then encodes it by adding his key without carrying the ten. He sends this numerical sequence to Mrs. Black (fig. 12.3, A), who takes her own key and adds it, again without carrying the ten (fig. 12.3, B). She sends this numerical sequence back to Mr. White, who subtracts his key without borrowing the ten (fig. 12.3, C). The result now goes back to Mrs. Black. The numerical sequence is encoded with only her key. She subtracts it and obtains the plaintext (fig. 12.3, D) Neither sender nor receiver had to know the other's key. The text was always exchanged in cipher. Mr. Gray again had no chance.

This cipher method without the exchange of a key works only if the encryption of sender and receiver can be reversed. If Mrs. Black first encodes with her key and Mr. White next encodes with his, the same ciphertext must emerge as in our illustration.

```
A:      s    e    e    y    o    u    t    o    m    o    r    r    o    w
       19   05   05   25   15   21   20   15   13   15   18   18   15   23
      +02   25   08   21   13   01   14   19   20   01   14   04   01   18
      ─────────────────────────────────────────────────────────────────
       11   20   03   46   28   22   34   24   33   16   22   12   16   31

B:      11   20   03   46   28   22   34   24   33   16   22   12   16   31
       +20   08   09   19   02   15   15   11   20   05   12   12   19   15
      ─────────────────────────────────────────────────────────────────
       31   28   02   55   20   37   49   35   53   11   34   24   25   46

C:      31   28   02   55   20   37   49   35   53   11   34   24   25   46
       -02   25   08   21   13   01   14   19   20   01   14   04   01   18
      ─────────────────────────────────────────────────────────────────
       39   03   04   34   17   36   35   26   33   10   20   20   24   38

D:      39   03   04   34   17   36   35   26   33   10   20   20   24   38
       -20   08   09   19   02   15   15   11   20   05   12   12   19   15
      ─────────────────────────────────────────────────────────────────
       19   05   05   25   15   21   20   15   13   15   18   18   15   23
        s    e    e    y    o    u    t    o    m    o    r    r    o    w
```

Fig. 12.3. Exchange of an encrypted message without an exchange of keys. A: plaintext, numerical plaintext, and the numerical key of Mr. White. Below the line, the ciphertext obtained by addition (without carrying the ten). B: the ciphertext just obtained is once more encoded, this time with Mrs. Black's key. C: Mr. White next subtracts his key. Now the ciphertext is encoded with only Mrs. Black's key. D: Mrs. Black subtracts her key and arrives at the plaintext. No key had to be exchanged.

My friend Sebastian von Hoerner has drawn my attention to the fact that Mr. Gray can intercept the encoded messages. If he compares the ciphertext sent to Mrs. Black in step A of figure 12.3 with the one sent back to Mr. White in step B, he might, by subtraction, discover Mrs. Black's key. Similarly the ciphertexts exchanged in steps B and C can reveal to him Mr. White's key.

There are simpler, safer, and therefore more important methods of coding for which secret keys need not be exchanged. Let us consider our model once more. Imagine a padlock with three keyholes and three keys (fig. 12.4). We have a large key N and two smaller ones, E and D. Each of these keys fits into only one keyhole. Anyone wishing to lock the padlock must use the large key and one of the two smaller ones—say, N and E. But the padlock cannot be opened again with these two keys. If it was locked with N and E, it can be unlocked with only N and D, and the other way around. With this miracle padlock, Mr. White and Mrs. Black can now exchange secret messages.

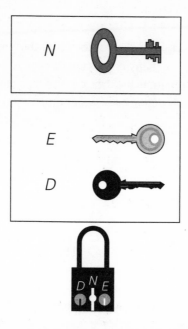

Fig. 12.4. The tools for asymmetrical encryption illustrated by padlock and keys. The padlock has three keyholes for three keys, marked N, E, and D. For locking and unlocking, the large key N and one of the two smaller ones, E or D, are needed. If the padlock was locked with keys N and E, it can be unlocked with only keys N and D.

Fig. 12.5. Diagram of an asymmetrical encryption. The padlock of figure 12.4 hangs on a box. Mrs. Black possesses the three keys, *N*, *E*, and *D*. Of the keys *N* and *E* she has given copies to all her friends. But she keeps *D*. No one except herself has that key. When Mr. White wishes to send a secret letter to Mrs. Black, he locks the padlock with keys *N* and *E*. After that he can no longer open the box himself. Only Mrs. Black can get at its contents with *N* and *D*.

Mrs. Black has acquired the padlock and the three keys from a reputable firm. She next has many copies cut of keys *N* and *E* and sends them to her friends and acquaintances. Mr. Gray, too, can obtain a set of these two keys. These are the *public keys*, accessible to anybody. But she keeps key *D* to herself. This is the *secret key*, which nobody, not even Mr. White, must have. She fits the three-keyhole lock to the box, which anybody may use who wishes to send her a message.

Let us now have Mr. White in figure 12.5 send a message to Mrs. Black. He takes his plaintext and places it in the box. He then locks it with Mrs. Black's public keys, that is, *N* and *E*. From that moment he can no longer access the contents of the box. The padlock locked with *N* and *E* can be unlocked with only *N* and *D*. This can be done by Mrs. Black alone, for only she possesses key *D*. Even the jealous Mr. Gray has no way of getting at the contents of the box. Mr. White and Mrs. Black do not possess the same tools, as they did with the box that had two identical keys. Mr. White has Mrs. Black's public keys, but these are known to everyone in town. Mrs. Black, however, has one key of which nobody has a copy. The situation is no longer symmetrical: we have *asymmetrical key management*.

Transmission of a signal with public and secret keys can be realized also in cryptology: there are methods that do not require agreement on a common key. In these procedures, numbers play an important role, because what is exchanged are not plaintexts and ciphertexts but plaintext and ciphertext numbers.

Transition from plaintext to plaintext number is simple. Each plaintext letter is replaced by its number in the alphabet. The transformation could also be effected with a Polybius table, but for the sake of simplicity we will stick with the numbers of the letters in the alphabet. Let us take as our plaintext the word *rose*, with its eight-digit plaintext number 18151905. This number is converted into a ciphertext number—we will soon see how—and the receiver, using another calculation procedure, derives from that the plaintext number, whose number pairs he next replaces by the plaintext letters. The secret lies in the mathematical transformation of plaintext number into ciphertext number, and vice versa.

THE RECIPE FOR ASYMMETRICAL ENCRYPTION

A recipe lists the ingredients from which we prepare a dish. Take two cups of flour, one pint of milk, two tablespoons of butter, and whatever else is needed. You do not have to ask why exactly two tablespoons of butter and not three, or why this dish does not also need a cup of ham, finely chopped. The author of the cookbook has tried out the dish—or so we hope. In dealing with the question of how Mr. White can send an encrypted message to Mrs. Black without a secret key having been agreed between them, we will at first similarly consider only the recipe and not its justification.

Take three keys, a large one that we will call N and two small ones, E and D. These keys will be numbers. But for visualization we may think of them also as real keys, as in figure 12.5. A simple example: let $N = 85$, $E = 5$, and $D = 13$. These are not random numbers that just occurred to me; there exists among them a special relation that is not instantly obvious. Such a relation also exists between $N = 33$, $E = 3$, and $D = 7$. We call such numbers *magic numbers*. $N = 20$, $E = 11$, and $D = 5$ are not magic numbers. How to find three magic numbers is described in appendix C. Thus, for instance, $N = 49,048,499$, $E = 61$, and $D = 2,409,781$ are magical. For practical application, large numbers are needed, numbers with more than a hundred digits. For our recipe I have chosen smaller ones, $N = 85$, $E = 5$, $D = 13$. These three magic numbers serve Mrs. Black and Mr. White as keys. Mrs. Black must guard one of the two numbers, E or D, very closely. She must not reveal this number to anyone, and if it is so long that she has to write it down, she should keep the note in her safe with her jewelry. While she has to guard the secret of D, if she has chosen D, she can proclaim E and N from the rooftops and send out postcards: "Let all who wish to write to me encode their messages with my public key numbers N and E (i.e., 85 and 5)."

This information also reaches Mr. White. Normally he writes slightly longer letters, such as "How did you like the concert last night?" But let us assume, for the sake of simplicity, that his plaintext today consists of just one letter, say, x. The message hardly seems to merit so much fuss, but it will show us the principle. The place of x in the alphabet is represented by the number 24. That is the plaintext number. Mr. White can now encrypt. He possesses the public keys N and E. He does not need to know anything else. Mrs. Black, moreover, possesses key D in addition to N and E, but that is no business of Mr. White's.

ENCRYPTING WITH N AND E

Write down the plaintext number E times, with multiplication signs between them.

During multiplication, subtract N as often as possible from the intermediate results, to prevent the product from becoming large. In the end, one number will be left that is smaller than N. This is the ciphertext number.

DECRYPTING WITH N AND D

Write down the ciphertext number D times, with multiplication signs between them. During multiplication, subtract N as often as possible, to prevent the product from becoming large. In the end, one number will be left that is smaller than N. This is the plaintext number.

MR. WHITE ENCODES, MRS. BLACK DECODES

The recipe demands that Mr. White raise the plaintext number (i.e., 24) to the power of E (in this case, 5; in other words $24^5 = 24 \times 24 \times 24 \times 24 \times 24$. But he does not really need that product; all he needs is the remainder after dividing it by N (i.e., 85). The product is 7,962,624; the remainder is **79**, which is the ciphertext number.

With very large numbers it is advisable to subtract 85 repeatedly from intermediate results, as recommended in the box on the previous page. This changes nothing with regard to the remainders, which ultimately alone matter, and the intermediate results thus remain small. A more elegant method of determining the remainder is demonstrated in the box that follows.

Whichever way he calculates. Mr. White gets the ciphertext **79**. This he sends quite openly to Mrs. Black. It is of no use to anyone, not even to the unauthorized Mr. Gray, because he does not know the secret key D. But there is nothing to stop Mr. Gray from also sending an encoded message to Mrs. Black. As he knows her public key numbers N and E, he can create a ciphertext number with them. This in turn cannot be read by Mr. White—after all, Mr. White cannot take the ciphertext number he himself created and transform it back into the plaintext number, just as he can no longer retrieve the letter from the box that he himself locked in figure 12.5.

As soon as Mrs. Black has received the ciphertext number **79**, she expectantly sets about decoding. She takes her secret key D—the number 13—out of her safe. Next she calculates the Dth (i.e., the thirteenth) power of 79, or 79^{13}. This is a laborious business, because the result is a number of twenty-five digits. Fortunately she can save herself some work. It is sufficient if she operates with the remainders with regard to N, that is, 85. After each multiplication she can divide by 85 and continue with the remainder, as explained in the box that follows. As a result, finally, she will get 24. This is the plaintext number that Mr. White encoded. It corresponds to the letter x.

This was a very short message. How does Mr. White proceed with longer letters? He could, of course, encrypt each letter individually. He could convert the plaintext *rose* into the four plaintext numbers 18, 15, 19, and 5 and encode each individual number in the manner described.

LARGE NUMBERS TAMED BY A SMALL POCKET CALCULATOR

Mrs. Black calculates $79 \times 79 = 6{,}241$. Dividing by 85, she gets 73.4235. The number 85 is therefore 73 times fully contained in 6,241. But 85×73 is only 6,205. This leaves a remainder, after division, of 36. In the *domain* of remnants of 85, therefore, $79 \times 79 \equiv 36$ (mod 85). Next she calculates $79 \times 79 \times 79 \times 79 \equiv 36 \times 36$ (mod 85); the remainder is 21. Hence $79 \times 79 \times 79 \times 79 \times 79 \times 79 \times 79 \times 79 \equiv 21 \times 21$ (mod 85) $\equiv 16$ (mod 85); and $79^{12} \equiv 21 \times 16 \equiv 81$ (mod 85). It follows that $79^{13} = 81 \times 79 = 6399 \equiv 24$ (mod 85). In the domain of remainders, Mrs. Black easily performs all her operations with a pocket calculator.

This produces the four ciphertext numbers **18, 70, 49** and **65**, which he then transmits to Mrs. Black in the form **18704965**. She could then break this up into two-figure groups and decode them individually with her secret number D, that is, 13. And the rose would blossom for her.

A word of caution. With letter-by-letter encryption each plaintext letter is represented by a two-digit number, which is then converted into a ciphertext number. This is nothing other than monalphabetic encoding. Every e of the plaintext is transformed into the same pair of numerals in the ciphertext. Mr. Gray therefore—without bothering about E or D— could decode the ciphertext simply by way of the frequency distribution of the groups of two in the ciphertext, just as one would decode a monalphabetic encryption. This method has another drawback. The letter a corresponds to the plaintext number 1. No matter how often you multiply this by itself, one always remains one. This means that a always remains a, which, for instance, would enable Mr. Gray to guess the word *abracadabra* if it happened to occur in Mr. White's letter. Encryption without transmission of a key is therefore not so simple. I chose this form of encryption only so we could keep to small numbers, where the operation is easier to follow.

Mr. White, however, can choose a better way by taking the numerical sequence 18151905—we already know that this is the name of the rose— as a single number, that is, a number of more than eighteen million. Now the method we have been using will work only if the number N is greater than the ciphertext number. I therefore choose a new set of magic numbers, N = 49,048,499, E = 61, and D = 2,409,781. Never mind where I got those numbers; I will explain it in appendix C.

Let us see how the method works with these three magic numbers. With such large numbers, you will no longer find it so easy to follow me on your pocket calculator. Remember that Mr. White has to perform sixty multiplications with his eight-digit plaintext number in order to obtain his ciphertext number. Mrs. Black, in order to determine the plaintext number, has to multiply more than two million times. The numbers involved are kept within bounds since it is only necessary to work in the domain of the remainders of N. I used my PC to spare you the work, and have encoded not only the plaintext word *rose* but also two similar words, using the same magic triad of numbers. The result is shown in figure 12.6. One can see that similar words are transformed into totally different ciphertext numbers and that even the simple letter *x* has an eight-digit ciphertext number corresponding to it. No matter how hard he tries, Mr. Gray will not discover that x.

But suppose Mr. White wishes to send a longer letter, one containing a hundred or more symbols? Let us assume his message has one hundred letters, that is, two hundred plaintext numerals. He would therefore have to have a magical number triad in which N is a number of at least two hundred digits. The calculations involved can be performed only by a computer.

Mrs. Black and Mr. White will therefore agree always to divide their messages into groups of four or five, which they will then individually encode, group by group, as we did with the word *rose*. The lengths of the numbers they have to deal with during encoding and decoding are determined by the number N. Even a single-letter text, such as *x*, can result in a large ciphertext number after encryption, as we saw in figure 12.6. After

N = 49048499, E = 61, D = 2409781		
plaintext	numerical plaintext	numerical ciphertext
rose	18151905	**10697935**
hose	8151905	**32147069**
host	8151920	**17555573**
x	24	**23985193**

Fig. 12.6. Encryption of four words, using the magic numbers N, E, and D.

we have learned how to find the magic numbers, we will discuss the question of whether Mr. Gray can break the secret of the code. We will see that with a small N he can break it easily enough. But if N has a length of a hundred digits or more, he will find it not only difficult but virtually impossible. The secret of the encryption described here involves numbers of a type that mathematicians for a long time believed were very interesting but of no practical value.

NUMBERS THAT CANNOT BE DIVIDED

In a time long since past, there used to be peasants with their flocks. They had to count their sheep to make sure none had been lost. Thus they discovered whole numbers or integers. Anyone taking a wife received additional animals as her dowry and would therefore have to learn to add two numbers together. If one's daughter married, she was given cattle and sheep to take with her into her marriage, so her father had to learn how to subtract. As he grew old and began to worry about leaving his livestock to his children fairly, he learned to divide. A peasant with twelve animals discovered that he could divide the animals only if he had two, three, four, or six children to leave them to; thirteen animals he could never distribute fairly—unless he only had only one child or thirteen children. Through such reflections, people learned to handle integers; they also learned that these numbers not only were greater and smaller than one another but also possessed some special characteristics.

It soon emerged that some very surprising and involved relations existed among integers, and this gave rise to the science of *number theory*. Number theory is concerned with the regularities among integers. A vast quantity of books and articles in journals shows the colorful variety and wealth of the world of integers. It is unlikely that the investigation of them will ever reach a conclusion.

Another example of a gigantic range of knowledge developing from a few initial rules is the game of chess. There are only a small number of rules about how a chessman can move or take another. But from these simple rules, strategies are developed that fill entire books. Classic games by great masters are published and republished in the chess literature. They are veritable works of art, and some even bear a name, such as "The Immortal," won by the Breslau mathematics master Adolf Andersen in the mid-nineteenth century. Yet even this masterpiece was only a series of applications of primitive rules, such as "A pawn moves straight and takes diagonally."

Whereas there is no general theory of chess, games with integers are governed by fixed theorems. In chapter 4 we made the acquaintance of calculation with remainders. This represents a part of number theory. Numbers can be added, and they can be multiplied. Their remainders can likewise be added and multiplied. Here we already have a theorem of number theory, albeit a very simple one. We will consider another area of number theory: *prime numbers*. These play a vital part in ciphers.

When two integers are multiplied, the result is an integer: 10 times 13 gives us 130. Dividing this number by 10 leaves no remainder. Dividing it by 2 or 5 or 13 likewise leaves no remainder. We call 130 a composite number. Ten is also composite, made up of 2 and 5. However, 13 has no factor. It is a prime number, divisible only by 1 and by itself, but these two primitive cases are of no interest to us. Two is a prime number, and so is 3. Four has a factor; 5 has none. One itself is not normally regarded as a prime number. The first few prime numbers are therefore 2, 3, 5. With the exception of 2, all prime numbers are odd numbers. Obviously, because otherwise they would have 2 as a factor. Figure 12.7 shows the prime numbers up to 1013. Does the series that we have stopped at 1013

2	3	5	7	11	13	17	19	23	29	31	37
41	43	47	53	59	61	67	71	73	79	83	89
97	101	103	107	109	113	127	131	137	139	149	151
157	163	167	173	179	181	191	193	197	199	211	223
227	229	233	239	241	251	257	263	269	271	277	281
283	293	307	311	313	317	331	337	347	349	353	359
367	373	379	383	389	397	401	409	419	421	431	433
439	443	449	457	461	463	467	479	487	491	499	503
509	521	523	541	547	557	563	569	571	577	587	593
613	617	619	631	641	643	647	653	659	661	673	677
683	691	701	709	719	727	733	739	743	751	757	761
769	773	787	797	809	811	821	823	827	829	839	853
857	859	863	877	881	883	887	907	911	919	929	937
941	947	953	967	971	977	983	991	997	1009	1013	

Fig. 12.7. **Prime numbers to 1013.**

go on? Are there an infinite number of prime numbers, or is there a biggest and final one, with all further numbers being divisible by smaller ones? This question was answered by the Greek mathematician Euclid about 300 B.C. The series of prime numbers has no end. We know therefore that our table of prime numbers can be continued at will.

WHY THERE ARE AN INFINITE NUMBER OF PRIME NUMBERS

Let us assume that there exists a greatest prime number, and let us call it G. We then multiply all the smaller prime numbers by one another and by G, and add 1. We call the result Y. This number is certainly greater than G, since G was multiplied by many integers and, moreover, 1 was added. Y is not divisible by any prime number smaller than G, nor by G itself, because division by G or by any of the smaller prime numbers leaves a remainder of 1. This proves that Y either must be a prime number itself or must be divisible by a prime number greater than G. In both cases a prime number greater than G must exist. Why, then, is there an infinite number of prime numbers? Because for any prime number we can always use this method to prove the existence of a greater one.

SIEVED NUMBERS

How can we find prime numbers beyond our table? A simple method for doing that was discovered by a Greek about 250 B.C.—Eratosthenes of Cyrene. He was the director of the famous library of Alexandria and the first person to determine the size of our globe. His method of finding prime numbers is still called the "sieve of Eratosthenes."

Let us determine the first prime numbers with him. Write all the numbers from 1 to 100 into a table. Now start with the second number, that is, 2, and underline every other number that follows it. Then start with 3 and underline every third number that follows it. When we get to 4 and are about to underline every fourth number following it, we find that this is not necessary, as all these numbers were already covered when we operated from 2. We therefore proceed to 5 and underline every fifth number following it. We do not have to bother about 6: these numbers are underlined

1	2	3	<u>4</u>	5	<u>6</u>	7	<u>8</u>	<u>9</u>	<u>10</u>	11	<u>12</u>	13	<u>14</u>	<u>15</u>
<u>16</u>	17	<u>18</u>	19	<u>20</u>	<u>21</u>	<u>22</u>	23	<u>24</u>	<u>25</u>	<u>26</u>	<u>27</u>	28	29	<u>30</u>
31	<u>32</u>	<u>33</u>	<u>34</u>	<u>35</u>	<u>36</u>	37	<u>38</u>	<u>39</u>	<u>40</u>	41	<u>42</u>	43	<u>44</u>	<u>45</u>
<u>46</u>	47	<u>48</u>	<u>49</u>	<u>50</u>	<u>51</u>	<u>52</u>	53	<u>54</u>	<u>55</u>	<u>56</u>	<u>57</u>	<u>58</u>	59	60
61	<u>62</u>	<u>63</u>	<u>64</u>	<u>65</u>	<u>66</u>	67	<u>68</u>	<u>69</u>	<u>70</u>	71	<u>72</u>	73	<u>74</u>	<u>75</u>
<u>76</u>	<u>77</u>	<u>78</u>	79	<u>80</u>	<u>81</u>	<u>82</u>	83	<u>84</u>	<u>85</u>	<u>86</u>	<u>87</u>	<u>88</u>	89	<u>90</u>
<u>91</u>	<u>92</u>	<u>93</u>	<u>94</u>	<u>95</u>	<u>96</u>	97	<u>98</u>	<u>99</u>	<u>100</u>					

Fig. 12.8. **Determination of prime numbers with the sieve of Eratosthenes.**

already. With 7 we again encounter numbers not yet underlined. The result is shown in figure 12.8. We will find that the underlining of numbers up to prime number distances of no more than 7 is enough to obtain *all* prime numbers under 100. Indeed, comparison with our prime numbers table confirms that the numbers not underlined are the prime numbers to 100. Admittedly, 1 stands at the beginning of our table, but it is not included in the prime numbers proper; it is not taken seriously as a prime number. If we wanted to find higher prime numbers, we would have to write down a longer string of numbers and start afresh with our underlining.

In 1903, the largest known prime number was 2,305,843,009,213,693,951. Whereas in the past such large prime numbers were only sporadically known, the American mathematician Derrick Norman Lehmer in 1914 published a complete list of prime numbers to 10,006,721. Figure 12.9 shows a small section of his extensive tables. The largest prime number discovered by computers in 1996 had 420,921 digits—but we know that the series continues into infinity.

9900601
9900623
9900641
9900643
9900661
9900677
9900689
9900697

Fig. 12.9. **Prime numbers between 9,900,600 and 9,900,700, according to Lehmer.**

It would be nice if, instead of this laborious sieving, we had a formula that would supply all prime numbers sequentially. There is a promising procedure that I will formulate in the language of our childhood number games: "Think of a number, subtract 1, multiply by the number you have thought of, and add 41!" Try it out yourself, starting with 1. The result is 41, because $1 - 1 = 0 \times 1 = 0 + 41 = 41$, a prime number. The next number, 2, gives 43, another prime number. Three gives 47, and 4 gives 53, again prime numbers. Comparison with our table, however, reveals that we have skipped some prime numbers. Not only do we lack the ones below 41, we also lack 59. Even though this rule does not provide all the prime numbers, does it at least invariably give us a prime number? Let us take 12. The result is 173, a prime number. Twenty gives us 421, again a prime number. Thirty and 40 give us 911 and 1,601, two more prime numbers.

Do we have here a universal formula for prime numbers? Disappointment starts with 41, which gives us 1,681—not a prime number, because $1,681 = 41 \times 41$. There simply is no formula that produces all prime numbers sequentially.

There are twenty-five prime numbers below 100, but only fourteen in the equally long span between 900 and 1,000. The decrease of prime numbers as we go up is irregular. Between 500 and 600 there are only thirteen. In the ten million range there are usually fewer than ten prime numbers among one hundred consecutive numbers. Thus there are only six prime numbers between 9,921,400 and 9,921,500 and only three between 9,893,200 and 9,893,300. In the nineteenth century, mathematicians discovered the law according to which prime numbers become scarcer as we count upward, but this law does not tell us where those prime numbers will be located.

There are other peculiarities in the distribution of prime numbers. Let us look again at the table in figure 12.7. Time and again we encounter prime numbers differing only by 2. They could not possibly be closer, because of any two numbers differing only by 1, one is an even number. And unless the even number happens to be 2, it is not a prime number. If the distance between two prime numbers equals 2, they are called *prime number twins*. In the table of figure 12.7, we notice 2\3, 5\7, 11\13, 17\19. One might think that this is a phenomenon occurring only with low numbers, where prime numbers follow each other more closely. But in the range between 800 and 900 our table shows 821\823, 827\829, 857\859, and 881\883. Twin pairs are found even in the range of millions.

In the short extract from Lehmer's table (fig. 12.9), there is the pair 9,900,641\9,900,643. Not long ago a twin pair was found with 11,713 digits. There seems to be no end to the sequence of twin pairs.

WHAT STILL AWAITS EXPLORATION

I often come across people who accept that in the natural sciences, no matter whether biology or astrophysics, new knowledge can be continually acquired through research, but who find it hard to accept that mathematics is by no means a completed field of knowledge and that new insights are being gained every day. We do not even yet fully understand integral numbers. Here is an example:

On June 7, 1742, the conference secretary of the Saint Petersburg Academy, Christian von Goldbach, in a letter informed the mathematician Leonhard Euler of a mathematical theorem about prime numbers. However, he was unable to prove the theorem, and no one to this day has succeeded in supplying the proof. That it why it is known as the *Goldbach Assumption* and not the Goldbach Theorem. The assumption states that every even number that is greater than 2 is the sum of two prime numbers. Simple examples: $20 = 3 + 17$, $24 = 5 + 19$, and $872 = 199 + 673$. Not one even number has been found, so far, that cannot be expressed as the sum of two prime numbers. But it cannot be ruled out that someday somebody will produce an even number to which the Goldbach Assumption does not apply. This would refute the assumption.

Another problem associated with prime numbers is their multiplication. It is easy to multiply two prime numbers. But if the numbers are large, it becomes impossible to tell from what constituents the product was formed. With small numbers this is easy. Anyone can see at once that 85 equals 5 times 17. But how can one tell, by looking at the number 1,009,961, that it is the result of the multiplication of the prime numbers 997 and 1,013? The numbers 991,847 and 49,048,499 are likewise the products of two prime numbers. Can you guess which two? Multiplication of two prime numbers is easy; separating the product into its prime factors is difficult. The fact that no one will discover the prime numbers concealed in a large N is the basis of the encryption of the correspondence between Mr. White and Mrs. Black by means of three magic numbers.

So far it has been virtually impossible, in the case of a two-hundred-digit number produced by the multiplication of two prime numbers, to reconstruct those prime numbers. But someday a mathematician may discover a procedure by which the factorizing of large numbers into two prime numbers can be not only accomplished but also accomplished quite quickly. There is talk of a new type of computer, of computers that operate on totally different principles—so-called *quantum computers* by means of which large numbers can be rapidly factored. If this is ever achieved, the method of public keys described above would suddenly become worthless.

PRIME NUMBER ENCRYPTION

The public-key system has been known only since 1978. That year, the February issue of a reputable American journal carried an article by three scientists from the Laboratory for Computer Sciences at the Massachusetts Institute of Technology.[1] It dealt with two problems.

The first concerned the question of how a document transmitted online could be signed in such a way that the receiver would be certain that the signature was authentic. In normal exchanges, a person signs by hand, and every recipient, whether a private individual or the Internal Revenue Service, can tell by comparing the signature with those provided earlier, whether it is genuine or not. If necessary, an expert is brought in to decide—for instance, in a court of law. But if a person "signs" a document on the typewriter, the recipient cannot know whether he has typed the name himself. The same problem arises with documents transmitted via telex or over the Internet. We will see how the three authors solved this problem.

The second was the problem of how to exchange encoded messages without parting with the secret key. This is the question we will address first, because it is the basis of the cipher system used by Mr. White and Mrs. Black. The authors of this epoch-making study are the mathematicians Ronald L. Rivest, Adi Shamir, and Leonard Adleman; accordingly this cryptosystem is nowadays known by their initials, RSA.

The system is based on the fact that one gets hold of three numbers, which earlier I called the magic numbers N, D, and E. The RSA team recommends that these be determined in the way described by me in appendix C. The authors take two prime numbers, p = 47 and q = 59, and multiply them. This gives them the big key,[2] N = 2,773. Next they choose E = 17 and, by the method given in appendix C, find D = 157. For illustration they use, as plaintext, the quotation placed by Shakespeare in Julius Caesar's mouth:

its all greek to me

Using the position of the letters in the alphabet, they transform this into a plaintext number, indicating the spaces by two zeros. They thus obtain, written in blocks of four:

0920 1900 0112 1200 0718 0505 1100 2015 0013 0500

They next encode the blocks of four. They raise the number of the first block to the power of E, that is, the power of 17. They therefore create 920^{17}. After each multiplication, they divide by N and keep only the remainder, modulo 2,773 (N). The final result is 948. So the first block is encrypted: 0920 has become **0948**. They continue in the same way until they have encrypted all the blocks:

0948 2342 1084 1444 2663 2390 0778 0774 0219 1655

This is the ciphertext. Take note that the RSA encoders did not use the number D. For the receiver, however, D is indispensable.

The receiver decodes by raising the individual blocks of four of the ciphertext to the power of D, that is, the power of 157. Dividing by N and keeping only the remainder, modulo 2,773, gets him to the plaintext. This is precisely the encoding and decoding Mr. White and Mrs. Black used for their correspondence.

In appendix C it is demonstrated that the secret of encryption lies mainly in the prime numbers p and q, from which N was produced. If Mr. Gray can factor the number N, which after all is public, into these two prime numbers, he will crack the code. But no simple recipe exists for factoring a number of about a hundred digits. There is no alternative, therefore, to dreary trial and error: one divides N by 2, 3, 5, 7, 11, . . . that is, by all prime numbers smaller than N.[3] The moment such a division leaves no remainder, one has identified a prime number as a factor. But, with a very large N, this can take forever.

In their article, the three RSA authors estimate that one would have to perform some 14 billion mathematical steps in order to factor a five-digit N into its prime numbers. With a 200-digit N, a 1978 computer would have needed a period of time on the order of the age of the universe. Even though computers have become faster, a 500-digit N requires a forty-digit number of mathematical operations—too much for even the most modern computers.

But some numbers can be factored more easily. Thus it proved possible in 1992 to factor a 157-digit number.[4] RSA users would be wise to avoid such exceptional numbers.

Supporters of RSA had a nasty shock at the beginning of the nineties. In August 1977, Rivest, Shamir, and Adleman published a 129-digit number in *Scientific American* and promised a prize of one hundred dollars to anyone finding the two prime numbers of which this number was made up.

The number was:

N =11438162575788886766923577997614661201021829672124236256256184293570693524573389783059712356395870505898907514
7599290026879543541

You have to imagine all the digits written in a row. If therefore someone receives messages encoded with N and E, and N is the 129-digit number above, then the ciphertexts will remain secret only so long as the prime numbers of N remain unknown. The \$100 went unclaimed for sixteen years.

In 1992, four mathematicians took up the problem. They split the task of factoring the numerical monster into partial operations and shared these among many small computers. They were joined by six hundred volunteers from twenty-five countries on five continents; the collaborators communicated over the Internet. The outcome of this collective effort was a 64-digit number p:

4905295108476509491478496199038981334177646384933878439908200577

Dividing N by p, we obtain q. With six hundred claiming a prize of a hundred dollars, each received sixteen cents.

As the number of digits grows, the time needed for factoring increases enormously. If one proceeds from a 129-digit number to a 300-digit number, the calculating time needed increases a hundred-thousandfold. That is what makes RSA encryption so attractive. What matters is not whether an encryption can be cracked but whether it can be cracked quickly. If Mr. White and Mrs. Black use a cipher to make a date for Thursday, it does not help the jealous Mr. Gray if his PC comes up with the decoded message thirty years later.

ASYMMETRICAL BUT FAST

The advantage of using a public key is offset by the disadvantage that operations with large numbers take time, even on fast computers. Despite the fact that one operates only in the domain of the remainders of the large number N, so that the numbers involved can never be greater than N itself, the numbers that arise during encoding and decoding are still large. But if encryption is to be secure, then N must be large. There is, however, an alternative that combines the speed of symmetrical encryption with the security of asymmetrical encryption.

Let us take, from an example of symmetrical encryption, the key worm of random numbers we used in figure 7.7 (page 137). In order for sender and receiver to be able to communicate, the sender must first transmit to the receiver the seed number for their random-number generators. This can be done by an RSA procedure, as follows:

Mrs. Black has an RSA program on her computer and has given her N and her public key E to all and sundry. Mr. White wishes to send her an encoded message. He writes the plaintext, replaces the letters by their numbers in the alphabet, and produces a numerical plaintext. Then he chooses a seed number and uses it to start up his random-number generator in order to create a long key worm. Next he produces a numerical ciphertext by the addition of his numerical plaintext and his key worm. So far this is of no use to Mrs. Black, since she does not know the seed number to use to produce the same key worm. Mr. White now uses his RSA program to encode the seed number for Mrs. Black with N and his public key E. He sends her first the RSA-encrypted seed number and second the numerical ciphertext produced by symmetrical encryption.

Mrs. Black decodes the seed number, using her secret D, and with it starts her random-number generator, producing the same key worm that Mr. White used. This she subtracts from the ciphertext and so obtains the numerical plaintext, which she can easily convert into a letter text. In this process, the secret key number D has not been transmitted at all, and the key to the symmetrical procedure, the seed number, has been transmitted only in encrypted form.

Mr. White can choose a new seed number for every message. Transmission then proceeds in two steps. With Mrs. Black's public numbers N and E, he encrypts the seed number he has used to create his keyword and places this number at the beginning of the text to be transmitted. It might form the first ten digits of the message to Mrs. Black. He follows this with his numerical secret message, encrypted with his key worm. Decoding the first ten digits of the message with her secret D, Mrs. Black thus obtains the seed number, which she uses to start the random-number generator that produces the necessary key worm. She subtracts the key worm from the ciphertext, gets the numerical plaintext, and from that she derives the plaintext in letter form.

This method is in wide use nowadays. The PGP (Pretty Good Privacy—see appendix D) encryption program transmits the key by RSA but encodes with a symmetrical method.

The world's banks communicate with one another by a cipher method called SWIFT, short for Society for Worldwide Interbank Telecommunication. Here, too, the method is symmetrical, but the key is transmitted by RSA. Encryption of the message proper is performed in the DES system.

Until now we have let Mr. White encrypt with N and his public key E and Mrs. Black decipher with N and her secret key D. In actual fact, E and D are absolutely equal. What has been encoded with E can be decoded only with D, and vice versa. Mrs. Black could not only use her secret D (and her public N) for decoding incoming messages, but could also use it to send encoded messages. Not only Mr. White but anybody else could then decode her messages with the publicly known key E (and N). What would be the use of this? What can be decoded with Mrs. Black's public E can only have been encoded with her secret D. Since she alone knows D, any ciphertext that can be decoded with E must originate from her. This is as secure a signature as if she had signed it with her own hand. We will deal with this in greater detail in the next chapter.

NOTES

1. Ronald L. Rivest, Adi Shamir, and Leonard Adleman, "A Method for Obtaining Digital Signatures and Public Key Cryptosystems," *Communications of the ACM* 21.2 (1978) 120.

2. In the practice of RSA encryption, only E and D are described as keys, not N. But in this book I call N a key as well; after all, any tool needed for opening a lock (an encryption) is a key. Anyone who knows E and D without knowing N stands helpless in front of a locked door.

3. One need not try all the prime numbers smaller than N. It is sufficient to try the prime numbers that are smaller than the square root of N. If the prime numbers between 0 and the square root of N are not contained in N, then the larger ones are not either.

4. Numbers a little below a high power of 2 can be factored more easily. In 1992, Arjen Lester and Dan Bernstein factored the number $2^{523} - 1$ into prime numbers. For this they required three weeks of computer time on a computer that contained more than sixteen thousand processors. Especially suitable for the creation of N are prime numbers p where $(p - 1) / 2$ is another prime number.

13. SMART CARDS, ONE-WAY FUNCTIONS, AND MOUSETRAPS

Anyone calling up the home page of the municipal savings bank in **** enters a virtual branch. At imaginary counters the customer can open an account, make transactions, trade securities. . . . Buy and sell orders get to the computer of the bank at the speed of light, but once there, they are processed manually.

—CHRISTOPH SEEGER, *Wirtschaftswoche*

AS CHILDREN WE HEARD the sad story recorded by the Brothers Grimm under the title "The Wolf and the Seven Little Goats." I have always wondered why there was no mention in the story of the father of the family. Had the billy goat left the old nanny goat with her seven kids for someone younger? Anyway, the climax of the story comes when the big bad wolf, his voice softened by chalk and his paw covered with fresh dough, knocks at the door and calls out, "Dear children, let me in. I am your mother and each of you shall have a present." The seven kids first want to see his paw, and when they see that it is snow-white, and because they hear the wolf speak in such a gentle voice, they believe it is their mother and let him in.

We know the rest of the story. It might have turned out differently if the old goat had not only warned her kids of the wolf's gruff voice and black paws but had also given them other, more unambiguous identity criteria.

It would have been best if the nanny goat and her kids had been able to read and write. Then the mother could have said, "When I get back, I'll slip a piece of paper through the door with my signature, so you can see if it is your mother or not." The kids could have relied on the slip of paper, just as we, and even courts of law, rely on hand-signed documents, though sometimes an expert must be called in to verify the authenticity of a signature by comparing it with earlier specimens.

The old nanny-goat could have arranged to slip her monogrammed handkerchief under the door. That, too, would have served as identification, since the wolf would have found it difficult to get hold of a similar handkerchief in a hurry.

Or she might have agreed on a password with her children, or on a combination of numbers the wolf could not guess—such as the date of birth of the vanished father of her children.

Today we might advise her to fit an electronic lock to the door, so that everyone living in the house could key in a certain sequence of numbers. In many countries, front doors are secured in this way—I have myself seen it repeatedly in Paris. The door opens only for the initiate. Without knowing the key, the wolf, even if the lock had only a three-digit combination, would have to try several hundred times before hitting on three numerals in the right sequence.

We therefore have three ways of identification. The mother either identifies herself by her *body*, such as her paw; by the *possession* of something, like a monogrammed handkerchief; or by some *knowledge*, such as a password. What matters is therefore either what she looks like, what she has, or what she knows.

WHO AM I?

In our daily lives we have to prove our identity again and again. If the identity check is performed by people, our appearance may be sufficient, provided the people know us personally; otherwise an unforgeable identity document with our photograph may be needed. The automatic machine at my bank that prints out the latest transactions of my account demands a plastic card. So long as this does not fall into the wrong hands, I can be sure that no one else will know the sad state of my account. But the automatic teller that dispenses cash is not satisfied with my plastic card; I also have to key in my secret PIN, my personal identification number, to convince it that the card was inserted into its slot by me and no one else.

When I want to use a computer at the Göttingen computing center, the screen first asks me who I am. I key in a shortened form of my name. The computer can now establish whether I am entitled to use the center's services. But since anyone could key in my abridged name, the computer next asks for my password. This, as it were, is my key, assigned to me by the computing center when, several years ago, I applied for permission to use its equipment. The password is a string of symbols, something like g7"kky=). If I wish to prevent someone else from sneaking into the computing center under my name, I have to keep it secret. It is unlikely that anyone would guess it.

My password consists of eight symbols, each of which can be a letter, a numeral, or a sign such as $, &, or =. There are several thousand billion possibilities. Even if a hacker tried to run through them, he would scarcely be able to hit on my password within his lifetime. Once the password was given to me, no record was kept of it anywhere at the computing center. How the computer recognizes me by it nevertheless, we will soon see. The password represents identification by knowledge. Only I know what it is, and once I have keyed it in, the computer knows that I am really myself.

But computers guarding more sensitive information, or buildings not accessible to the public, must be protected against unauthorized intruders more reliably than by a plastic card or an ID with a photograph or a password. This applies to prisons or to laboratories that have to be protected against industrial espionage, and it applies even more to storage places where, within the framework of nuclear disarmament, weapons-grade plutonium is kept.

That is why physical characteristics are included in electronic identification. The most secure characteristic of a person is the pattern of little veins on his or her retina. There are special devices that explore a person's eye with an infrared beam. The computer connected to the device compares the retinal pattern with a sample in its memory. Unless they tally, the person cannot get at the plutonium.

In terms of security, the retinal method ranks above fingerprints. For fingerprints the person under examination places his hand on a glass plate. The pattern of skin lines is compared with the print stored in the computer. Improved models in addition test for a pulse in the finger, to make sure that they are being shown the fingerprint of a living person and not one produced by a hacker who has taken his hobby too literally.

Fingerprints are not as secure as retinal patterns; if a person has burned his finger, the computer might not recognize him.

Voice comparison, as practiced by the old nanny goat, is a customary technique in criminal investigation. A blackmailer on the telephone may be identified by voice comparison. One's voice can also be used for identification by a computer. The computer compares a voice with the stored voice patterns of persons who have authorized access. This method is subject to failure. If a person has a cold or speaks into the microphone while an aircraft is flying overhead, he may not be recognized by the computer.

Every Morse operator has his own "handwriting." A certain rhythm — for instance, the way he keys the *d* (long, short, long) or the *u* (short, short, long), or the interval between letters — is characteristic of the man at the key. This was important during the two world wars, because an experienced receiver could tell by the rhythm if a different operator was suddenly at the other end. Thus he could tell if a spy, who until then had lived undisturbed in the enemy's country, sending his espionage reports, had been discovered. If an enemy operator then transmitted misleading information from the captured transmitter, this could be spotted by his different "handwriting." Even if the blown spy was "turned" and made to send false reports by his own hand, he could modify his rhythm to alert his own people not to trust the signal.

This feature is nowadays used in a modified form for computer identification, since not only the keying of Morse signs but also the rhythm of a keyboard are characteristic of the user. Thus the typical typing rhythms of authorized persons are stored in computer memory. The person examined must enter a short text. The computer measures speed and time differences and again compares these with patterns in its memory.

The same principle can be used by a computer for signatures. As two signatures of the same person are never quite identical, a program is needed that differentiates between significant and insignificant differences. A characteristic feature could be the places where the writer pauses or the speed at which he completes his signature.

Even though we have no intention of robbing other people's accounts or getting access to plutonium, we have to identify ourselves time and again, to confirm that we are entitled to park our car in our employer's parking lot or to shop in a store without cash.

THE PLASTIC CARD

Once we paid for nearly everything with real money. Nowadays our wallets are full of plastic cards.

First came the plastic card with raised numbers and letters—the number of the card, the cardholder's name, and perhaps also an address. No electric supply was needed for machine-reading the card. It gained rapid acceptance throughout the world. Credit cards of this type led to a flood of receipts and transfer instructions on paper, so the handling of them and the evaluating of their accounts was not cheap. Then cards appeared with a magnetic strip about a half inch wide, which normally carried the blind-pressed information once more in electronic form.

In the Eurocheck card, the blind-pressing has been replaced by printing. The magnetic strip can be machine-read. It can, moreover, contain additional information, such as when the card was last used. If we use the card to get the balance of our account, we insert it into a reading device at the bank. The device reads the magnetic strip, determines whether the card belongs to an account held at that bank, and prints out the most recent account activity. But not only banks content themselves with this simple card; many businesses will hand over goods to anyone who has such a card, provided that their reading devices can read the data on the magnetic strip. The customer has only to sign a slip.

So long as we are dealing merely with account statements, there is nothing to object to. Matters are different when you make a purchase with your credit card. In principle, the magnetic strip can be read not only by the machine in the store but by anybody. There are gadgets that measure the magnetic field along the strip. An unauthorized reader of my credit card could then transfer this information to the magnetic strip of another card and at my expense dine in style at some exclusive restaurant. All things considered, the simple magnetic strip does not give me a lot of security. If temporarily it falls into the wrong hands, or if I lose it altogether and fail to notify the credit card company in time, I could discover alarming activity on my account.

When matters get serious, my bank therefore does not rely on the magnetic strip alone. While the automatic teller can decide whether the card permits access to my account, it cannot know whether the card has been inserted by its rightful owner. I must identify myself additionally by knowledge, and that is why the bank has given me a secret PIN.

THE SECRET NUMBER: A SIMPLE VERSION

I now show how the customer can be protected. I will not go into the details of how banks today manage this; I will use a simple model to demonstrate how, in principle, a secret number can provide security against access by unauthorized persons. Mind you, I would not entrust any money to the bank of my example. Real banks, fortunately, use much more complicated methods.

The secret number is called the personal identification number, PIN for short. In addition to the magnetic strip the automatic teller expects me to key in my PIN correctly. Of course it would be nonsense to have my PIN incorporated in the magnetic strip. If it were, the unauthorized person who has copied my card would also, with his reading device, be able to read my PIN and present himself as me at the ATM.

One possibility would be to store the PINs for all accounts in the bank's computer (fig. 13.1). When the machine reads my account number on my card, it could then examine whether the PIN that I keyed in agreed with the one in its memory. If so, it would disgorge money; if not, it might give me another chance or two to key in the correct PIN. If I failed to do that, it would raise the alarm or retain my card. Either way, it would not dispense any money. A simple and safe procedure?

Not as safe as it looks. Suppose the PINs of all accounts were stored somewhere in the bank. Many employees would have access to the bank's computer, and a few would also have access to the customers' PINs. No problem, because in a real bank, as we know, all the staff are honest. In my imaginary model bank, however, there is one employee who was sacked because at the last staff party he flirted too much with the manager's wife. Supposing he quickly printed out the list of PINs in order to use them later?

The PINs stored in the bank's computer do not protect the customer. If a dishonest employee gets hold of my card, he can, knowing my PIN, clean out my account.

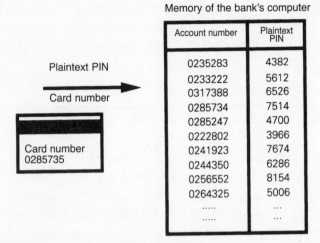

Fig. 13.1. **Simple access to a bank with a magnetic-strip card and PIN. The card numbers and PINs of all customers are stored in the bank's computer. The computer compares the card number read and the plaintext PIN keyed in by the customer with the data stored in its memory. If the PIN matches the card number, the machine can pay out the money requested.**

ENCODED PINs

This is where cryptology can help. When the bank assigns my PIN to me, it simultaneously encodes it, converting my plaintext PIN into a cipher-text PIN. I receive the plaintext PIN, while the bank stores my ciphertext PIN in its computer.

Below is a simple illustration, again far removed from what really happens in a modern bank, and I will use a simple cipher method—addition of a key number to my PIN. This is such a primitive method that no bank would practice it, but it will help us understand the principle.

The bank assigns a plaintext PIN to me, say, 2163. It has one key number, applicable to all its customers and guarded as a close secret: say, *4637*. It now adds this key number to my PIN, without carrying the ten:

Plaintext PIN	2163
Key number	*4637*
Ciphertext PIN	**6790**

HOW DO I KEEP MY PIN SECRET?

My bank cash card has a PIN. I also have two credit cards, each of which has its PIN. In order to be able to telephone home from abroad without additional hotel telephone charges, my credit card companies have also each given me a secret number for the use of their special telephone service. That makes five secret numbers I have to keep in my head. I was urgently told that I must not keep them written down on a piece of paper in the same wallet. I do not do that anyway. But since I cannot remember all my PINs, I carry them in encoded form in my wallet, indeed with my credit cards.

Encoding is quite simple. Let us assume the secret numbers are 3810, 5741, 6739, 8422, and 6284. I next think of a four-digit key number, which I must remember. We will also see how one can choose a number that can be reconstructed from memory at any time. Suppose I choose 6921 as my key number. I write down my five secret numbers and add my key number to each of them, without carrying ten.

$$3810 \quad 5741 \quad 6739 \quad 8422 \quad 6284$$
$$\textit{6921} \quad \textit{6921} \quad \textit{6921} \quad \textit{6921} \quad \textit{6921}$$
$$\mathbf{9731} \quad \mathbf{1662} \quad \mathbf{2650} \quad \mathbf{4343} \quad \mathbf{2105}$$

The bottom line shows my secret numbers in encoded form, and these I can confidently place in my wallet. I can even indicate to which card each belongs.

When I subtract the key number, my PINs awaken to new life:

$$\mathbf{9731} \quad \mathbf{1662} \quad \mathbf{2650} \quad \mathbf{4343} \quad \mathbf{2105}$$
$$\textit{6921} \quad \textit{6921} \quad \textit{6921} \quad \textit{6921} \quad \textit{6921}$$
$$3810 \quad 5741 \quad 6739 \quad 8422 \quad 6284$$

Instead of having to remember five numbers, I only have to remember one, my key number. But there is a simpler way. It is enough if I remember some word for constructing and remembering my key number. Let me write it down in one line, letter by letter:

P A B L O P I C A S S O

Now I write numerals under the letters, according to the alphabet: 1 and 2 under the two As, 3 under B, 4 under C, and so on. With numbers larger than 10, I omit the tens, simply writing 0, 1, and 2 for 10, 11, and 12.

P A B L O P I C A S S O
9 1 3 6 7 0 5 4 2 1 2 8

In this way I have turned Pablo Picasso into the number 913670542128; its first four letters represent my secret key number *9136*. If therefore you cannot remember your key number, memorize Pablo Picasso or some other long word. From it you can reconstruct your key number at any time.

The drawback of this method is that if anyone knows one of your real PINs, he can subtract from it your encoded PIN and thereby arrive at your key number, which then leads him to the rest of your PINs.

Once the bank has informed me of my plaintext PIN, its computer automatically destroys it. No one at the bank now knows my plaintext PIN. Only my ciphertext PIN is stored there. And only a person who knows the key number can discover my plaintext PIN by subtracting the key number (again without carrying ten) from the ciphertext PIN stored at the bank. This key number is treated as top secret at the bank.

I now go to the automatic teller with my card and the plaintext PIN assigned to me (fig. 13.2). I insert the card and key in my plaintext PIN. The bank's computer adds its key number to the PIN I have keyed in, again without carrying ten. It arrives, as before, at **6790** and compares the result with my ciphertext PIN. If they agree, the machine disgorges my cash.

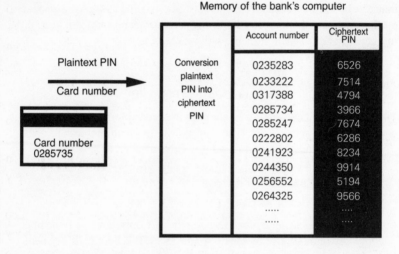

Fig. 13.2. **Withdrawal with magnetic-strip card and plaintext PIN at a higher level of security. The bank's computer possesses an encoding method by which it can convert my plaintext PIN into a ciphertext PIN. Upon issuing a card to the customer, it assigns a plaintext PIN to the customer and deletes the plaintext PIN from its memory. Now only the card number and the ciphertext PIN is stored for every customer. Those wishing to withdraw money from the automatic teller insert their magnetic card and key in their plaintext PIN. This is encoded by the computer, and the ciphertext PIN thus obtained is compared with the stored ciphertext PIN. When card number and ciphertext PIN match, the machine can dispense money.**

The dishonest bank employee now has a problem. Although all customers' ciphertext PINs are stored, they are useless to him if he does not know the key number. Under no circumstances should he learn the key number. This should be kept in a place to which perhaps the manager alone has access, and he should not betray it even to his wife. But somewhere there exists that number with which the plaintext PINs of all the bank's customers can be calculated.

To avoid this, so-called one-way functions are used. Before we deal with these, we must make a brief excursion into mathematics.

MATHEMATICAL MOUSETRAPS

A mouse can easily get at the cheese in a trap. Once in the trap, the mouse cannot get out again. It is easy for Mr. White, using the RSA method, to encode a plaintext with Mrs. Black's public key. But if he loses his plaintext, there is no way for him to read it again. What he has encoded he can no longer decode. It is the same as with the mouse in the trap: easy in one direction, impossible in the other.

Since plaintext and ciphertext are easily converted into numbers, we can also say: Turning a plaintext number into a ciphertext number is no problem, but to retrieve from it the original plaintext number is difficult. Transitions from one number into another that are easy in one direction and difficult in the opposite direction are called *one-way functions*. They occur on many occasions.

When Galileo turned a statement containing a scientific discovery into an anagram, the transition from plaintext to ciphertext was a one-way function. It is easy to turn a poem into an anagram; all you have to do is arrange the letters in alphabetic order. But then try to turn the anagram into a poem. Transition to an anagram is a one-way function. With the RSA procedure, the ciphertext is a one-way function of the plaintext. To multiply two large prime numbers by each other is relatively simple, but it is virtually impossible to factor such a number into its constituents. This is precisely why the RSA method is so secure. As we will be using the RSA method in different ways, I'll describe it again in the box that follows.

What use are one-way functions? Why should I worry if Mr. White can no longer read messages he himself encoded? But I would worry if the PIN that I need for withdrawing money from the ATM were known to someone other than myself. More than that—I do not even want the bank to know it. Once the PIN has been communicated to me, it should be

---

RSA WITH THE MAGIC NUMBERS N, D, AND E, IN BRIEF

1. Encryption of a numerical plaintext P with the magic numbers N and E (or with N and D): Write down $P \times P \times P \times P \times P$ . . . until P has been written down E times (or D times). Multiply and from the result keep subtracting the number N until the result is smaller than N. This remainder is the numerical ciphertext C.

2. Decoding with N and D (or with N and E): If C has been created by encryption of N and E, it is encrypted once more with N and D in the manner described above. The result is the numerical plaintext P. If C was obtained by encryption with N and D, it is encrypted once more with N and E.

3. One-way function using RSA: If a secret number C is created from a number P by means of N and E, no one who is not in possession of D can retrieve P from C.

---

deleted from the bank's computer. At the same time I want the bank's computer to recognize me by it. This is possible thanks to a one-way function. But we can achieve this objective only in several stages.

MY BANK ACCOUNT IS PROTECTED BY A ONE-WAY FUNCTION

Before, I let the bank encode my PIN by a very simple method. Instead it could encrypt my plaintext PIN by an RSA procedure, as described in chapter 12.

Let us recall: there are three magic numbers in the RSA method—a large one (N) and two small ones (E and D). What has been encoded with N and E cannot be decoded with N and E. So far we have used the RSA method only for messages that we have to encode and that subsequently have to be decoded by the receiver. Now we will use it, but only halfway. We will encode, with no intention of decoding. From a plaintext number we will arrive at a ciphertext number by means of the keys N and E. This transition is a one-way function—and that is all we need. That is why there will be no more mention of the key D.

The bank is in possession of N and E. With these it encodes my plaintext PIN, which gives it my ciphertext PIN, which it stores. It informs me of my plaintext PIN and deletes it on its computer. Apart from myself, there is now no one on earth who knows my plaintext PIN. A bank employee can at most come across my ciphertext PIN. With that he can do nothing, because the way from the ciphertext PIN to the plaintext PIN is blocked. This is the point of a one-way function.

Now to my side of the transaction. When I disclose to the machine my plaintext PIN, it uses the bank's one-way function to work out my ciphertext PIN and compares this with the one stored in its memory. If the two match, the machine gives me the money I want—naturally by instantly debiting my account with the amount.

Is this procedure really perfect? Security experts would not be too happy about the way my model bank operates. The reason is the electrical link between the keyboard of the automatic teller and the bank's computer. If someone taps this line, he can discover my plaintext PIN. Such tapping is not very difficult. The electrical pulses carrying my PIN down the wire create electromagnetic waves, similar to radio waves. The cable links act as antennas and radiate these waves in all directions. They can be intercepted even hundreds of yards away. With a suitable receiver anyone can gain possession of my plaintext PIN. If such a person also got hold of my cash card, he could gain access to my account from any automatic teller. This weakness of simple magnetic cards can be overcome if plaintext PINs are transmitted down the wires only in encoded form. This is what happens with real banks. But different methods will be used before long.

The magnetic strip on a card consists of iron oxide. It was once said that magnetic-strip cards therefore are only as smart as iron oxide.

THE COMPUTER IN THE BANK CARD

When I first had occasion to use an electronic computer in the mid-fifties, this machine filled a whole room. It stored its numbers on a big drum that carried a magnetic layer. Writing and reading heads probed the rotating drum. Nowadays our phone cards have built-in computers whose memories are a multiple of that of the drum of that dinosaur from the computer Stone Age. The entire chip, as these minute things are called, takes up no more than twenty square millimeters of the card. If it were any bigger, it would break when the card is bent. From the outside we see several separate gold-colored metal faces, the contacts. These are the computer's connections to the outside world. Through them it receives its operating current from the ATM, through them it receives data from the ATM, and through them it supplies data to the ATM. The computer chip proper sits in a depression routed out from the card's material, below its metallic surface. When we insert the card into the public telephone, the card receives current through its contact faces. In many countries cash cards issued by banks still have just a simple magnetic strip; but soon they too will be equipped with a microchip. Its memory will then be read from and written into. Instead of a magnetic strip there will be tiny condensers whose electrical charge will retain whatever has been fed into them in binary numbers. A charged condenser is a 1, an uncharged one a 0. A series of minute condensers can store in the form of binary numbers such data as the card number, the name of the bank, and the name of the account holder. They do not lose their charges even after years. The computer can change their state of charge, and thus stored numbers can be replaced by others. But the computer in such a *smart card* can do more than store data; it can calculate.

Here is roughly what will happen in my simple model of a bank. When it issues my cash card with chip to me, it also informs me of my PIN. This it encodes with a one-way function, say, using an RSA cipher. It takes a number N, as required for the RSA method. N therefore must be the product of two very large prime numbers. In my model bank, this N will be the same for all customers, but the bank calculates an individual key number E for every customer, as performed in appendix C in the determination of the three magic numbers. It therefore has a number E also for me. That is my key number. With it the bank's computer encodes my plaintext PIN to arrive at my ciphertext PIN. The N, my ciphertext PIN, and my E are written into the memory of my card. After this, my plaintext PIN and my ciphertext PIN are deleted at the bank. The bank retains only my key number E in its memory.

I now go to the automatic teller, insert my card in the slot, and key in my plaintext PIN. The chip in my card, now supplied with electricity and capable of operating, encodes my plaintext PIN by the RSA method with the N valid for all customers and with my personal E, and it compares the result with my ciphertext PIN, which is stored in it (fig. 13.3). If the two numbers agree, I have accomplished the first step. It is confirmed that I am the rightful owner of the card.

Now comes the next question. Does the chip in my card give me authorized access to an account at the bank? The bank's computer tests my card. As in an examination, the card is asked a question, and it must answer correctly. The bank's computer gives the card a random number. My chip thereupon encodes this number with N and with my key number E and sends the result, the encoded random number, back to the bank's computer. That computer meanwhile has likewise encoded the random number with N and with my key number E, which is known to it, and now tests whether my card has come to the same result. If it has, then it provides access to my account.

Let us recapitulate. I know my plaintext PIN, but my card knows only the generally known N, my ciphertext PIN encoded with N and E, and my key number E. Note that a member of the bank staff who may have got hold of the list of stored key numbers E is unable to produce a card that would be a copy of mine. After all, he does not know my plaintext PIN, and not even my ciphertext PIN is stored in the bank's memory. Moreover, when I withdraw money, my plaintext PIN is not transmitted between me and the bank's computer. If the ATM has been tampered with it could, when I key in my PIN, pass it on not only to my chip but also to some other PC. What is it, then, that passes down the wire between me and the bank's computer? Only new random numbers and their encryptions.

THE PLASTIC CARD AS WALLET

Bank clerk Mitchell loves his job. Work at the bank is interesting and varied, especially at such moments as this. Facing him is a customer who evidently intends to close his account, because he has just asked for the entire amount, nearly fifty thousand dollars, to be paid out to him in cash. In a back room the customer has Mitchell count out the money for him. Is he going to pocket it all, or will he take it away in a plastic bag? He has no attaché case with him. While the customer is counting, Mitchell notices that the man, rather anxious at first, becomes increasingly cheer-

Fig. 13.3. (Facing page) Withdrawal of money from an automatic teller with a chip card. When issuing the customer's card, the bank wrote on it the key numbers N and E that can be used for encryption by the RSA method. The bank also assigns a plaintext PIN to the customer, which it encodes with N and E. This gives it the customer's ciphertext PIN, which it likewise writes on his card but deletes on its own computer. The bank's computer therefore holds only the account number and the individual key E of each customer.

When the customer uses the automatic teller, he inserts his chip card and keys in his plaintext PIN. The chip on the card encodes the plaintext PIN with N and E. This gives it the customer's ciphertext PIN, which it compares with the ciphertext PIN placed in its memory by the bank. Agreement between the two confirms that customer and card belong together. Next a random-number generator starts working in the bank's computer. It gives a random number to the chip in the card. The card encodes the number with N and E and sends the result back to the bank's computer, which meanwhile has likewise encoded the number with N and the customer's key number E. If the chip and the bank's computer have come to the same result with the encryption of the random number, nothing now bars the dispensing of money.

ful. When the last fifty-dollar bill lies on the table between them, the customer beams. "Wonderful," he says. "You can put it back into my account now. I just wanted to make sure it was all there."

Wherever the money that a customer has deposited may be, it certainly will not stay at the bank for long. We are used to settling our bills without cash. We do not keep our banknotes and coins in a sock. So long as our business stays within the law, we do not have to carry our money across borders in a briefcase; we can have our bank transfer it anywhere in the world, to Honolulu or Sidney. If I make out a five-thousand-dollar check to Mr. Kwan-Ngok Yu in Hong Kong, my bank is not going to send him a parcel full of dollar bills, because in reality I have no money at the bank at all—a number in a book or in a computer, nothing more, records what the bank owes me. My remittance consists of the bank's informing the financial institution in Hong Kong: "Pay your customer Mr. Kwan-Ngok Yu five thousand dollars. We now owe you this amount." Simultaneously, of course, it debits my account by five thousand dollars.

Some transactions we do make in cash. We all carry money because we do not use a credit card or write a check when we buy a movie ticket or get on a bus. Everyday payments continue to be made in cash. Besides, cash is anonymous. A dollar bill does not tell you who handled it before me. This anonymity protects my private life.

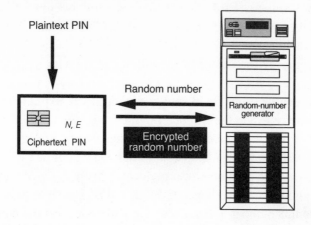

Memory of the
bank's computer

Account number	E
0235283	540254482
0233222	493716048
0317388	601825925
0285734	615948260
0285247	604826048
0222802	259269369
0241923	371604937
0244350	159370482
0256552	592693692
0264325	581369247
.....	.....
.....	.....

Cryptological methods have made it possible for me to carry an electronic five-hundred-dollar bill on my person. Just as the state of my account at the bank, it is no more than a number held on a portable computer. If electronic money is to become established, it must be as simple as possible for the user. Upon request the bank's customer receives a charged money card, that is, the card is charged with a definite amount, just as a phone card is charged with units. The customer goes to a store, makes a purchase, and pays for it by inserting his card into the reading device. The cost of his purchase is automatically subtracted from the amount stored on his card. The dealer, in turn, is connected to the dealer's bank, which credits his account with the amount in question. When the amount stored on the card is used up, the customer can have it "filled" again by the customer's bank, naturally with his account to be debited.

To illustrate the principle of such a method, I will explain the operations taking place inside the computer in the card, in the dealer's reading device, and in the bank's computer by means of my imaginary model bank. In the past, I would walk up to the teller and withdraw cash. Instead, the bank now writes a number into my card; this is my electronic cash, every bit as good as a five-hundred-dollar bill. If I wish to make a purchase, I give this number to the dealer. He will verify that the number he has received is really worth its value in money. When he delivers the number to the bank, the bank should credit his account with five hundred dollars.

How does this work? After all, there are no end of numbers. If numbers are to function as currency, surely anyone has an unlimited amount at his disposal. Much the same could have been said when paper money was introduced. If paper is going to be money, then everybody will be rich, since there is an unlimited amount of paper. But we know that not every scrap of paper is worth money. Only paper furnished with special characteristics, for instance, with forgery-proof printing, is worth money. The same is true of electronic money, where payment is made with numbers. Only specially prepared numbers are forgery-proof and suitable for use in the place of cash.

Let us consider the simple model explained in figure 13.4. The bank uses an RSA method. It has three magic numbers, N, E, and D. What is encoded with N and D can be decoded only with N and E. I want an electronic five-hundred-dollar bill from my bank. First of all the bank debits my account by the sum of five hundred dollars. Next it chooses a random number for me, say, 1997. In actual fact the bank would take a much larger number, one with twenty digits or more. This it writes down twice in succession, obtaining a new number, in my case **19971997**. The double number it then encodes with its secret number D. The result—let us assume it is **59274100698**—is my electronic five-hundred-dollar bill. The bank's computer enters it into the memory of my smart card.

The number protects against forgery. Any dealer I present it to in payment can convince himself of that. Suppose I go to an electronics store

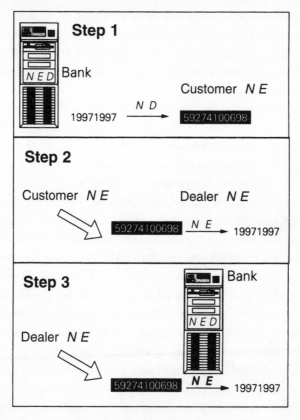

Fig. 13.4. The life of an electronic banknote of $500 value. The bank possesses three keys: the large key N and a key E for $500 bills—these two are public—and a secret key D for $500 bills.

Step 1. The bank produces a forgery-proof number, consisting of two identical numbers written one after the other, say, 19971997. We will call it the *double number*. The bank encodes this double number with the key N and the secret key D. The result is 59274100698. The bank puts this number on its list of electronic $500 bills issued, debits the customer's account by $500, and hands the number over to him. This number is an electronic $500 bill.

Step 2. The customer takes the number to a dealer. The dealer's electronic reading device checks to see if it really is a $500 bill by decoding it with N and E. If the result is a double number, the dealer knows that it is genuine and takes that amount from the customer's card. The number is now stored in the dealer's electronic reader. The money transfer is concluded, and the dealer can hand over the merchandise to the customer.

Step 3. The dealer takes the number to the bank. The bank verifies that it is genuine, again by decoding with N and E, and also makes sure from its list that the number has not already been cashed in. Next the bank credits the dealer's account with $500 and deletes the double number from the list of electronic banknotes issued but not yet cashed.

and buy a television set at the price of exactly five hundred dollars. For payment I insert my card in the reading device at the checkout counter. The device finds on the card the number **59274100698** that I received from my bank. Let us recall: the number resulted from the bank's encoding a double number with its N and secret key D. Now the dealer's reading device decodes the number with N and the public key E. This should give him my double number 19971997. If the decoded number consists of two numbers written one after the other, the electronic reader deletes the five hundred dollars on my card. I am allowed to leave the store with my purchase, since the dealer now knows that my electronic money is genuine. If in the memory of my card there had been an invented number, it would not have produced a double number upon decoding.

Next the dealer sends my electronic five hundred dollars — that is, the number **59274100698** — to the bank. The bank, for its part, wishes to know if the money is genuine; just as the dealer did, it tests to see if decoding with E produces a double number. If so, the bank credits the dealer's account with five hundred dollars. Everything is in order: I have my television set, my card is lighter by five hundred dollars, and the dealer's account has been credited with that sum.

However, the bank must make sure that the dealer will not cash in my number more than once. For that it keeps a list of money issued, that is, of the numbers used. On payment, it checks to see that a number has not been used already.

Of all these transactions you, the bank's customer, are totally unaware. All you know is that your five hundred dollars have gone.

In June 1998, the *New York Times* reported that a consulting firm had succeeded in deciphering the secret numbers of smart cards. The firm's special device measures the energy consumption of the chip during the time that the card performs calculations with the secret number. Consumption varies with every operation, and every variation, even though the differences are of the magnitude of millionth parts of a second, can be measured. Using his firm's instruments to obtain such data, twenty-five-year old Paul Koch in San Francisco eventually learns the secret number — bad news for manufacturers. In their race for the security of smart cards, encoders and decoders will be exploring ever new roads in the future. Let us hope that the encoders always keep one step ahead.

I have presented the method in simplified form, using as an example a money card that contained exactly five hundred dollars and explaining

Fig. 13.5. A smart card of Deutsche Bank.

how this exact amount was used for payment. In real life the electronic card would be exhausted in several small steps—by shopping, buying gas, and so on. Moreover, the bank in our example knows that the five hundred dollars that went to the dealer came from me, because it had specifically prepared the double number for me. Unlike a cash transaction, the method described does not protect my anonymity. But I only outlined the basic aspects; there are improvements that I do not propose to discuss in detail. All I wanted to do was show how electronic money can be brought into circulation from a customer's account, all without the threat of fraud.

Electronic wallets are in use today. Banks and savings institutions issue a card with a built-in chip (fig. 13.5) that initially—in the case of German banks—is loaded with 400 marks or, roughly, 300 dollars. At the store the customer inserts his card in an electronic reader that deletes from it the appropriate amount and simultaneously credits that amount to the dealer. The customer needs no PIN and does not have anything to sign. The dealer does not have to ask the bank first whether or not the customer has overdrawn his account, since, at the time of the card's issue, the bank already debited the customer's account by 400 marks. The card is every bit as good as cash. If the customer loses it, it is as if he has lost cash. And anyone finding it has in effect found cash.

"It's so easy"—I read in a prospectus of Deutsche Bank—"to fill up your Deutsche Bank SmartCard. At terminals or automatic tellers marked with the SmartCard symbol, just insert your SmartCard. The machine will tell you the balance of your electronic wallet as well as the maximum amount you can add to it. Key in the sum you wish to add and your PIN (identical with your EC Card or Customer Card PIN). The amount is automatically withdrawn from your personal account." With banking transactions it is always wise to ask about bank charges. Here I read: "Filling up at Deutsche Bank machines is free of charge for you; at the machines of other institutions there is a regular charge of two deutsche marks." (That's about $1.20.)

Are these "electronic wallets," along with cash cards and credit cards, with their new computer technology, really secure? Or can someone use my card to lead a high life at my expense? Just as safecrackers are continually trying to discover ways of cracking the allegedly unassailable security of each new type of safe, so electronic safecrackers are busily seeking ways to penetrate the secrets of smart cards in order to get at other people's money. Time and again we hear about these things in the media, since stories that our money is at risk make for better journalism than do reassurances that our electronic money is protected.

There is no doubt that electronic money presents us with new problems. Calculation of key numbers costs computer time. The world's great credit card companies have issued altogether some eight hundred million credit cards. A machine can produce a new card every second and a half. If all cards are renewed every two years, twenty machines have to be kept running around the clock. If existing cards are converted to the RSA method and 155-digit prime numbers are used to create the key number N, something like two hundred machines will have to work year in, year out, producing key numbers and cards. There is therefore some talk about assigning the same key to several customers scattered about the globe— a disturbing thought.[1]

Electronic wallets are gaining ground. It was estimated that by the end of 1997, some sixty million EC Cards and bank cards with a rechargeable chip would be issued in Germany and that one hundred thousand recharging locations would be set up.[2] One can imagine citizens standing rather helplessly with their electronic wallets in front of these different electronic readers. In addition to the smart card issued by

German credit institutions, the German Telecom, the German railways, and the Association of German Transport Operators are planning to issue a Paycard that can be filled up (at the cost of two telephone units) at any public cardphone. These will be joined by the P-Card launched by the Electronic Banking System (EBS). Which card will be decoded by which electronic reader, or whether it will be possible to use a MoneyCard also for making telephone calls—remains to be seen. At present German cards do not work either in Belgium or in Austria.

The future will show whether the public will accept the plastic electronic wallet.

ELECTRONIC SIGNATURES

What you sign is valid. Admittedly there are contracts from which, even though I have signed, I can withdraw. But as a rule I have to keep to whatever I have put my signature to. In important matters, such as the purchase of real estate, the law requires the presence of a notary, who makes sure that I really am the person who signs my name. The document then will also bear his signature. That everything was aboveboard is recognized even when the signatories are no longer alive. In the event of doubt, experts compare the signature with those on other documents to decide whether or not it is genuine.

The drawback of a signature is that, in order for its authenticity to be verified, the original is needed. With a little effort anyone can copy a signature from one document and use it on another. If you send a fax from your computer, your signature is scanned into your computer and can be used on another document. Only an expert can then—perhaps—tell from the fax if there has been any cheating. After all, the signature is quite genuine; it merely stands under the wrong document. It is therefore possible to transmit a text by telegram or fax to any corner of the earth, but the recipient cannot be sure whether the electronically transmitted signature is genuine or false. In this situation, too, cryptology can help.

Figure 13.6 again illustrates the principle with the model of a box with a padlock needing more than one key. Mr. Alt possesses the three keys N, E, and D. Since N and E are public, any receiver of the box possesses them. On receiving the box, the receiver knows that the paper

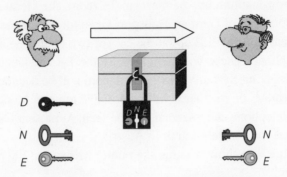

Fig. 13.6. An electronic signature illustrated by our example of a box with a double lock. Mr. Alt types a letter to the notary Mr. Mayerhofer, but he does not sign in his own hand. He places the paper in the box and locks the padlock with the large key N and his secret key D. Mr. Mayerhofer unlocks it with Mr. Alt's public keys N and E. Since N and E can open only what has been locked with N and D, Mr. Mayerhofer knows that the message must come from Mr. Alt. That is as certain as if Mr. Alt had signed in his own hand.

was placed in the box by Mr. Alt and no one else, since the padlock can be unlocked only with Mr. Alt's key E. Let us consider a realistic example.

Mr. Alt is spending his vacation in Thailand. One evening, his attorney and notary Mr. Mayerhofer calls him from Munich to remind him that his fixed-interest agreement for a loan he took out for the purchase of his apartment block ends in a few days' time. Unless Mr. Alt immediately signs a new loan agreement, the 150,000 marks become payable. That is why Mr. Mayerhofer is sending a new loan agreement by fax. Although he is empowered to sign on Mr. Alt's behalf, he would nevertheless like to have his consent within twenty-four hours. Only then will he be able to conclude the new agreement for his client. Mr. Alt wants to give his attorney the green light. But the attorney wants to be sure that the green light really comes from Mr. Alt and not from some Mr. Gray, who may be interfering in Mr. Alt's business. For such contingencies Mr. Alt has an RSA encryption at his disposal. The public keys are the numbers N and E, which of course are known also to the notary, but the secret key D is known to Mr. Alt alone. Mr. Alt gets down to business and writes the following text:

Ihere byins truct mrmay erhof erres ident inmun ichun gerer stree ttoco nclud eonmy behal faloa nagre ement foron ehund redan dfift ythou sandm arksl eopol daltx

Needless to say, this text will not help Mr. Mayerhofer. Because he cannot tell whether the signature is genuine, he cannot be sure that the telegram is from Mr. Alt. If, for instance, on a swim in the Gulf of Siam Mr. Alt had an encounter with a shark, his heirs could accuse the notary of having concluded an agreement without authorization, since a telegraphed signature is worth nothing. That is why Mr. Alt now encodes the message with N and his secret key D and sends it to Mr. Mayerhofer. What has been gained by this?

Let us bear in mind that the keys E and D can be equally applied. Encoding as a rule is with N and E, decoding with N and D. But the reverse is also true. The message that Mr. Alt has encoded with N and his secret key D can be decoded by anybody, including the notary, with N and Mr. Alt's public key E. The point, however, is not to keep the message secret but to authenticate the signature. If decoding results in a meaningful text, the notary sees that the telegram must come from Mr. Alt, since what can be decoded with N and E can only have been encoded with N and D. Since no one except Mr. Alt has D, not even Mr. Gray, no one except Mr. Alt can turn any plaintext into a ciphertext that, upon decoding with N and E, will produce a meaningful text.

In this manner it is possible electronically, with RSA encryption, to transmit a document so that the recipient knows who it comes from—just as surely as if it bore the sender's signature in the sender's own hand.

Electronic signatures have been used for a number of years in banking, and especially in business with major companies. A bank and a company doing business will have contractually agreed to recognize electronic signatures.

ELECTRONIC IDs

Mr. Mayerhofer the notary may be satisfied with Mr. Alt's electronic signature. He has known him for years and received the electronic key numbers N and E from him personally. But your signature alone may not always satisfy a notary. If you are buying or selling an apartment, he will want to see your passport or identity card, if he does not know you personally. These documents prove that you are you. They tell the notary that the right person is signing his or her name.

How can this level of certainty be achieved with an electronic signature?

Matters with an identity card are much the same. The card was issued by some office that first had to be convinced that you were the one who applied for the identity card, that you were registered with the police at your place of residence, and that the passport photograph submitted with the application was a photograph of you. All this the office confirmed on your document. For electronic identity cards an authority also needs to be set up: a *certification center*.

Let us replay the exchange of messages between Mr. Alt in Thailand and the notary Mr. Mayerhofer in Munich but change the scenario. The two men have not met before. Mr. Alt would like the notary, who was recommended by friends, to work for him, moreover to begin immediately. For that Mr. Mayerhofer needs a power of attorney from Mr. Alt. Mr. Alt has already applied to the certification center for a signature-key certificate. He personally went to the center, identified himself, and submitted his RSA numbers N and E. The center established that it really was Mr. Alt who wanted the certificate, confirming that Mr. Alt was Mr. Alt and that he possessed the public key E and that his encryption was based on an RSA method using the number N. Mr. Alt's identity document can be printed by the center on a sheet of paper or transmitted by fax or by telegram. So far, this identity card is not much use. After all, Mr. Gray could make such a document for himself and pretend to be Mr. Alt. The notary has to be sure that the identity card was in fact issued by the certification center.

We already know how this can be achieved: the center must electronically sign the identity card. For that purpose the center has its own RSA procedure. Its N and its public key E are generally known. The center now encrypts all identity cards it issues with its secret key D. Mr. Alt sends to the notary, by telegram or over the Internet, a message encoded with his secret key, together with his electronic identity card. The notary first decodes the identity card with the center's public key. If he succeeds in decoding it, he knows that it is genuine. At the same time he learns Mr. Alt's public key. With that he can decode the message, secure in the knowledge that the message is from Mr. Alt.

With this example I have gotten ahead of the actual state of affairs. In the United States, the necessary infrastructure is now being created for the recognition of electronic signatures, for instance in the renewal of drivers' licenses. According to the September 1, 1998, issue of the *New York Times*, some states, including California, Texas, and Utah, have already enacted legislation to this effect. In most other states, however, this is not yet the case. There are still some problems about making the recognition of electronic signatures compatible with the Statute of Frauds, which is derived from old English law. This is probably why Allan F. Farnsworth, a leading contract law professor at Columbia University, still advises that important and complicated contracts be signed by hand. "I think the safe thing to do is to do it in the old-fashioned way." Sooner or later, however, the necessary conditions for the acceptance of electronic signatures will be created throughout the world. Our banks, however, have long been using a similar method to identify themselves to one another for international payments. SWIFT, their certification center, is based in Belgium.

Number theory, a branch of pure mathematics, has until recently been a field that fascinated only those directly concerned with it; it was not believed to have any practical application. This has changed. We are moving toward an information society in which the transmission of messages around the globe is becoming increasingly important. Already the RSA method helps protect our money. With it, encoded signatures will soon be recognized as signatures in courts of law all over the world. And all this will be based on numbers so large that no one can divide them into their factors.

The smallest number that no one has so far been able to factor has 140 digits. The American company that distributes the RSA method puts seven thousand dollars into a fund each year. From this fund a prize will be paid to anyone who discovers the factors of what, at that time, is the smallest unfactored number. Since the last win, seventeen thousand dollars have accumulated, and the sum is growing every year. The next winner will receive four-sevenths of the jackpot. The remaining amount will then grow again, until a new winner comes up.

It is not only this prize money that makes mathematicians throughout the world search for methods of factoring large numbers. The challenge itself draws them. For more than ten years there has been the method of *elliptical curves*; this methods works provided one of the factors contained in the large number is not too large itself. The largest factor found by this method is a prime number of 47 digits. Mathematicians have also developed another method, called by them the *square sieve*, echoing the sieve of Eratosthenes. In April 1996, the square sieve made it possible to factor a number of 130 digits.

But those who rely on RSA are now being threatened from another direction. Physicists in their laboratories are trying to utilize properties of atoms that are determined not by classical physics but by quantum mechanics. In this connection an entirely new kind of computer is being developed. It will store and process data in binary form, just as our present computers do, but while in present computers the ones and zeros of the binary system are created by open and closed electronic switches, by charged and uncharged capacitors, or by variable magnetic fields on a hard disk, the creation of ones and zeros will be performed by different quantum states of molecules. In a quantum computer, radio pulses will flip molecules from one state into another. Such computing will be much faster than what is available to us today. Teams at several American universities are busy developing the quantum computer. Their success, if it comes, should have immediate consequences for cryptology. A few years ago a scientist at Bell Laboratories, Peter Shor, invented a method by which, using a quantum computer, one can factor large numbers at lightning speed.

Should we therefore worry about our money in the bank? Could somebody in the future strip us of all our savings with a forged electronic signature? So far no quantum computer exists. If it arrives, then it will not only make easier the factoring of large numbers, it will also, by creating longer key numbers, make decoding more difficult.

To factor a large number and thereby crack an RSA encryption will remain a mathematical problem that can be tackled only by large-scale teamwork and not by someone in a lonely attic. That is why our RSA-protected assets will continue to be as safe against theft as the gold in Fort Knox. At least we hope so.

NOTES

1. *New Scientist* (Oct. 12, 1996) 21.
2. *Wirtschaftswoche* 48 (Nov. 21, 1996) 188ff.

APPENDIX A
A HOMEMADE ENCRYPTING MACHINE

I N 1989, THE LONDON JOURNALIST Robert Matthews (whom we met on page 137) published a guide for the production and operation of a simple encryption device. It consisted of two paper strips that were stuck together at their upper and lower ends to form a loop and that could then be rotated against each other on a cylinder. Matthews suggested the use of a narrow-gauge film can. Instead, I have used the casing of a pencil sharpener (fig. A.1). The two strips are shown in figure A.2.

No matter what you use as a cylinder, copy figure A.2 on a sheet of paper. According to the size of your cylinder, enlarge or reduce the table. Next cut along the vertical line. You now have two parts, one with two and the other with four columns. If you have made the copies on the right scale, you will not find it difficult to place the two cut strips around the cylinder in such a way that they fit accurately and can be rotated one against the other. Now tape the ends together. The left strip has two columns and carries the alphabet (with no distinction between I and J, so there are only twenty-five letters); the right strip has four columns of numbers and an arrow pointing left. On the left strip, each letter has a number.

We can now, as with the Vigenère method, work with a finite keyword; or we can, in the manner of the *one-time pad* (see chapter 7) use as long a string of random numbers as we wish.

Fig. A.1. A homemade cipher machine. The paper strips produced in accordance with figure A.2 have been wound around a cylindrical pencil sharpener. They can be rotated one against the other.

Let us start with a simple keyword, *ONCE*. With the help of the left strip we can turn this into a key number, consisting of *13 12 02 04* according to the four letters of the keyword. Next we encode the plaintext "rose." We rotate the right strip until the line with the key number *13* is aligned with the first plaintext letter, that is, *r*. The arrow on the right strip then points to the first ciphertext letter, **E**. Now we rotate the second key number, *12*, to match the second plaintext letter, *o*. The arrow now points to **A**. Continuing like this, we get the ciphertext **EAUI**. The general rule for this encryption is: Bring the plaintext letter and key number in line, and the arrow will point to the ciphertext letter.

Decoding is done analogously. The decoder knows the key—the numerical sequence *13 12 02 04*—and has the ciphertext **EAUI** before him. He aligns the arrow with the first ciphertext letter, **E**; the key number *13* gives him *r*. We continue like this until **EAUI** again becomes "rose." General rule for decoding: Align the arrow with the ciphertext letter, and the key number gives you the plaintext letter.

Operating with a keyword or key number of any length—something

0	A	1	26	51	76
1	B	←	25	50	75
2	C	24	49	74	99
3	D	23	48	73	98
4	E	22	47	72	97
5	F	21	46	71	96
6	G	20	45	70	95
7	H	19	44	69	94
8	I	18	43	68	93
9	K	17	42	67	92
10	L	16	41	66	91
11	M	15	40	65	90
12	N	14	39	64	89
13	O	13	38	63	88
14	P	12	37	62	87
15	Q	11	36	61	86
16	R	10	35	60	85
17	S	9	34	59	84
18	T	8	33	58	83
19	U	7	32	57	82
20	V	6	31	56	81
21	W	5	30	55	80
22	X	4	29	54	79
23	Y	3	28	53	78
24	Z	2	27	52	77

Fig. A.2. **The table shown here should be enlarged or reduced on a copier so that it fits accurately on a cylinder like the one shown in figure A.1. The table should then be cut along the line marked. The two strips are fitted on the cylinder and their ends taped together.**

like the sequence of number pairs from figure 7.6—is no different. If we again use the opening of Carl Sagan's *Contact* as a key worm, as we did in chapter 7, then we have to assign key letters to the plaintext with the help of the left strip.

APPENDIX B
YOUR COMPUTER AS ENIGMA

THE INFORMATION SCIENTIST Marian Kassovic of the University of Hamburg has written a program with which you can turn your computer into Enigma. For your personal use you can download it from the Internet. All you need is an IBM-compatible computer and access to the Internet—or a friend with access to the Internet. Using a file transfer protocol or most Web browsers, you can get it under the address: ftp://agn-www.informatik.unihamburg.de/pub/cryptsim/simulators/. Once you have the program stored in a directory on your hard disk, key in *enigma22*.

This creates several new files. Two of them end in *.doc*. The file *swissn.doc* explains to you how Enigma worked, senigma.doc is the instruction for running the Enigma program *senigma.exe*. This you should read carefully. Unfortunately for the English-speaking reader, these two documents are in German. If you cannot read them, continue and try to learn to manage the program by trial and error. You can next go into action and key in *senigma*, whereupon the diagram of Enigma appears on your screen. The machine's keyboard is that of your PC. On the screen twenty-six fields light up; these correspond to the little lamps of Enigma. Above them, in windows, you can see the letters of the rotors. You now have to set up your Enigma. To do that, type /. In case you have forgotten what the *senigma.doc* instruction told you, the procedure is once more explained. You can opt for a three-rotor or four-rotor Enigma. You next fit three of the possible eight rotors in the machine and choose the sequence in which these are installled. If you decide in favor of the four-rotor machine, you can additionally install one of the Greek drums (B and C for the Beta and Gamma rotors) and the appropriate thin reflecting rotor. Choose the ring setting and cable connections and next bring the rotors into their basic position. If you key in *1*, two fields in the left part of your screen will indicate how you have set your Enigma. Now you can encrypt.

Enter your plaintext. You will observe how with each letter the right-hand rotor advances by one step and how every now and then the middle rotor moves. Simultaneously your plaintext and the ciphertext appear in two lines at the bottom of your screen. You will find that the ciphertext you obtain again produces the plaintext if keyed in with the same initial position of the rotors. You can also test the characteristics of the four-rotor Enigma described on pages 192-93. If the Greek drum Beta of the original Enigma (marked B in the program) shows the letter A in the window, and if the reflecting rotor (marked B in the program) is installed, then the four-rotor machine encrypts like a three-rotor machine whose rotors have the same initial position as the three movable rotors of the four-rotor machine.

TAKE TWO PRIME NUMBERS, to be called p and q. In the encryption example on page 218 they were the numbers 5 and 17. In the example on page 221, $p = 48{,}611$ and $q = 1{,}009$. Once these two numbers have been chosen, they are multiplied by each other and the first magic number N is obtained. In the first example, $N = 85$, in the second $N = 49{,}048{,}499$. Next we calculate an auxiliary number, to be called z. We obtain z by reducing both p and q by 1 and multiplying the results. In the first example $z = (p - 1)(q - 1) = 64$, in the second $z = 48{,}610 \times 1{,}008 = 48{,}998{,}880$. The number z helps us determine the two key numbers E and D. With one of these numbers, let us say E, this is simple; it need only have the property of not sharing a factor with z. The number z is divisible by 4, because p and q should be odd numbers (nobody would think of making one of them equal the prime number 2, because in that case the secret would be out at once—as we shall see.) But if p and q are odd, then $p - 1$ and $q - 1$ are even, and z has the factor 4. It follows that E must be an odd number, because otherwise it would share the factor 2 with z.

Anyone wanting to make things easy for himself simply chooses a prime number smaller than z and, by division, checks whether it is contained in z. If it is, he tries another prime number; if not, he can make that number his E. In our first example, we chose $E = 5$, in our second example $E = 61$. Both 5 and 61 are prime numbers not contained in the z associated with them.

We now have the two public key numbers N and E. The most important number, of course, is the third, the secret key number D, and getting that requires a little more effort. The number D must have the following properties: multiplied by E, it must, when divided by z, leave the remainder 1, that means: $E \times D \equiv 1 \pmod{z}$. First I demonstrate the calculation of D by the simple example of $z = 64$.

Take $z = 64$ and $E = 5$, divide the larger number by the smaller, and determine the remainder. In our case $z = 12E + 4$. The remainder is 4. We next divide E by the remainder 4. $E = 1 \times 4 + 1$, so the remainder is 1. If the remainder is 1, I have finished. If I have chosen E so that it shares no factors with z, then sooner or later I will arrive at a remainder 1. Now comes the second part: I start with the last equation and write it so that the 1 is on the left side: $1 = E - 1 \times 4$. I replace the 4 by the remainder of the preceding equation—that is, $1 = E - (z - 12E)$—and rearrange: $1 = -z + 13E$. Our requirement that $E \times D$ must lie within the domain of the remainders of z equals 1 is met. If we go over to the remainders and add $z = 64$ on both sides, we receive within the domain of remainders $1 \equiv 13E \pmod{z}$. Hence $D = 13$.

How to sum up this number magic in a simple formula that will allow us to discover the secret D in other cases? Call z the first remainder and E the second remainder. This may sound a little stupid, for why should they be remainders when we have not even divided yet? But we will see that the rule can best be formulated this way. A little while ago we divided the first remainder z by the second remainder E, getting the third remainder 4. Then we divided the second remainder E by the third remainder 4, getting the fourth remainder 1. We can therefore state the following rule:

Divide the first remainder by the second to get the third; then the second by the third to get the fourth, and so on. From the third remainder on, each remainder is determined by the division of the next-to-last remainder by the last remainder, until you arrive at 1. Then you start on the final equation, writing the 1 on the left side and all the rest on the right, and replace all remainders arising by the preceding formulas, until finally the 1 is expressed by the first and second remainder, that is, by z and E. If you then go to the domain of remainders with regard to z, the summand that contains z as a factor disappears. D is then the factor of E.

Let's do this again in the example where $z = 48998880$ and $E = 61$. The first remainder is z, the second E. Division of the first by the second, $z = 803{,}260E + 20$, gives us the third remainder 20. Division of the second remainder by the third, $E = 3 \times 20 + 1$ gives us 1 as the third remainder. And this is it. Substituting from the end: $1 = E - 3 \times 20 = E - 3 (z - 803{,}260E) = -3z + 2{,}409{,}781E$, hence $1 = -3z + 2{,}409{,}781E$ or $1 \equiv 2{,}409{,}781E \pmod{z}$. Hence the secret $D = 2{,}409{,}781$.

In this way we determine a magic triad of numbers. I have not proved that encryption with numbers determined in this manner really functions—in other words, that encryption with N and E will, in the way described in chapter 12, turn any plaintext number into a ciphertext number that, with the aid of N and D, can be converted back into the plaintext number. This would require mathematical proof, which the reader can find in the books by Friedrich L. Bauer and Albrecht Beutelspacher I've included under "Further Reading."

Apart from a little mathematics, the determination of the secret key number D is no particular problem. Does this not suggest that Mr. Gray, knowing the public key numbers N and E, could also discover the secret D? By no means. Remember that for calculating z we used not N or E but the two prime numbers p and q, of which N consists. We arrived at the auxiliary number z by multiplying the two prime numbers, each of them reduced by 1. Those Mr. Gray does not know, because they are strictly secret. The secret of encryption is in the factoring of the number N into the product of two prime numbers. In the case of $N = 85$, this factoring is easy; any schoolboy can tell that 85 is divisible by 5, and if he does divide it by five, he gets the prime number 17. With the knowledge of the two prime numbers he can calculate z, and from the publicly known E he can determine D in the same manner as we did above. The cipher is cracked. To repeat: the code is broken when the two prime numbers concealed in N have been found. This is easy with 85 but much more difficult with $N = 49048499$, and practically impossible with numbers of more than a hundred digits.

A final observation. I have explained how, when p and q and hence also N are established, the number E is chosen and D calculated. I might equally well have chosen D and calculated E. E and D are entirely interchangeable. In this book we have always used E as the public key and D as the secret key, but we could just as easily have chosen D as the public key and E as the secret key.

APPENDIX D
PGP, THE ENCRYPTION PROGRAM
FROM THE INTERNET

I t costs nothing, you do not have to be a computer genius, and you do not need a particularly sophisticated computer. On my 386 computer dating from 1990 the program runs superbly. I even got it to work on my ancient IBM-PC PS/2-30, which stands in my basement and which none of my friends wants even as a gift.

There are many locations on the Internet where you can download PGP programs. Take any search program and ask for PGP. I got mine from the students of Mannheim University. The address on the Web is: http://www.uni-mannheim.de/studorg/gahg/PGP/. There you will find several programs marked by *pgp* and some symbols following it. At the end there is *.zip*. I copied *pgp263i.zip* onto my disk, but I also own the version *pgp262ii.zip* that a friend gave me.

The extension *.zip* means that this is a compressed program that you have to decompress before use. For this there is a little program called *pkunzip.exe*, which you either have in your computer already or can get from a friend. Put *pgp263i.zip* into a directory you have created for PGP. Call the directory PGP. The *pkunzip.exe* program should also be in that directory, unless you have so arranged your computer that auxiliary programs are always available regardless of the directory you are working in. You now issue the command *pkunzip pgp263i.zip*. Things are now happening on your screen. A whole number of names appears and scrolls upward to make room for new names. More than twenty new files have come into being from the compressed program. This is the program for PGP (Pretty Good Privacy).

You will also find PGP program versions on the CDs that come with the books by Claus Schönleber and Philip Zimmermann mentioned in my "Further Reading." The book by Simson Garfinkel contains a 3.5" diskette with two program versions for DOS and UNIX operating systems.

INSTALLING PGP

An English operating instruction will be found in the files *pgpdoc1.txt* and *pgpdoc2.txt*. For readers who want to know only the principle, I'll describe a few simple applications of the program.

Like any RSA program, PGP requires the three magic key numbers: the N that is valid for all users, your own public $E,$ and your own secret D. Only then is the program able to encode and decode. You do not personally have to determine your key numbers by the method described in appendix C; the program does that for you. Enter *pgp -kg* (there has to be a space before the hyphen). After a lengthy explanation that need not interest you at the moment, the program offers you a choice of key numbers. You can choose short key numbers, longer ones, or very long ones. (In the case of my old PC in the basement, the program first demands that in the directory I create a subdirectory called *temp*. It presumably needs this to store intermediate data.) Accordingly the encryptions are hard to crack, or harder still, or very hard. You decide on your own secrecy level. Now you are required to enter your user ID by which the computer will recognize you next time. Enter an abridged form of your name. Mrs. Black would simply choose *black*. The user ID is nothing very secret yet; the secrecy comes now, because the computer asks you to choose a password, a secret sign that no one else must know. Enter a combination of letters and numerals that no one could guess—say, *xyzoed78*. But you will have to remember this password. As a check the computer makes you enter the password a second time.

Now for the three magic keys. You still need a public E and a secret D. For that the computer makes you key in a lengthy text. From the rhythm of your keying in, the program determines an *E* and the *D* that belongs to it. Just type away—perhaps a poem you remember from your school days. After some time the program tells you that this will do. It begins to calculate. Dots and asterisks appear on the screen in one or more lines. Then the program has finished. Your two key numbers have been determined. Your public key is in a file that bears the name *pubring.pgp*. To read it, you have to key in *pgp -kv*. On your screen you will now find a combination of letters, something like *pub 512/59184C2D 1996/09/22/black*. The public key named *512/59184C2D* was created on September 22, 1996, and belongs to Black.

But to exchange encrypted messages with others, you have to do more than this. You have to give your public key to others and get to know as many public keys of others as possible. For that you create a list. Copy the data in your *pubring.pgp* file onto a diskette and in the diskette give the file a different name, say, *list.pgp*. Exchange this list with your correspondents who use the same PGP program.

So far, we have installed PGP for only one user. Using the two computers standing in my office, I now describe how several people with PGP can exchange messages once they have installed PGP on their computers in the manner described above.

I install a PGP program on each computer. For one computer I slip into the role of Mrs. Black, enter *black* as the user ID and choose a password—for the sake of simplicity *b0b0b0b0*. On the other computer, I do the same in the role of Mr. White: user ID *white*, password *w0w0w0w0*. For both computers I choose the same secrecy level.Upon being prompted, I type in a lengthy text on both computers, and the program determines keys *E* and *D* for users White and Black. All I have to do now is tell each computer the public key of the other. So far each computer has only its own public key in its file *pubring.pgp*, but it has this file also on a diskette under the name *list.pgp*. White and Black now exchange diskettes and copy the file *list.pgp* into their PGP directory. Next, each enters *pgp -ka list.pgp pubring.pgp*. The program searches the file *list.pgp* for the public keys it does not yet have. Mr. White's program finds Mrs. Black's public key and adds it to its file *pubring.pgp*. The Black program does the same. Each now has the other's public key.

ENCODING WITH PGP

Mr. White wishes to send the message "tomorrow at eight at the station" to Mrs. Black in encrypted form. With a text program, ideally with the DOS editor, he keys the message into his computer, gives the file a name, for example, *letter1.txt*, and brings it into his PGP directory. Then he enters *pgp -e letter1.txt black*. The word *black* tells the computer to use the public key of Mrs. Black. The encoded letter appears in the directory, now called *letter1.pgp*. Mr. White now copies this encoded message to a diskette and sends it to Mrs. Black.

DECODING WITH PGP

Mrs. Black inserts the diskette into her computer and copies the encoded message to her PGP directory. Then she enters *pgp letter1.pgp*. Since Mrs. Black's secret key is needed for decoding, the program must make sure that the person at the computer really is Mrs. Black. It demands her password. She enters it, and before her the *letter1.txt* appears in plaintext.

SIGNING WITH PGP

The letter that Mr. Alt sent to Mr. Mayerhofer required an electronic signature. With PGP the procedure would be as follows. Mr. Alt writes his message with a text editor, names it *mssge.txt*, and moves it to the PGP directory. He next enters *pgp -s mssge.txt alt*. We know that "alt" is his user ID. Since an electronic signature requires his secret key number, the program asks for his password. He enters it, and a file *mssge.pgp* is created, encoded with Mr. Alt's secret key.

If Mr. Mayerhofer has Mr. Alt's public key in his *pubring.pgp* file, the computer tells Mr. Mayerhofer that the document can come only from Mr. Alt, since decoding has been successful with Mr. Alt's public key. It also creates a file named *mssge.pgp*, which contains the plaintext and which Mr. Mayerhofer can read on his computer with a text editor.

FURTHER READING

FROM THE EXTENSIVE LITERATURE of cryptology, I list only a few books, arranged in increasing order of difficulty. The first book requires the least mathematics.

Kahn, David. *The Codebreakers*. New York: Macmillan, 1967; Scribner, 1996. This standard work in English covers the history of cryptology. It has become a classic.

———. *Kahn on Codes: Secrets of the New Cryptology*. New York: Macmillan, 1983. A collection of articles on different cryptological topics.

———. *Seizing the Enigma*. Boston: Souvenir Press, 1991. The full Enigma story from the Polish contribution to Bletchley Park.

Hinsley, F. H., and A. Stripp. *Code Breakers: The Inside Story of Bletchley Park*. Oxford: Oxford University Press, 1993. Several contributors remember their time at Bletchley Park and how this vast operation was run.

Hodges, Andrew. *Alan Turing: The Enigma*. London: Burrett Books, 1983. This biography deals in detail with the work done at Bletchley Park in World War II.

Kozaczuk, Wladislaw. *Geheimoperation Wicher* (Secret Operation *Wicher*). Koblenz: Bernhard Graefe Verlag, 1989. The story of the Polish Enigma code breakers from 1929 to the end of the war. In German.

Gaines, Helen Fouché. *Cryptanalysis: A Story of Ciphers and Their Solution*. 1939. New York: Dover, 1956. Cryptology before the Enigma era.

Beutelspacher, Albrecht. *Cryptology*. Cambridge: Cambridge University Press, 1994. This little book provides an introduction but demands a fair amount of mathematical competence.

Bauer, Friedrich L. *Decrypted Secrets: Methods and Maxims of Cryptology*. New York: Springer Verlag, 1997. In a review, David Kahn, the "pope" of the story of cryptology, called this the best book on the subject he had read. Bauer gives mathematical formulas, explanations of the different cipher methods, and many stories and anecdotes.

Schönleber, Claus. *Verschlüsselungsverfahren für PC-Daten*. (Encryption Methods for PC Data.) Poing: Franzis Verlag, 1995. A factual introduction to cryptology, in German. Accompanying this book is a CD-ROM with 123 megabytes of files of texts on cryptology and programs largely collected from the Internet. The preface speaks of a "colorful bazaar of programs and items of daily use." The user can indeed browse and burrow in the different directories. But the user is on his own, since the author in the book hardly deals with the contents of the CD. Some of the files can be used straightaway, but most are compressed for reasons of space. The files ending in *.zip* are handled with the *pkunzip* program in the way described in appendix D. Files compressed by another method end in *.gz*. I have not looked at all the files but found the PGP program discussed in appendix D.

Whereas the above books are concerned with general questions of cryptology, the following two works are specially devoted to the PGP program:

Garfinkel, Simson. *PGP: Pretty Good Privacy.* Sebastopol, CA: O'Reilly, 1995. A very detailed and lovingly written instruction for the use of the PGP program, which comes with the book on a diskette.

Zimmermann, Philip. *The Official PGP User's Guide.* Cambridge, MA: MIT Press, 1995.

In conclusion, I recommend to the reader if he happens to be in Munich, a visit to the permanent exhibition "Informatics and Automation" at the Deutsches Museum. In the "Coding" section, there are a large number of exhibits, including a German naval Enigma, a *Schlüsselzusatz Lorenz* (see chapter 11), and a modern version of Thomas Jefferson's cipher machine.

INDEX

(Roman numerals refer to color plates.)